'One Man, Three Lives' tells the in[*well-travelled man. Frederick Cope* *most turbulent years, including a sp* *He was clearly an astute observer o*̤ *providing assistance to China at a time of great turmoil. Read Frederick Cope's story to find out more about a truly global citizen.*
   Rana Mitter, Professor of Modern History and Politics of China; Director of the University of Oxford China Centre; Vice-Master of St Cross College

Frederick Cope endures torture and solitary confinement as a Japanese prisoner of war in China. On his release, he ends up in South Africa, where he starts a new life as a farmer. But his trials aren't over yet. Here, he is up against the Great Depression, bush fires, and unpredictable weather which repeatedly destroy the crops which are his livelihood. This book is a testament to his humour, fortitude and strength of spirit in the face of constant adversity. This is an inspiring memoir for anyone facing challenges in their life and seeking words of wisdom to pull them through it.
   Stephanie J Hale, Founder of Oxford Literary Consultancy UK; formerly journalist and news reader and previous Assistant Director of Oxford University's creative writing programme, author

This is a moving story of an intrepid and indomitable man whose life deeply inspired his daughter, Tonia, the author of this book. Such was this inspiration that it impelled her to research thoroughly her father's life, the fruit of which we have in these pages. Fred lived in three continents and had wide experience over his 89 years. This makes for fascinating historical reading. Tonia also gets her readers really caught up in her Dad's intriguing character and life journey. His quest for meaning, truth and peace is moving to follow and was rewarded in his last days. His legacy most certainly lives on in Tonia's very productive life.
   Carol and Michael Cassidy – Michael is founder of African Enterprise, an Africa-wide organisation with headquarters in Pietermaritzburg, South Africa, and a prolific author

i

If you had written this story as fiction people would have said it was too far-fetched! It could be said that no one person would have had such varying experiences in three different countries, or been able to start again after so many mishaps.
  Grace Townshend, Principal medical writer Watermeadow Medical, Oxford

Everyone has an interesting story to tell but some lives are more epic than others. That is certainly true of the author's father, Frederick Cope. The chosen title 'One Man Three Lives' is apt because the lives he lived in three continents read like the stories of three different men. His successes and tribulations in England, China and South Africa were of a different character. Her father understood oppression. In 1966 he was horrified by the launch of Mao's Cultural Revolution and foresaw its cruel effects on the lives of Chinese friends. Fred liked to quote Lord Acton, 'Power corrupts and absolute power corrupts absolutely', and wrestled with the oppression of Apartheid South Africa.
Anyone interested in how an independent minded person keeps their integrity in different cultural settings will be inspired by this story. Tonia has thoroughly researched the background and told her father's story with warmth and honesty. I first met Tonia through the charity she founded - the Thembisa Trust. The author shares her father's optimistic internationalism.
  Sylvia Vetta, journalist and author whose books include *Brushstrokes in Time* set against real events in China 1963-1993. (Oxford, UK)

Reading books has filled many hours of my life with pleasure, but in editing a section of this book I found I just had to read the rest of the book. I have learned much that has been new to me, not only about England and China, but also about my own country, South Africa. It has been as if I was re-visiting places that are pleasant memories of my past. There are snatches of history, world and local that I never learned in school. There are photographs and word pictures that evoke nostalgia like the lovely Cosmos flowers, like the Drakensberg. There are people here that Tonia brings to life, as if I know them well.
  Frederick Borchers, Editor of the South African section of *One Man Three Lives*, Durban, South Africa

One Man Three Lives
The Man Who Would Never Give Up

*A biography of Frederick Cope
by his daughter,
Tonia Cope Bowley*

COSMOS PRESS

Copyright © Tonia Cope Bowley 2017

The moral right of the author has been asserted.

ISBN paperback: 978-0-9935332-0-4
ISBN eBook: 978-0-9935332-1-1

EBook design by IngramSpark
Cover design by Oxford Literacy Consultancy

All rights reserved. No part of this publication may be reproduced, stored in retrieval systems, or transmitted in any form or by any means without the prior permission in writing of the publisher, nor be otherwise circulated in any form of binding or cover other than that in which it is published and without a similar condition including this condition being imposed on the subsequent purchaser.

First published in Great Britain in 2017

www.toniacopebowley.co.uk

CONTENT

Preface 1
Setting the scene 2
Stephen's perspective 6

ENGLAND 9
Yorkshire 10
The Great War 1914–1918: Fred's involvement 21
Qualifications and experience 26
    The Consultant 48
    Venture into Manufacturing – Esmerene, a New wool 49
Hard times 59
    Sights on China 61
    World Traveller 65

CHINA 71
    Skating over Apects of Chinese History 73
Shanghai 75
    Historical Spotlight on the Treaty Ports 77
    Man of Wonder 82
Suzhou 86
South China 1930-1942 90
    Industrial Consultant Based in Hong Kong 93
    Growing Aggression – Japan's Sights on China 98
Canton (Guangzhou) 110
The Yangtze River 126
China's war with Japan 134
    Shameen 137
Closing years in China 142
    Civilian Prisoner of the Japanese 145
    Solitary Confinement 147
Exchange Prisoner 153
    Life Aboard the Tatuta Maru 156
    Prisoner Exchange at Lourenco Marques 158

SOUTH AFRICA 163
Cathedral Peak 164
Ethel 175

Fred and Ethel are wed 207
   Early Married Years 215
   It's a Girl 217
   The Ostrich Feather Factory 219
   Running Oban 226
Farming at Rosedale 228
   Cracks in the Marriage 248
Van Reenen District and Village 249
   Oxen Power 253
   The Green Lantern Inn 254
   Aspects of the Early History of South Africa 256
   The Inferno 259
Fred's Philosophy and values 263
   TOTT 263
   Secrets of a Leather Suitcase – F.C.3 264
   The Night Sky 273
   Is There Anybody There? 274
The writing is on the wall 275
Port Shepstone 276
   Body, Mind and Spirit Fred's Search for Truth 276
   Ethel's Crisis 280
Pietermaritzburg 281
   The Last Move 286
   England after 50 Years 287
Closing years 288
   Transformation 290
   Last Words 290
   Orion 291

REFLECTIONS 294

APPENDIX 307
   Credits 307
   Sources and Recommended Reading 309
   Canton Contacts 313
   Outline of Experience 320

TIMELINE 322
About the Author 326

*In gratitude for the lives of my parents
Frederick and Ethel Cope*

And

*For Stephen Bowley, my husband, for his
companionship, encouragement and insightful
contributions towards understanding my
father's life*

PREFACE

Each life has its own mystery, its own tale to be told.
Philip Yancey

Some 33 years elapsed after my father died before I picked up my pen in an attempt to record something of Frederick Cope's remarkable life story. My first stumbling words signalled a journey just beginning. I did not have any idea of its length and breadth, nor of the paths that I would follow. Perhaps most noteworthy is what I have discovered and learnt along the way.

The ensuing years have provided one adventure after another. Time and again, my journey has been enhanced by others who have journeyed alongside me. These people are acknowledged later. My primary co-adventurer is my husband, Stephen Bowley. In many ways Stephen is similar to my father (whom he never met). His sense of humour, together with his broad interest and expertise in matters geographical, planning and consultancy have not only kept me on track but led me to discover facts and places I'd otherwise have overlooked. Together we explored aspects of Yorkshire, China and South Africa and endlessly tossed ideas back and forth.

To foster understanding of where, when, how and why my father lived as he did in three very dissimilar countries I have incorporated contextual snippets. In no way do I intend these to be a comprehensive history of any period included here. The TIMELINE on the last pages will help you navigate Fred's life in the context of world events.

I hope you will enjoy and be stimulated in following Fred's journey – the worlds in which he sojourned, his humour and irrepressible optimism.

Esmerene Tonia Cope Bowley
Oxfordshire, 2017

SETTING THE SCENE

*The last thing that we find in writing a book
is to know what we must put first.*
Blaise Pascal

It was a bright African Sunday afternoon with not a cloud in the sky. Dad emerged from what I called his 'den'. By the glow on his face I knew something significant was coming.

> *How about it? Shall we try sailing our yacht today?*

For what seemed forever, in every spare moment, Dad had laboured over that little model yacht. He had designed and built it from scratch, sails and all. Sometimes he'd invite me into his den to help him. Help, in Dad's terms, meant my watching him work on the yacht while he told endless stories of some strange and far away land called China. Some of the stories seemed far-fetched, bizarre – perhaps untrue. But I believed Daddy. He was an honest man so if he said something was true it must be true.

I have to confess that sometimes I'd drift off into my own Alice-in-Wonderland dream world while pretending to listen. How I wish now that I had listened better.

Dad disappeared back into his den but soon reappeared proudly holding the yacht up high.

> *Come on, let's go to our favourite rock pool and try her out. We'll call her Joan.*

As we walked down the tree-avenue that Dad had planted a few years earlier, I offered to carry Joan. Not a chance! Dad protested that I might drop her. We soon got to the rock pool above the kloof (South African word for rocky valley or a gorge where the valley is deep). There was one last thing to do before trusting Joan to the water. A long stretch of string should be tied onto her so we wouldn't lose her.

We don't want her to sail out of sight and not come back.

Dad was watching the water flowing over the edge. Lucky me! I got to hold the string while Daddy launched her. Hurrah! Joan sailed.

That was a prompt for another story.

Not that many years ago, I was Commodore of the Canton Yacht Club. It was situated at a beautiful spot on the Pearl River at the edge of a large Chinese city called Canton, (known today as Guangzhou). I was the proud owner of an ocean-going yacht – the original Joan. Joan and I sailed up and down the China coast, to and from Hong Kong and up and down rivers like the Yangtze. The Yangtze was my favourite. I especially enjoyed the challenge of navigating the steep and dangerous Three Gorges. Many important and interesting people travelled with us from time to time.

Dad paused. For a moment his face clouded. Puzzled, I almost let go of Joan's string! He continued:

That got me into serious trouble later.
Why? I ventured.
I'll tell you some day. Let's enjoy sailing Joan for now.

Little by little, like the early stages in constructing a jigsaw puzzle, Dad's life began to take shape in my youthful mind. He was a staunch and proud Yorkshireman with accent to prove it. In his mid thirties, times were hard in England so he had packed up, boarded a slow boat to China and settled there for over fifteen years. Then times got bad – very bad. It was before and during WWII that Japan was invading China. For two years, Dad was a prisoner of the Japanese. This included nine months when he was held in solitary confinement. Then Britain joined the fight against Japan. Heads were rolling, but, in the end, Dad got lucky. With assistance from the British Government, and the Red Cross, he boarded the Tatuta Maru, a crowded war-time prisoner exchange ship bound for Lourenco Marques (Maputo) where the plan was he would board another ship bound for England. But he never got that far! Instead he landed up in South Africa to start his 'third' life. As his daughter, I am part of that third!

I often think about my father's life. Mother and I badgered him again and again to write his story. We thought he was doing so when he spent hours alone with his pen and paper. Then, in 1979, Dad died. In our grief we searched his papers hoping to find what he had written about his life. But no, we found not a word. Then one day, we came across a carefully-guarded box. It revealed many secrets: old passports; letters of thanks; copies of magazines he'd edited; a resume of his work experiences; a booklet on *World Crisis – A Way Out* that he had written in 1933.

As I sit chewing this over in Pret, my favourite watering hole in Oxford, my mental arithmetic tells me that thirty-three years have gone by since Dad left this world.

Now is the time.

I suddenly speak my thoughts out loud, surprising both myself and those around me. For, ever since the day Mother and I found that carefully-guarded box, I'd known that Dad had left to me the task of telling his story. And it is a story that must be told.

For many years I have researched various aspects of Dad's life. In fact, the shelf in my study is threatening to buckle under the weight of the accumulated papers! There rests a lot of exciting stuff, but not everything has fallen into place. As I set out to tell this story I resolve not to fabricate. Where there are gaps in Dad's history, I will say so. Quite literally, Dad had three lives, in three countries, in three continents.

Sailing Dad's model yacht at Rosedale
Photo from Tonia's childhood album

Tonia Cope Bowley
Oxfordshire, England
Setting the Scene was written on 22 November 2012

STEPHEN'S PERSPECTIVE

A little perspective, like a little humour, goes a long way.
Allen Klein

Tonia's book is an intensely personal story of her father's long life. His life in China as an industrial consultant in the 1920s to 1940s, imprisonment by the invading Japanese and release as an exchange prisoner of war is unique and of general historic interest. Fred Cope had immigrated to China following the collapse of his textiles business in Yorkshire in the economic depression after WW1.

In August 1942, he was en route to England on a prisoner exchange ship from Shanghai. He never made it home due to illness and was disembarked at Lourenço Marques in Mozambique. The book tells how just four months later he was married and starting a family life in South Africa at the age of 52!

Fred died the year before Tonia and I met in 1980 and I regret not meeting him – we would have got on very well. Through this book, I have learned more about his life and times. I hope readers will gain insights into his life, and of the circumstances in the first half of the 20th Century, spanning two World Wars and periods of economic depression that necessitated migration and building new lives.

ENGLAND

Source: University of Texas Libraries http://www.lib.utexas.edu/maps/faq.html

Yorkshire

God's Own County

Wakefield

Eee-bah-gum! It's a boy!

It is possible these were the first words Frederick Cope heard as he slipped into 'God's Own County', on 5 May 1890 in Wakefield, the county town of the West Riding of Yorkshire. Fred was his parents' second son. Perhaps they had been hoping for a girl and were surprised by a second boy. Who knows?

Certainly Eee-bah-gum was an integral part of Fred's vocabulary. This frequently-used Northern expression means:
    'Eee' – an exclamation of surprise or amazement
    'Bah-gum' – who would have thought that?
He couldn't have known it then, but Fred came from a long line of Copes. And all his life he would fulfil the Cope motto:

Always be ready – be present with your mind

THE SURNAME COPE

The name COPE is of early medieval English origin derived from the Old English word CAPE as in the cape that you may wear.

During the Middle Ages, people were unable to read or write and there were no numbered houses, so signs were needed for identification. When men went into battle, heavily armed, they were difficult to recognise. It became the custom for them to decorate their helmets with distinctive crests – the forerunner of coat-of-arms – which accompanied the development of surnames. Of the numerous Cope coat-of-arms, at least one bears this family motto:

Aequo adeste animo

*Always be ready
Be present with your mind*

Early Years

The 1891 census records the Cope family as living at 17 Johnston Street, behind St Andrew's Church, Wakefield (in the background of this picture). Most houses have long since been replaced by a pleasant park accessed via Back Peterson Road.

The first home Fred remembered was at 94 Stanley Road, in the Municipal Borough of Northgate – a tiny back-to-back house near to the junction with Greenhill Road (approximate location indicated on the map section of 1914 as held in the Local Studies Library in Wakefield).

Fred lived with his father, John Henry Cope, employed in the confectionary business, his mother Martha Cope and brother John Henry (Harry) who was some four years older than him. That house has long since been demolished along with many other back-to-backs.

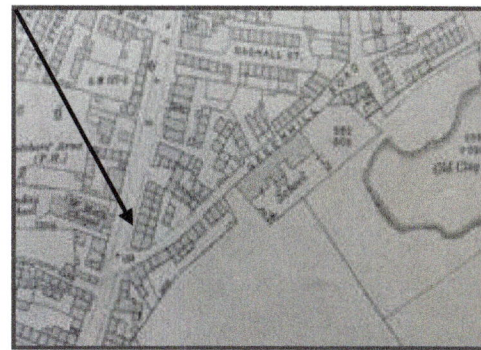

As photographed in 2013, the Albion Inn stands on the 94 Stanley Road site. At the end of the nineteenth century, more than 10% of the population was very poor and many lived in back-to-back housing. It seems that the Copes fell into this category.

> **BACK-TO-BACK TERRACED HOUSES**
>
> Back-to-backs often share a rear wall. Numerous back-to-back houses, two or three storeys high, were built in English cities for working class people during the 19th century. These high density houses were generally of low quality, some having only two rooms, one on each floor. They were notoriously ill-lit and poorly ventilated and sanitation was of a low standard.

My father, Fred, seldom spoke of his early days but it was clear he was very fond of his dad. When Fred was nearly six years old, his father, then 33, fell ill with pneumonia. Fred recalled his London uncle, Samuel Cope, coming to visit, and the sad and shocking day when he told them that John Henry, their father, had died (21 April, 1896). This came as a terrible shock to the boy Fred.

After his father died, it was Fred's job to help his mother around their home. One of his jobs was cleaning out the grate and fetching the coal in the early mornings before going to school. School was never a problem for Fred. He had a sharp and enquiring mind and soaked up information like a sponge.

In those days, infant mortality was high. Alice Robbins Cope, Fred's little sister, born in 1891, lived for only one year. Clifford, Fred's half brother, died at three. Of Martha's four children, only Harry and Fred survived into adulthood.

Yorkshire, the largest of the English counties, was fundamental in shaping Fred.

A Brief History of Yorkshire

Yorkshire has a long and colourful history. It was first occupied around 8000BC following the retreat of the Ice Age. During the first 1000 years AD, it was successively occupied by the Romans, Angles and Vikings. Many words in the Yorkshire dialect have their origin in old Norsk, the language of the Vikings. The name *Yorkshire* dates to 1065. The county was originally made up of three Ridings – West, North and East. The term *Riding*, meaning a third part, is a term loaned from Old Norsk.

The period from about 1066 until around the 1500s was particularly violent and bloody. The Wars of the Roses, a series of wars over the throne of England, fought between supporters of the houses of Lancaster (Red Rose) and York (White Rose) are of note – the Lancastrian claimant, Henry Tudor, was victorious and marked the start of the Tudor dynasty.

Within the Yorkshire borders are vast stretches of unspoiled countryside in the Yorkshire Dales and North York Moors. These are considered to be among the greenest in England. Yorkshire has sometimes been nicknamed *God's Own County* and is the largest of the English counties.

In the 16th century, as Yorkshire towns recovered from the wars, the wool industry flourished in cities like Leeds, Wakefield and Halifax. Sheffield became famous for its cutlery. In 1780, William Wilberforce, Member of Parliament for Hull, and later for Yorkshire, was influential in the abolition of the slave trade and slavery itself in the British Empire.

By 1832, conditions in industrial towns were dirty, unsanitary and overcrowded with resultant outbreaks of cholera. The late 19th century saw improvements, but by the 1920s and 1930s things were difficult. Coal and textile industries declined, resulting in mass unemployment. On the other hand, local authorities started demolishing the worst slums and the first council houses were built.

In 1974, Local Government reforms re-partitioned Yorkshire into North, West and East Yorkshire. Traditionalists still use the name *Ridings*.

Wakefield in Fred's Day

In 1888, two years before Fred was born, Wakefield became the county headquarters and administrative centre of the West Riding County Council, with city status being granted the same year. It is located on the eastern edge of the Pennines, south-east of Leeds, and on the banks of the lower Calder River. Wakefield is at the junction of major north-south routes to Sheffield, Leeds and Doncaster and west-east routes to Huddersfield and Pontefract. In the Middle Ages, it was dubbed the "Merrie City".

From the fourteenth century, Wakefield was a prosperous town and by the start of 1800 an established market town trading in wool and grain. Its rich reserves of coal underpinned the local economy. Many of the buildings built in the 19th century have stood the test of time such as the Court House (1810), County Hall (1880) and Wakefield Library on Drury Lane (1906).

Electricity

Electricity gradually replaced the use of coal in homes. The smut and grime disappeared but not the Wakefield enterprising spirit, camaraderie, individuality, energy. These characteristics were embedded in Fred.

Although electricity had been studied for centuries, it was only in the late nineteenth century that it was applied to industrial and residential use, thus transforming society. It gave people more time to enjoy life as it cut down on the amount of work they had to do. Household appliances made work easier, while electric lights enabled people to stay up longer in the evenings.

Early on, electricity and its applications captured Fred's imagination, enthusiasm and direction.

St Andrew's Church, Wakefield

St Andrew's played a significant part in the lives of the Cope family. Fred's mother, Martha, married John Henry Cope in 1885 at Chorlton near Manchester. He died at the age of 33. On 21 April, 1896, she was remarried at St Andrew's to William Parkinson, 28. Their son, Clifford Cope Parkinson, born on 11th March 1900, and was baptised at St Andrew's on Easter Sunday, 15th April 1900. Fred's baptism followed on 1st June 1900.

Years later, Frederick Bolland (Dick) Cope, Fred's nephew, was living nearby with his father, Harry, and mother. He too was baptised at St Andrew's.
For some years Fred was a choir boy, though as an adult the church no longer played a part in his life.

In an effort to discover more of Fred's early years, we visited St Andrew's in October 2013 and found it with the bell tower under re-construction. This symbolised Fred's life – always under construction!

In keeping with the needs of the times, the church has been modernised. True to the noticeboard we found a warm welcome in the Coffee Shop. The vicar, Dawn Ingham, was serving teas. On learning of my mission – to research for my father's biography – she took us on a tour of the church

The rigid pews have been replaced by comfortable, modern chairs enabling a variety of uses of the space. The vicar lives in Johnston Street, the street where Fred's parents started their married life.

The interior of the church is divided into two. High up on the dividing wall, looking similar to stained glass windows, are colourful batiks representing the four seasons, designed by a parishioner and mounted during 2008.

Not much was gleaned about Fred's years at St Andrew's (now St Andrew and St Mary). Fred would have approved of the positive way in which that church has, in our ever-changing world, adapted according to the needs of the local people. He was never one for standing still and clinging to the past.

By the time Fred was twenty, he was a qualified electrical engineer. At that stage he was living with his mother, step-father and household servant, Polly Kendall, from Lincolnshire at 198 Bentinck Villas, Stanley Road, Wakefield. This house is still there. It is not far from their old address but is a more substantial property, indicating their increased prosperity. It was those years that set a solid foundation for the rest of his life. He always embraced change and seized new opportunities.

It seems Fred learnt early on that:

The secret of change is to focus all of your energy, not on fighting the old, but on building the new.
Socrates

Technical Education – Leeds University

It was time to explore the Redbrick University. What a vast and interesting campus: a mix of ancient and modern; traditional and leading edge. Today it is amongst the world's 100 best universities with around 33,600 students. Founded in 1904, its origins go back to 1831 when the Leeds Medical School was established. Then in 1874, as the wool and textile industries competed with Europe, the Yorkshire College of Science came into being.

Of special interest are the old buildings of The Cloth Workers' Court. I suspect this was an area that stimulated Fred's interest in textiles, which were to play a role in his life wherever he went.

Fred's CV

At the start of his 'third life', when seeking a new job in South Africa, Fred prepared, on his old portable type writer, his *Outline of Experience* (CV in today's terms) covering his work in England and China. His time at Leeds University receives prominent mention as in the extract below.

```
BACKGROUND.    Technical education -- Leeds University.
               Training -- under W.B. Woodhouse Esqr.,(Engineer
               and Managing Director of The Yorkshire Electric
Power Company; a member of the Council, and a past President of
the Institution of Electrical Engineers.)
```

The history of Leeds University is rich and diverse.

Adjoining the Campus is St George's Fields. Today this cemetery is a tree-lined park with the headstones gathered together and laid flat or placed standing in groups beneath the trees.

In its early years, the Medical School was an overcrowded parish church graveyard.

Body snatching for the supply of cadavers for students to dissect was the order of the day. But by the 1830s, the state of the cemetery, and the body snatching, so displeased the Leeds elite that Leeds General Cemetery Company was formed. Shares at £25 were sold. The resulting private cemetery is where numerous Leeds folk of note are buried.

Most of the old buildings (some pictured here) would have been in use in Fred's student days.

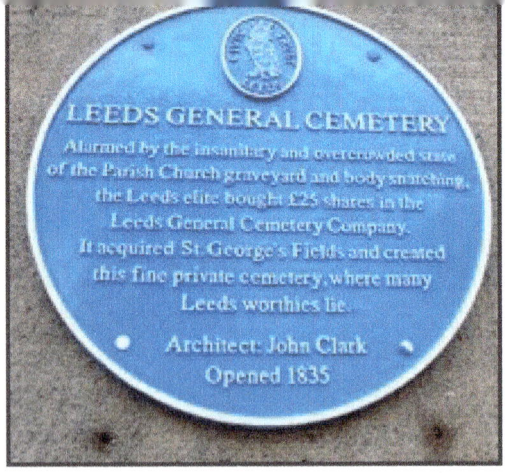

Electrical Training

Fred studied at Leeds part-time under Mr W. B. Woodhouse, Engineer and Managing Director of the Yorkshire Electric Power Company. Woodhouse was Fred's role model – a man of integrity, vision and national influence and a leading authority on electricity.

Woodhouse was president of the Institute of Electrical Engineers in 1923 and 1924 and a president of the Arthington Horticultural show. His articles published in the journal of Electrical Engineers include *Electrical Growth in 1907* and *Notes on Overhead Line Construction*. The Yorkshire Post and Leeds Mercury reported on his Memorial Service, held on 5 April 1940. A vast number attended including many throughout the country. It was said:

Many men are expert and efficient, but it is only the few to whom it is given to be pioneers and leaders. Woodhouse was a man who possessed imagination, foresight and courage to a very high degree ... He was a quiet, kindly, humane man who served on the Council of Bramhope Church, Leeds, and that of Leeds University.

Throughout Fred's life he often referred to Woodhouse with admiration and gratitude. In 1910, Woodhouse took Fred on for a year's probation as a Junior Assistant Engineer. The agreement was signed by Fred and his step-father, William Parkinson. A year later, on 17 February 1911, W. B. Woodhouse showed his satisfaction with Fred's work.

> THIS IS TO CERTIFY that Frederick Cope has completed his period of service with the Company under this Agreement and has during that time carried out his work to the full satisfaction of the Company.
>
> 17/2/11.   *WBWoodhouse*
>   Resident Engineer.

Fred's expertise in electricity was to prove vital. For instance, in his years in China, his in-depth knowledge of electricity and the workings of industry enabled him to survive in a dire situation but also to provide for hundreds of others. Meanwhile, at that point, along with thousands of others in Britain and the world, there came a major disruption to Fred's career path.

A Reflection on WW1

During 2014, the hundredth anniversary of the start of 'The Great War' was widely commemorated with men and women honoured for their bravery and dedication, generals for their strategy. In a refreshing article (The Guardian, Monday 28th July 2014), Adam Hochschild hailed the peacemakers – those who had worked to prevent that war. He wrote:

> *No one intended to create what Winston Churchill would later call a "crippled, broken world"... More than 9 million troops were killed and as many as 10 million civilians ... Millions of people became homeless refugees. Some 21 million soldiers were wounded ... Before he died, Harry Patch, Britain's last surviving veteran said this: 'It was not worth even one life.'*

Hochschild goes on to question why there are no plaques to commemorate these peacemakers. Why?

THE GREAT WAR 1914-1918: FRED'S INVOLVEMENT

WW1 Soldier Winchester

The wars of peoples will be more terrible than those of kings.
Winston Churchill 1901

Only on rare occasions did Fred speak about his experiences in World War One in the military. However, in his *Outline of Experience* (extract at the bottom of the page) he refers to his involvement in WW1.

Military Service

When war broke out on 28 July 1914, Fred was an ambitious young man of 24 working as assistant to W. B. Woodhouse who, during the war years, was an advisor to the Ministry of Munitions and to the Admiralty. The work was of national importance. It covered power problems in connection with shell and filling factories, and was of Top Secret Priority One classification.

WAR PRODUCTION AND NATIONAL SERVICE.   When not on military service in the last War, the writer was an assistant to W.B. Woodhouse who, as an adviser to the Ministry of Munitions and to the Admiralty, supervised in his district the speeding up policy of work of national importance, work of Priority One classification.   This experience covered power problems in connection with National shell, and filling factories.
For a period the writer was posted to Armstrong Whitworth's Barlow Airship factory where R.33 was under construction.
Later, engaged on statistics and reports.
Deputed to travel and explain the working of the Heat, Light, and Fuel Control Order to the various Urban and Rural Councils in Yorkshire.
Afterwards, continued with electrical distribution.

Some time in the early part of WWI, Fred became part of the war machine. He spoke infrequently about war. Conversations were brief, always ending abruptly with the line:

In war, horrendous things are done.

Fred's mood would then darken and he was best left alone.

I recall Fred saying he was on the Western Front, in and out of those ghastly trenches. He'd witnessed the death of friends and scores of others randomly killed.

At some point Fred was wounded – shot in his lower left arm and wrist. Although in agony at the time of this gunshot, he was determined to recover. That incident sent him home to recuperate, ended his military career, and as a consequence of his injury he had life-long limited use of his left hand. In compensation, he was granted a small war veteran's pension for life. Years later, during his 'third-life', I recall his indignant, yet humorous, outburst on the occasion a letter arrived, from the Pensions Office in London, informing him of a reduction of his pension:

It's a mean test, not a means test.

All in all, Fred was grateful that he was able to leave frontline warfare behind him: the trenches, the stenches, the rats, the lice, the plagues, the patrols, the tensions, the boredom, the senseless daily deaths and the barbed wire surrounds.

He was alive!

Fred was keen to get back to work.

Beyond what he wrote in his *Outline of Experience*, Fred left no details as to when and where he served, his rank, regiment and the duration of his WW1 involvement. To date, extensive research into Fred's military service history has not borne fruit. Whilst there is a possibility of finding these details at some time in the future as more records are put online, at this juncture I assume that Frederick Cope's records held in the British Army Service Records 1914-1920, were amongst the 'Burnt Documents' destroyed when a German incendiary bomb that landed on the War Office Record Store in Arnside Street, London, during an air raid in September 1940. The fire destroyed two thirds of the 6.5 million records (WO 363).

The Chelsea Pension Records (WO 364) were held elsewhere and escaped the Arnside Street bombing, but the surviving WW1 Ministry of Pensions (PIN series) files now hold only 22,000 records out of some 3 million they once contained. Over the years, the Government has weeded out those it did not need to keep. Surviving records are accessible through Findmypast.com but there seems to be no trace of a Frederick Cope born in Wakefield in 1890.

Armstrong Whitworth's at Barlow

Fred's time at Barlow was challenging. His efforts ensuring a steady power supply for the factory where the R33 Airship was to be built seemed to him to be of far greater significance than trench warfare.

Armstrong Whitworth had the contract to build the R33. This operation, in the West Riding of Yorkshire (now in North Yorkshire), is 3 miles south-east from the Selby railway station.

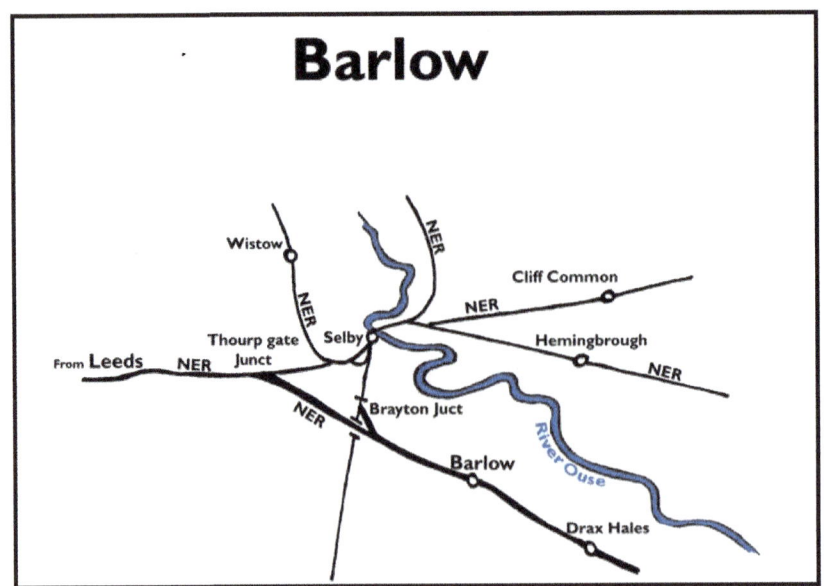

Barlow is a small rural village, currently a dormitory village for Selby, York and Leeds commuters. The R33 factory site later became a munitions depot. The land on which both of these were sited now lies under the ash tip of the nearby Drax power station. Until 1964, Barlow had a railway station on the Selby to Goole branch.

Barlow Railway Station – 23 April 1961

The R33 Class of British Airship

The R33, a WWI patrol airship, hides interesting stories.

From 1916, this rigid airship was planned, built and tested for the Royal Naval Air Service at Barlow – the first of this design. From 1918, it was used by the Royal Air Force.

The British landed a stroke of luck on the night of 23rd/24th September 1916 when a German airship, the Zeppelin L-33, was damaged by anti-aircraft fire, intercepted and brought down at Great Wigborough, Essex with hardly any damage to the airship. It was embedded in the latest German technology. Over the next five months, a top-secret record was made of every feature. The British designers, still at the planning stage, were able to modernise their design based on these findings. The construction of the ship began in the summer of 1918.

The R33 was in service for ten years. Amongst its many adventures was its survival of a horrifying incident when ripped from its mooring mast in a gale.

In July 1919, the R33 carried out endurance flights over the main cities of the Midlands and the North of England – Sheffield, Bradford, Manchester, Liverpool, North Wales, the Isle of Man, and the Irish coast. In May 1920, the R33 flew over the peace procession in London, towing an enormous banner advertising Victory Bonds. A band on board played over the cities from the upper gun platform. Finally, during 1928, the R33 was dismantled.

> **EARLY EXPERIENCE.** After qualifying in Electrical Power Generation and Distribution, the writer held various positions as an assistant engineer on The Yorkshire Electric Power Co., which is a statutory Company, distributing electricity over an area of over 2000 square miles.
> One of these positions was particular experience insomuch as it conducted a series of special investigations into the working of a large variety of industries. The investigations were undertaken for the purpose of ascertaining efficiency methods, and methods for increasing the rate of production. The industries comprised small Power Stations and Tramways; Worsted, Woollen, Cotton, and Silk Mills in their spinning, doubling, weaving, knitting, and dyeing sections of the Textile Industry; Collieries; heavy and light Engineering works, Chemical, Glass blowing, and Fertiliser factories; Flour mills; Electrical furnaces etc.
> The work in most instances required a close study of the raw materials and the processes involved.

QUALIFICATIONS AND EXPERIENCE

Once Fred had recovered from his war wounds and the traumas of war, he resumed his studies while employed by the Yorkshire Electric Power Company. He was a motivated and hard worker. In 1918 he qualified in Electrical Power Generation and was accepted as a graduate member of the Institute of Electrical Engineers (IEE) with his business address as Southgate Chambers, Wakefield.

In 1920 Fred was accepted as an Associate Member of the IEE and could then add the letters A.M.I.E.E. after his name. Years later, when living in China, Fred used the IEE London address as his British contact point.

```
TELEPHONE : 24298
P. O. BOX 366

Frederick Cope   A.M.I.E.E. M.A. MIN. E.E.
                 CHARTERED ELECTRICAL ENGINEER
    CONSULTANT.

  8th Floor,
Pedder Building,      EFFICIENCY ENGINEERING.
  Hong Kong.          INDUSTRIAL ECONOMICS.
```

```
Present Address.
    c/o. The Institution of Electrical Engineers.
        Savoy Place, Victoria Embankment,
                    London, W.C. 2.
```

IEE (pronounced I-double-E or I-E-E) was a British professional organisation founded in 1871, originally known as the Society of Telegraph Engineers. Since then it has had several mergers and name changes. In 1889 it became the Institution of Electrical Engineers and in 1921 received its charter. From then on Fred used the title, Chartered Electrical Engineer. Membership and Associate membership of the IEE is documented in the bound volumes. Fred's name appears as an Associate Member, with his address as Southgate Chambers, Wakefield, in the lists of 1919, 1921, 1923, 1925 and 1927. He later appears at this address: Box 366, Hong Kong, China in lists of 1930, 1933, 1935, 1937, 1939, 1946, and 1948. His name does not appear in later lists. From 1942, he lived in South Africa and after some years he let his membership lapse.

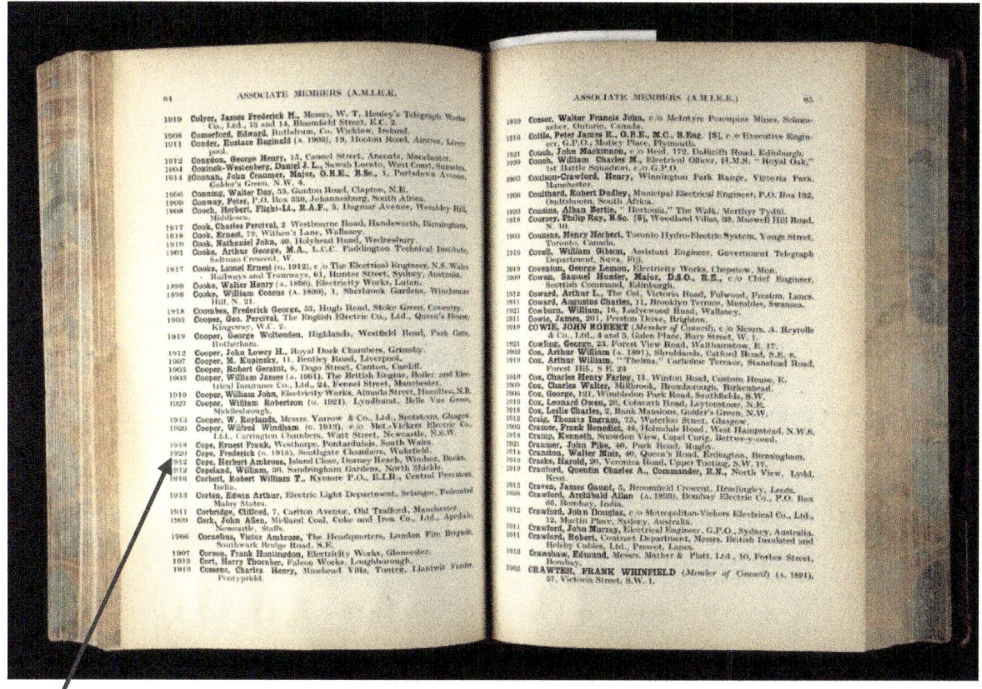

Frederick Cope's entry in Journal of Electrical Engineers Yearbook 1920

27

Assistant Engineer

Once he had qualified in Electrical Power Generation, Fred became the assistant engineer for the Yorkshire Electric Power Company. The scope of the job was wide ranging and challenging. It involved distributing electricity in an area of over 2000 square miles.

Fred revelled in investigating the new and improving on the old where possible. He assessed and promoted efficiency operations in a whole range of industries in order to increase production. These included: small power stations; tramways; textiles (worsted, woollen, cotton and silk mills in spinning, weaving, knitting and dying); collieries; heavy and light engineering works; chemical plants; glass blowing; fertiliser factories; flour mills and electrical furnaces.

Departmental Head

In 1918, Fred became a Departmental Head in the Yorkshire Electric Power Company. This involved him in varied work in and around Yorkshire's industrial towns such as Port of Goole, Castleford, Ossett, Selby, Otley, Sowerby Bridge and Bingley.

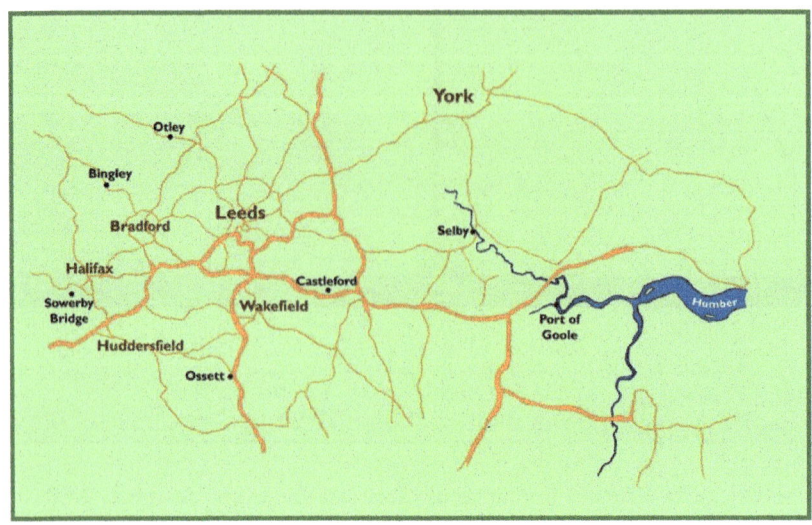

ELECTRIC SUPPLY MANAGEMENT. As a departmental head of The Yorkshire Electric Power Co., the writer's experience covered the development and management of a number of electrical undertakings in Yorkshire. These undertakings were operated under Provisional Orders of the Electric Lighting Acts and comprised such industrial towns as the port of Goole, Castleford, Ossett, Selby, Otley, Sowerby Bridge, Bingley etc.

Getting to grips with the nature of the raw materials and the processes involved was right up Fred's street.

But times were tough. Those were days of strict rationing, not only of food but with all utilities, energy resources included. These were monitored under strict controls.

Fred was commissioned to explain to Urban and Rural Councils throughout Yorkshire the workings of The Control Order for Heat, Light and Fuel.

Once that job was completed, Fred returned to his work on electrical distribution.

The Coal Board, Board of Trade, displayed notices similar to:

SAVE ELECTRICITY AND GAS
Thus
SAVE COAL

In the national interests
the coal controller desires
to point out that
every light must be turned off
when not actually required.
...
HELP TO SAVE COAL

British Coal is the
KEY TO VICTORY

From the story thus far, one might conclude that Fred was a dull and boring workaholic. Oh no! He knew the meaning of all work and no play makes Jack a dull boy. He was a lad with a passion for exploring the countryside with his pals.

Around 1918, Fred moved into lodgings near to Aberford Road, a more rural environment.

Aberford Road area - 2013

Bonzo, the Bus and the Butcher

Fred was an animal lover – especially dogs. With countryside on his doorstep, he decided it was time to acquire his very own dog – a pure white, highly intelligent and trainable bull terrier. The puppy arrived. Fred named him Bonzo.

Training began in earnest on day one. Fred and Bonzo became firm friends and during the evenings and weekends long exploratory walks were the norm.

In fact, Fred was so fond of Bonzo that many years later, in South Africa, he managed to find, buy and train his second Bonzo – as in this photograph.

Fred trained his dog well. Bonzo was intelligent, obedient and full of tricks, which Fred delighted in demonstrating to his pals for their amusement.

Fred's South African Bonzo – about 1952

Whenever he went by bus to the butcher, Bonzo accompanied him. There, of his own accord, as he waited outside for Fred, Bonzo would, when he spotted a customer, dance on his hind legs then sit up in begging position with a hungry appealing look on his face cocking first one ear and then the other. If he did not secure a titbit that way, he would wink! This performance won him many friends and their generosity was always rewarded by a vigorously wagging tail. Bonzo developed new tricks of his own.

One day, when Fred was out all day, a bored Bonzo escaped from the house and headed straight for the bus stop. As the door opened, he boarded the bus with a confident leap. The astonished driver, not finding Fred with his dog, tried to coax Bonzo off the bus to no avail. Bonzo settled down next to the driver where he could see out of the door. As the bus came to the butcher's stop, he leapt off and took up his usual place near the butcher's door. He performed for the shoppers until he'd had his fill of meat.

Satisfied, he headed back to the bus stop for his return journey home.

Fred was surprised to find him asleep on the door step and wondered why Bonzo wouldn't eat his dinner!

This bus trip to the butcher became Bonzo's habit. Eventually, Fred pieced the facts together. The accounts of the butcher and his customers, the bus drivers, and passengers on the bus painted the story.

An Aberford Road bus stop - 2013

The locals grew fond of Bonzo. Fred's meat bills diminished.

Countryside, Traditions and History

From early on, Fred explored his county, Wakefield on the West Riding, a county of breathtaking contrasts. The grim disorder of Victorian towns with areas of dirt and ugliness was offset by magnificent natural beauty and grandeur. On countryside ventures, Fred was usually accompanied by Bonzo.

Waterways

Fred was captivated by the waterway systems – the rivers and the navigations built initially to ship coal. Commercial shipping continued until 1986. Today, as well as commercial traffic, some routes are used for leisure pursuits. In 2013, Stephen and I set out to follow some of Fred's exploring footsteps.

Wakefield lies in the proximity of the River Calder and the Aire and Calder Navigation – a complex meandering of rivers and canal systems. By 1704 the Calder, with its numerous locks, was navigable as far as Wakefield. Steam tugs were introduced in 1831.

Stanley Ferry

This was one of Fred's favourite local spots. He spoke of the marvels of the navigation systems – the engineering aspects and resulting trade. This aqueduct, built between 1836 and 1839, takes the Aire and Calder navigation over the river Calder.

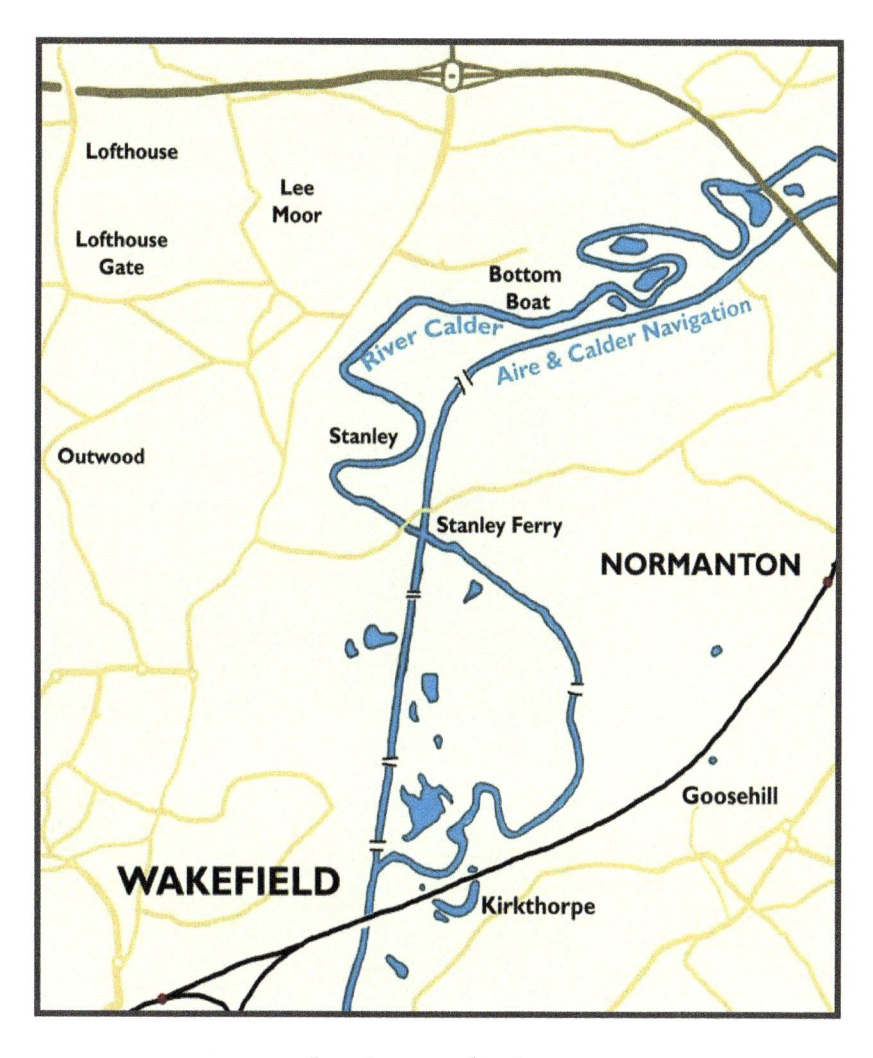

*Location map showing
waterways on Wakefield's doorstep
and places associated with Fred whilst living in
Yorkshire*

Stanley Ferry provided us with a taste of Yorkshire humour.

What's in a word?

Meanings of **Audacity** include: daring, boldness, courage, bravery, nerve, cheek and over-confidence. In my book all these meanings are in keeping with aspects of Fred's character.

Tyke
In the Yorkshire dialect, Tyke is a nickname for a Yorkshireman. It originates from the Viking word for dog – tika – and gives rise to the expression:
   Yer mucky little tyke – an expression often used by Fred in his South African days.

36

Ilkley Moor

This moorland, one of Fred's favourite places, lies between Ilkley and Keighley in the West Riding of Yorkshire (W. Yorkshire). It is a site of Special Scientific Interest as a habitat for ground-nesting birds. Ilkley Moor is perhaps best known for the humorous song, On Ilkla Moor Baht 'at' – a dialect song sung for generations and originating sometime after 1850 (Arnold Kellett). It has become Yorkshire's county anthem. I learnt the lyrics from my farmer father during his 'third life'. He loved to make me squirm as he sang the verses about the worms and the ducks which could some day eat 'me' up!

On Ilkla Mooar baht 'at

Lyrics in Yorkshire dialect	Words in Standard English
Wheear 'ast tha bin sin' ah saw thee, ah saw thee? On Ilkla Mooar baht 'at Wheear 'ast tha bin sin' ah saw thee, ah saw thee? Wheear 'ast tha bin sin' ah saw thee? On Ilkla Mooar baht 'at On Ilkla Mooar baht 'at On Ilkla Mooar baht 'at	Where have you been since I saw you, I saw you? On Ilkley Moor without a hat Where have you been since I saw you, I saw you? Where have you been since I saw you? On Ilkley Moor without a hat On Ilkley Moor without a hat On Ilkley Moor without a hat
Tha's been a cooartin' Mary Jane Tha's bahn' to catch thy deeath o' cowd Then us'll ha' to bury thee	You've been courting Mary Jane You're bound to catch your death of cold Then we will have to bury you
Then t'worms'll come an' eyt thee up	Then the worms will come and eat you up
Then t'ducks'll come an' eyt up t'worms	Then the ducks will come and eat up worms
Then us'll go an' eyt up t'ducks	Then we will go and eat up ducks
Then us'll all ha' etten thee	Then we will all have eaten you
That's wheear we get us ooan back	That's where we get our own back

Yorkshire Pudding

Yorkshire folks' 'earts are like their puddings:
crisp outside, but soft within.

While on the subject of Yorkshire traditions, I must mention Fred's love of Yorkshire pudding, which no one could make as good as his mother! In Fred's 'third life', when we were having Sunday dinner, he would quote an old Yorkshire favourite:

Thems that eat most Yorkshire pudding gets most meat!

He'd go on to say:

When I was a child we were hard up. Meat was scarce. I failed to appreciate that if I ate lots of Yorkshire pudding I'd have little room for meat. The economics of Yorkshire!

In South Africa on Sundays, Dad would say a Yorkshire grace:

God bless us all, and make us able

Yorkshire Pudding

As far as I can trace, the exact origin of Yorkshire pudding is not known. A recipe appeared in 1737 in the book: *The Whole Duty of a Woman*. A decade later *Hanna Glasse*, one of the most famous food writers of the time, included Yorkshire pudding in her cookery book:
The Art of Cookery Made Plain and Easy
This popular book spread the word on Yorkshire pudding which became a Standard English addition to a dish served with roast meat, vegetables and gravy. Crispy on the outside and custardy on the inside, Yorkshire pudding has become widely popular. Originally made in an oblong dish and cut into squares, today it is often made in patty-tins with this result.

Ta eat all t' stuff 'at's on this table!

Regret

In spite of my best efforts in trying to locate photographs of my father in his youth, I have drawn a blank.

This photograph of Fred in the late 1950s at Rosedale, his farm in South Africa near the village of Van Reenen, reveals his typical farmer's attire: a cap and bow-tie!

Fred wore an 'at' when there was the slightest chill in the air. In South Africa, years later, he wore a traditional flat cap, the kind that is still made and sold today.

The African farm workers gave him the nickname 'bow-tie'.

North Riding Coast

Whitby Harbour

Fred got to know the North Riding Coast well after his mother and step-father moved to Scarborough. His visits to her were often by train as far as Whitby. There, on the quayside, he would indulge in the best fish and chips in the world (as he delighted in telling me years later!).

Fred would then board a coastal train from Whitby to Scarborough. The line, opened in 1885, was dismantled in 1968. Today, the Scarborough to Whitby Rail Trail (or 'Cinder Track' as it is sometimes known) is a bridleway for horses, cyclists and walkers.

Whitby

Earliest records show Whitby as a permanent settlement in 656 AD.

This historic seaside town on the east coast of the North Riding (North Yorkshire) is situated at the mouth of the River Esk. It has a long maritime, fishing and tourism heritage enhanced by the arrival of the railway in 1839, which all contribute towards the current local economy.

Caedmon, the earliest recognised English poet, lived in what are now the ruins of Whitby Abbey.

In 1078 the settlement gained the name Whitby derived from "white settlement" in Old Norse.

The port was developed in the 18th century and became a centre for shipbuilding and whaling. Whitby 'Jet Jewellery' manufacture began in this period.

Whitby is linked to the rest of Yorkshire and NE England primarily through national rail and road links.

Scarborough
North Riding of Yorkshire (North Yorkshire)

In October 2013, we visited Scarborough in search of the house where Fred's mother and step-father had lived: Brynfield, Cross Lane, Scalby Mills. Fred stayed there on trips to England from China.

Finding Cross Lane was easy – north of central Scarborough, close to the golf course and the sea. But there we found no house with the name Brynfield.

In 1976 my parents travelled to England. It was Dad's first visit in almost 50 years and mother's very first visit. We'd driven to Scarborough and found Cross Lane. Dad was convinced that the house in the photograph was their old home. That visit unearthed long-buried memories like those of his mother who lived to 91.

Cross Lane in 2013

Happy days in Scarborough – Fred with his daughter – 1976

There he stood on 'his' Yorkshire Coast, drinking it all in. Often I heard him recite:

> *I must go down to the sea again,*
> *to the lonely sea and the sky;*
> *I left my shoes and socks there –*
> *I wonder if they're dry.*

Fred was overjoyed to be back in the land of his birth. So much had changed in 50 years. Progress and impressive improvements, yes! But not all was good. Often he would turn to poetry to express the way he felt:

> *England, with all thy faults,*
> *I love thee still.*
> *My country!*
> *Where English minds and manners may be found,*
> *Shall be constrain'd to love thee.*
> (William Cowper)

Exploring the historic sites like the castle was a must as was the fun of the entertainment for the crowds.

Of course Fred made sure that we ate fish and chips on the beach!

44

Anne Bronte's Grave – 1849

On our way up to the castle, we stumbled across 'Paradise'! A peep through the opening revealed an old graveyard. This was part of Dad's history. I recall in his farming days in South Africa, in the evenings, he and mother would read by gas light and paraffin lamps. The books included those of the Brontë sisters.

45

Scarborough – A Potted history

One thread of thought is that Scarborough was originally named Skarðaborg after a Viking raider, Thorgils Skarthiby, around 966. Evidence suggests earlier Stone Age and Bronze Age settlements.

During the Middle Ages, Scarborough Fair, a six-week trading festival, attracting merchants from all over Europe, was permitted in a royal charter of 1253. The fair was held annually for 500 years and is commemorated in the song, 'Scarborough Fair', with first lines:

Are you going to Scarborough Fair?
— parsley, sage, rosemary and thyme....
Remember me to the one who lives there,
For once she was a true love of mine.

In 1626, acidic water was discovered in a stream emerging from a cliff that ran to the south of the town. This gave birth to the Spa, making Scarborough Britain's first seaside resort. The first rolling bathing machines were on the sands by 1735.

In 1845, the opening of the Scarborough–York railway led to an increased flow of visitors. The same year, Scarborough's first hotel was opened – the name 'hotel' being derived from the word 'hostel'.
During the First World War, the town was bombarded by German warships.

In 1930, 'Lawrie' Mitchell–Henry caught on rod-and-line a tunny weighing 560 pounds (250 kg) marking the start of the Big-game tunny fishing off Scarborough.

In 2010, the town, as nominated by the Academy of Urbanism, won the 'Great Town Award' beating Chester and Cambridge.

Today, Scarborough has around 50,000 inhabitants – the largest holiday resort on the Yorkshire coast. The older part of the town lies around the Harbour protected by a rocky headland. As well as a long established fishing industry, the town has a growing digital and creative economy. Inhabitants are known as 'Scarborians'.

Donkey rides on the East Riding coast as popular as in Fred's day

CONSULTANT AND EFFICIENCY ENGINEER.	Experience in private Consulting in Wakefield, England. The experience here covered arbitrations, valuations of electric plants for legal transfer and similar purposes; advising on electric supply, also Company directors on new industrial undertakings and on extensions to old plants; efficiency work, mainly in the textile industries, which covered design of progressive layouts, efficient application of power, and specially arranged methods of manufacture
ORGANISATION AND MANAGEMENT.	During the same period the writer organised factories from the grass site to the working unit, complete with departmental systems, records, accounts etc. Ownership of industrial interests during this period, a period of ever changing economic and financial conditions, provided considerable experience in factory costing, general financial, industrial, and commercial factory management.

The Consultant

I have not established exactly when Fred moved on from his job with the Yorkshire Electricity Company. However, the experience he had gained had provided Fred with the skills and confidence to take the bold step of moving into the world of private consultancy. He set up office at 9 Southgate, Wakefield.

The original buildings have long since been demolished, rebuilt and/or modernised.

In that period of ever-changing, challenging, economic and financial circumstances, Fred provided industrial support and guidance on commercial factory development and management. His consultancy work included:

Arbitration – a process of resolving disputes outside the courtroom where parties agree to be bound by the arbitration decision, legally binding on both sides.

Valuation of electric plants for legal transfer – the estimate of the worth of the property / plant could include the market value, fair value, and intrinsic value.

Advising on electricity supply – this included purchasing of energy, its transportation, costs, determining the right load, etc.

Advising Company Directors on new industrial enterprises and extensions of old plants – providing a brief on responsibilities in new undertakings such as plant acquisition and maintenance, integration in the factory, health and safety aspects and so on.

Work efficiency (mainly in textile industries)

At that juncture Fred's interest was focused on textiles. He invested energy in learning about virtually every aspect of wool.

Venture into Manufacturing – Esmerene, a New wool

Fred wasn't one for settling into a hum-drum rut. His entrepreneurial spirit surfaced and with his experience and interests this led him to explore the possibility of entering the world of textile manufacture – wool and its products.

The Story of Wool – Most Valued Fabric in the World

Woolly skins of wild sheep were first used by primitive man to protect him from heat, cold, wind and rain. By 10000 BC he had domesticated sheep. Some Northern European tribes had spun and woven wool cloth even before this time.

British Wool

More than any other commodity produced in Britain, wool is central to its heritage. Since the Bronze Age, around 1900 BC, wool was woven into cloth. When the Romans invaded in 55 BC, the wool industry was well established. By the 8th century, Britain was exporting woollen fabrics to the Continent and by the 13th century, English cloth had gained an international reputation. At the end of the 15th century, England was mainly a nation of sheep farmers and cloth manufacturers. Through selective cross-breeding and blending wool with other fabrics, wool has been adapted to meet modern needs. Today there are almost 1000 million sheep in the world. 30 million are in the UK.

The West Riding Wool and Textile Industries

By 1770, the cloth conurbation of Yorkshire had taken shape – Leeds, Bradford, Halifax, Huddersfield and Wakefield. During the 18th and 19th centuries, the West Riding was in the forefront of textile and woollen manufacturing. For example, Leeds was a centre for manufacturing woollen cloth and the leading finishing centre and by the 20th century, Leeds led the world in this global trade.

Bradford became the world centre of woollen and worsted manufacture with the Wool Exchange having some 3000 dealers. This included local buyers and sellers with those from the Colonies and the Far East.

During the Industrial Revolution, Yorkshire textile factories introduced power looms. This met with strong opposition from those who feared for their jobs. The Luddites attacked mills, destroyed machinery and threatened manufacturers. The Government intervened with force to stop the unrest, executing some of the protesters. Watts's steam engines provided power for all mechanical processes, and women and girls were employed in the weaving process.

Wool must be sorted, cleaned, graded, seeds and burrs removed, and dyed before being made into cloth. Woven woollen cloth is made from short fibres while worsted uses longer fibres. Yarn used for knitting is single and continuous. No other material has all the qualities of wool.

Fred's *Outline of Experience* mentions his ownership of industrial interests in Yorkshire. Years later, in South Africa, not only did he speak of his 'woollen factory in Yorkshire', but he based a new venture there on his experiences in Yorkshire's textiles – more of that later. The year was 1919. Fred was 29 and living at Brynfield near Aberford Road, Stanley, in the vicinity of Wakefield. He'd had over ten years' experience in electricity and industry. Manufacturing and trade had picked up since the end of WW1. It was time to follow his textile interests.

Windhill Mill, Lofthouse – Woollen and Worsted Factory

According to records in the West Riding Registry of Deeds (Vol 14; page 979, number 354), it was on 19 March 1919 Frederick Cope signed an agreement to buy into Windhill Mill Company near to Lofthouse in the township of Stanley cum Wrenthorpe. The vendor, John Sharphouse, entered into a partnership retaining one part of the business, while Frederick Cope and Harold Moorhouse, for £1182 14s, bought the other part of over 12 acres. On the same day, Fred signed for a mortgage to cover this cost witnessed by solicitor W. H. Burton, Wakefield.

Fred was living his dream in a Yorkshire textile factory – the county's most important industry in an area ideal for sheep. Before long, he was experimenting with new types of yarn.

Photo (2013) of a poster in the Three Bags Full wool shop, The Piece Hall, Halifax

Life has a habit of dishing up the unexpected! On 20 April 1920, a little over a year after buying into Windhill Mill, John Sharphouse died. In his will, William Sharphouse and Oliver Sharphouse were named as the trustees and executers.

For Fred there was no turning back. Business was to continue as usual so on 19 October 1920 he re-registered Windhill Mill. Once again Frederick Cope and Harold Moorhouse were the borrowers. Fred's address was given as 9 Southgate, Wakefield. William Sharphouse and Oliver Sharphouse were the mortgagees.

Wool and Wool Products

The Piece Hall

Built in 1779 with 300 separate rooms, the Piece Hall was set around a courtyard. Built by Halifax merchants and manufacturers it was one of the largest Piece Halls in Yorkshire illustrating the vital importance of the wool trade before the industrialisation of the 1800s.

Originally designed for trading locally made "pieces" of cloth, it has, for over 230 years, been at the heart of the commercial, civic and cultural life of Halifax.

The Piece Hall tells the story of working class people in Georgian times – the enterprise, ambition and importance of the wool trade in this country and beyond. Although several other towns had cloth halls, the Piece Hall was most well-regarded. It is the only surviving cloth hall in Britain. In 1928 it was scheduled as an Ancient Monument and in 1954 as a Grade 1 Listed Building. It is currently undergoing major renovation and due to re-open in 2016.

A visit to the Three Bags Full wool shop paid off. There in a bin was a job lot of Bouclé wool which, according to the lady of the shop, was from a batch long concealed in an old factory.

54

Bouclé is created by combining two different types of yarn. The spindle feed rates of the yarns differ. The tension of one is looser than that of the other. The result is a yarn with a looped effect and used in knitting and textiles. The name Bouclé is derived from the French, boucler, which means 'to curl'. Today there are increasing numbers of varieties of Bouclé, which are widely used in knitting and crochet, homemade and fashion clothing.

But what, you may ask, is so significant about Bouclé? Why include it in this biography? Where and how did Bouclé originate? Who was the inventor of this 'loopy' yarn?

Fred's Invention – Esmerene Wool

Fred had long played around with the idea of creating a new type of yarn. Eventually, he experimented with combining wool with an artificial silk thread. One of the threads was spun with a looser tension than the other.

The resulting yarn with its looped effect was promising, innovative, and worth a trial run, he thought. So he introduced the model to the shop floor workers at Windhill Mill for a test run. The result was stunning.

But what should this new yarn be named? Quick thinking was required. He suggested that the names of two secretaries at Windhill Mill – Esme and Rene – be combined to form a new name for his invention: *Esmerene*. His idea was unanimously accepted, so Esmerene became the name.

Mass production followed and marketing Esmerene became priority. Windhill Mill opened an office in Regent Street in London to facilitate advertising and processing orders. As Esmerene became known, orders came in from local traders and firms abroad as far away as Australia. Several advertisements for Esmerene are recorded in Trove Digitised Newspapers (example below).

ADVERTISEMENT for ESMERENE
The Argos, Melbourne, Australia - Monday 2 March 1925

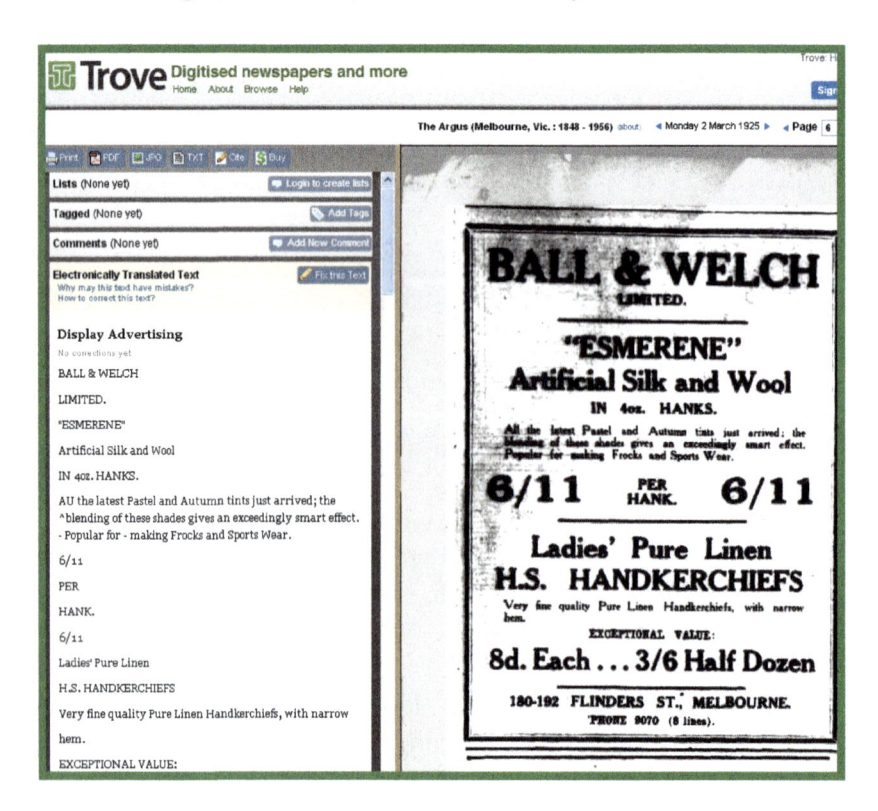

Ball & Welsh, a firm of drapers, was established in the 1850s on the Australian Gold Fields. Other stores opened later in several Australian cities. The Melbourne store was for a time the city's leading family draper. Ball & Welsh was bought out in 1970 and the stores closed in 1976 due to declining profits. In another Ball and Welsh advert, 18 March 1925, are these words:

> *Esmerene – Artificial Silk and Wool 6/11*
> *Splendid range of autumn rainbow shades blended*
> *together, gives a beautiful effect when knitted ...*

Reading this took me back to my childhood in South Africa. Baby clothes at that time were knitted in Bouclé (Esmerene) pastel shades. I loved the silvery thread and bumpy texture of the wool. I recall my father looking intently at a ball of Bouclé baby wool and telling me (and all who cared to listen) that this yarn was **his creation** – he'd invented it in Yorkshire many years before. Did anyone believe Fred – that talkative Yorkshireman trying his hand as a South African farmer? I suspect most thought he was spinning a yarn and certainly not one made of artificial silk and wool. I for one did believe him. After all, at his suggestion, my first name carries forward the name of that yarn: *Esmerene*.

Involvement with Freemasons and Rotary

Fred was a man who concerned himself not only with his own needs but also had a concern for others less fortunate. He was passionate about world affairs, a businessman and an ardent entrepreneur. It is not surprising therefore that he joined the Freemasons and Rotarians where, in the company of like-minded people, he was able to fulfil some of his concerns for society.

A Freemason

Minimum requirements for becoming a Freemason include that the candidate must be a mature adult, free, and considered to be of good character. Most Grand Lodges require the candidate to declare a belief in a Supreme Being and to be concerned with moral and spiritual values.

Around the time Fred bought into Windhill Mill he joined the Freemasons. The Grand Lodge Certificate, 14 October 1920, shows Frederick Cope was initiated into Chantry Lodge Wakefield, No. 4065. Years later, 18 December 1940, during the Japanese invasion of China, while resident in Canton, he joined Jubilee Chapter No. 2013, Hong Kong.

A Rotarian

Rotary is a non political and non sectarian organisation. Rotarians meet for companionship and service. Members are usually involved in business or the professions and are expected to follow the aims and objectives of Rotary in their everyday life. This includes providing service through fellowship; upholding high business ethics; promoting world understanding and goodwill and peace. The primary motto: Service above self. The secondary motto: One profits most who serves best.

In 1923 Fred joined the Rotary Club of Wakefield.

HARD TIMES

Affliction is a good man's shining time.
Edward Young

From 1850 to 1914, Yorkshire was prosperous and known as The Workshop of the World. With the outbreak of the First World War thousands of Yorkshire men volunteered for action. Soon, the war was claiming huge numbers of lives. In 1916, conscription was introduced. During the war, the economy was at full stretch with women and girls replacing the absent men in factories – making both textiles and bombs.

After the end of WWI, there was a short-lived post-war boom. However, English industry had lost its competitive edge due to international competition. Yorkshire's importance in the national economy declined. Hardship and bitterness were the order of the day in the coal mining areas. In 1921, the post-war boom collapsed. The West Riding output from the textile industries had diminished significantly due to the general fall in the worldwide trade. Along with hundreds of other small enterprises, Windhill Mill was in trouble.

The writing was on the wall, Fred observed. On 22 March 1921 Windhill Mill Company was re-mortgaged. Frederick Cope and Harold Moorhouse are listed on the schedule and Frederick Cope is named as one of the witnesses.

Voluntary Liquidation

Unfortunately, mortgaging did not get Windhill Mill off the hook. In spite of the success of products like Esmerene, by 1925 the owners, realising the extent of the diminishing returns, decided to go for voluntary liquidation.

> HM. Seal of the Windmill Co Ltd. John F.Crabtree & H.Moorhouse, Directors; C.Wilkinson, Secretary.
>
> Vol.26 page 963, number 391
>
> Windhill Mill Company Ltd Registered 24 Mar 1921 at 11.15 forenoon
>
> Indenture of Mortgage dated 22 Mar 1921 between Windhill Mill Company Ltd 9 Southgate of the one part & London Joint City & Midland Bank Ltd & regarding the Windhill Mill Company & all buildings listed on the schedule & Frederick Cope & Harold Moorhouse as before. Witnesses: John F Crabtree, Windhill Mill Co & C.Wilkinson, Frederick Cope. John Frederick Crabtree, Chairman of Directors.

So, as recorded in The London Gazette, 22 October 1925, at an extraordinary general meeting, the company concluded that it could no longer continue in business, and would seek to be wound up voluntarily.

On 10 November 1925 a meeting was held with creditors in the Metropole Hotel, Kings Street, Leeds. On 8 December 1926 notice was given that on 14 January 1927 the liquidator's report giving the terms of the liquidation would be delivered.

The London Gazette, 14 December 1926

> The Companies Acts, 1908 to 1917.
> The WINDHILL MILL COMPANY Limited.
> (In Voluntary Liquidation.)
>
> NOTICE is hereby given, that a General Meeting of the Members of the above named Company will be held at the offices of Charles L. Townend and Co., Incorporated Accountants, Permanent Chambers, Halifax, Yorks., on Friday, the fourteenth day of January, 1927, at eleven o'clock in the morning precisely, to receive the report of the Liquidator, showing how the winding-up of the Company has been conducted and its property disposed of, to hear any explanation that may be furnished by the Liquidator, and to pass an Extraordinary Resolution as to the disposal of the books, accounts and documents of the Company.—Dated this 8th day of December, 1926.
> (031)   CHARLES L. TOWNEND, Liquidator.

Esmerene: Fore-runner of Bouclé?

Fred's nephew, Dick Cope, remembered 'Fred's factory going bust'. He recalled that it was bought by a reputable firm, but which firm was that?

Every lead I have followed as a result of that conversation has drawn a blank. My Wakefield researcher has found nothing. Hours of sifting through the Internet have been just as fruitless. I have written to several contemporary firms who sell assorted Bouclé products, especially those who claim to have a 'history'. Most have not replied. When I have unearthed 'their history' it has, understandably, revealed only details of that firm's Bouclé brand,. I have not chanced upon anyone claiming to know the origin of Bouclé yet alone of Esmerene. So, unless at some point in the future history beams on a different light, I conclude that my father was right: Bouclé is Esmerene's successor.

Sights on China

The sun shines hot and if we use delay
Cold biting winds mars our hoped-for hay.
Shakespeare

For some years Fred had been aware of the declining British textile industry and indeed the decline of British industry generally. Yes, Esmerene was a success but the markets were waning. He saw that Windhill Mill had a limited lifespan. What was he to do? There was scant prospect for an entrepreneur in declining Britain.

Some colleagues had left England and rooted in China where opportunities were plentiful for people of experience. So when Fred received a letter from a contemporary working for a prosperous firm in China saying:

> *If you come to China and set up as an Independent Industrial Consultant, we will guarantee you enough work to get you on your feet.*

Snippets of Chinese History Floated through Fred's Head

Always interested in world affairs, he was aware of recent conditions in China and fascinated by its lengthy history. It is the country with the longest continuous civilisation in the world, a fact supported by archeological finds that show the civilisation dates back at least to 3,000 BC.

Fred was aware that modern-day China was no thornless rose. And that Britain, its history intermingled with that of China, was responsible for some shameful episodes involving opium trade and smuggling dating back to the early 1800s. The mid 1800s had seen Britain brutally bullying its way to secure trade with China. Also, Britain had been after lands and mines too.

For thousands of years China's rule was under dynasties. These were underpinned by the orderly Confucian philosophy. However, the twentieth century saw a major change evolving. For instance, in 1900, communities in the North spurred on by drought, famine and pitiful poverty no longer had faith in the state and rebelled with considerable violence – known as the Boxer uprising. Change was moving on apace.

Fred was aware of these dramatic changes and of leaders of influence like Sun Yat-sen, Chiang Kai-shek and Mao Zedong.

What will happen in China? he wondered.

Moving on from Yorkshire

Not one to shrink from a challenge, Fred decided to burn his Yorkshire boats. He booked a passage on a 'slow boat to China', the Malwa, a P&O Liner leaving London on 25 February 1927. Once the liquidation of Windhill Mill was finalised (14 January 1927), Fred wound up his affairs. He disposed of the effects in his Southgate Consultancy and private lodging. What he wanted to keep he moved to his mother's home in Scarborough. The hardest task of all was re-settling and parting from Bonzo. Of course, Bonzo was left in good hands.

Slow Boat to China

In no time at all, Fred was on his way to London to board the Malwa. It was an exhilarating, if not a daunting, prospect. He had done his homework on the liner.

MALWA

MALWA was launched on October 10th 1908 by Caird & Co, Greenock for the Peninsular & Oriental Steam Navigation Co (P&O Line). At 10,883 tons, 562ft long, with a 61.2ft beam; depth of 24.6ft, two impressive funnels and two masts she was a fine ship. Accommodation was for 407 in 1st class and 200 in 2nd class.

Malwa's history
January 29th 1909: Maiden voyage from Tilbury to Columbo, Melbourne and Sydney.
1910 in collision with the British steamer Nairn off Columbo
1917 requisitioned for use as a troopship.
September 24th 1920 she resumed passenger service
December 16th 1932 she was sold for breaking up in Japan.

Fred travelled 2nd class to Shanghai. On the route, he took the opportunity to explore the ports where Malwa docked: Southampton, Plymouth, Tangier, Gibraltar, Marseilles, Malta, Port Said, Aden, Bombay, Colombo, Penang, Singapore and Hong Kong. After Fred disembarked in Shanghai, Malwa sailed on to Yokohama and Kobe. On the passenger list, Fred's country of permanent residence is recorded as China – clearly he'd emigrated.

Fred was in his element. He had long wanted to travel and extend his knowledge of the world, its places, peoples, economics and politics. The freedom of sailing the seas and meeting new people was a good beginning. He had put behind him the Windhill Mill experience and was looking forward to a creative new start – but why in China?

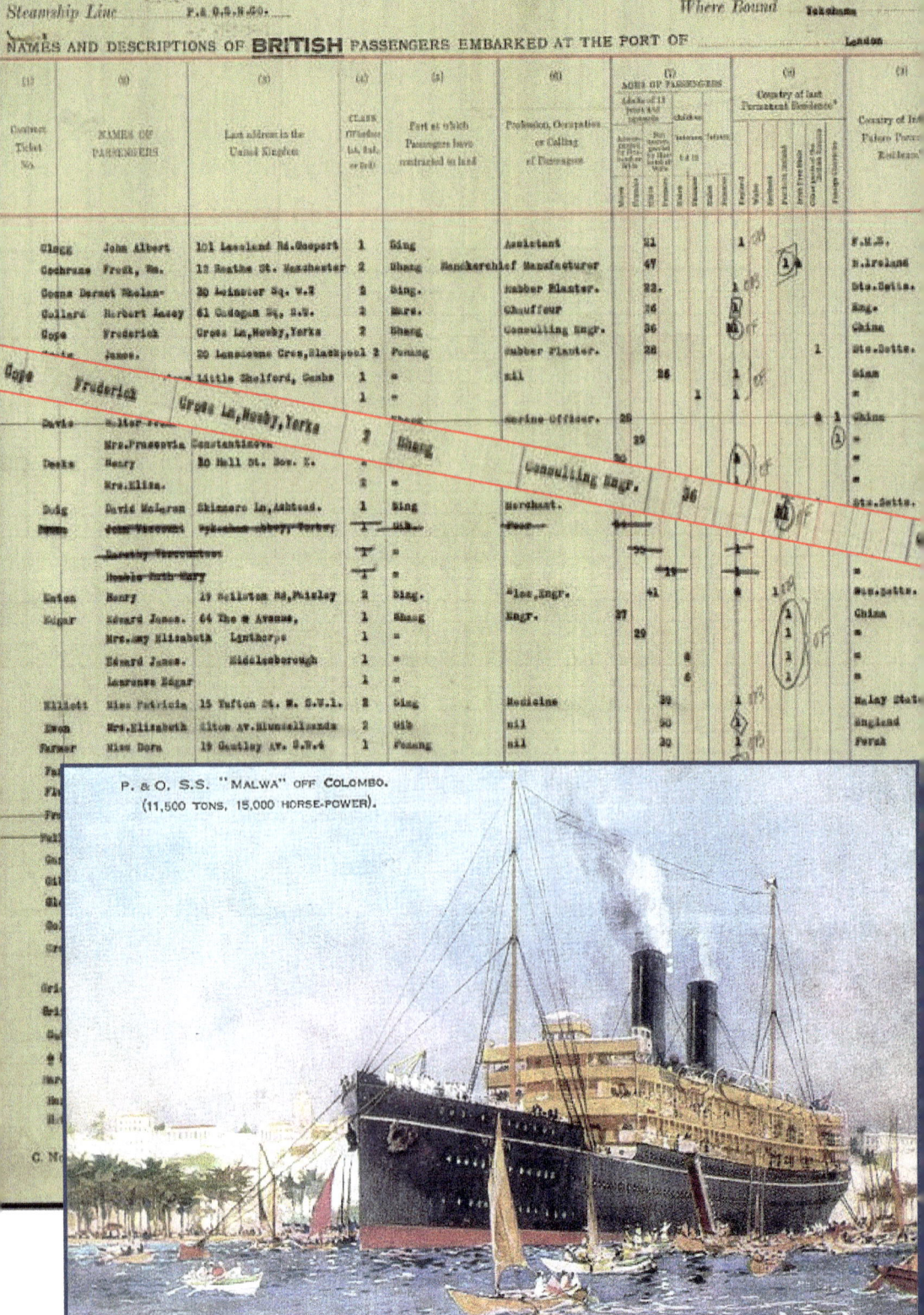

Name of Ship "MALWA" Date of Departure 25th Feb.1927 19
Steamship Line P.&O.S.N.Co. Where Bound Yokohama

NAMES AND DESCRIPTIONS OF BRITISH PASSENGERS EMBARKED AT THE PORT OF London

Contract Ticket No.	NAMES OF PASSENGERS	Last address in the United Kingdom	CLASS	Port at which Passengers have contracted to land	Profession, Occupation or Calling of Passengers	Ages			Country of last Permanent Residence	Country of Intended Future Permanent Residence
	Clegg John Albert	101 Leesland Rd.,Gosport	1	Sing	Assistant	21		1		F.M.S.
	Cochrane Fredk, Wm.	12 Heathe St. Manchester	2	Shang	Handkerchief Manufacturer	47			1	N.Ireland
	Coons Dermot Whelan-	30 Leinster Sq. W.2	1	Sing	Rubber Planter	32				Sts.Setts.
	Collard Herbert Lacey	61 Cadogan Sq. S.W.	1	Mrs.	Chauffeur	26				Eng.
	Cope Frederick	Cross Ln,Mossby,Yorks	2	Shang	Consulting Engr.	36				China
	~~Cain~~ James	20 Lansdowne Cres,Blackpool 2		Penang	Rubber Planter	28		1		Sts.Setts.
		Little Shelford, Cambs	1	"	nil		25	1		Siam
			1	"				1		"
	Davis Walter Fre-				Marine Officer	26			1	China
	Mrs.Prascovia Constantinovn		2	Shang		29			2	"
	Deeks Henry	20 Hull St. Bow, E.		"		30				"
	Mrs.Eliza		2	"						"
	Doig David Malgren	Skinners Ln, Ashtead	1	Sing	Merchant					Sts.Setts.
	~~Down~~ ~~John Vancouver~~	~~Wykeham Abbey, Torkey~~	1	Gib	~~Peer~~					"
	~~Dorothy Vancouver~~		1	"			15			"
	~~Honble Ruth Mary~~		1	"						"
	Eaton Henry	19 Neilston Rd,Paisley	2	Sing.	Elec.Engr.	41		1	1	Sts.Setts.
	Edgar Edward James	64 The Avenue, Linthorpe	1	Shang	Engr.	37		1	1	China
	Mrs.Amy Elizabeth Linthorpe		1	"		29		1	1	"
	Edward James	Middlesborough	1	"			8		1	"
	Lawrence Edgar		1	"			6		1	"
	Elliott Miss Patricia	15 Tufton St. W. S.W.1.	2	Sing	Medicine	30		1		Malay State
	Ewen Mrs.Elizabeth	Alton Av. Blundellsands	2	Gib	nil	50				England
	Farmer Miss Dora	19 Gantley Av. S.W.4	1	Penang	nil	30		1		Perak

P. & O. S.S. "MALWA" OFF COLOMBO.
(11,500 TONS, 15,000 HORSE-POWER).

© P&O Heritage Collection www.poheritage.com

Britons in the Far East

British interests in China had evolved over centuries. After acquiring Hong Kong in 1841 and, following the Treaty of Nanking (Nanjing) in1859 when the treaty ports of Shanghai, Amoy, and Foochow & Ningpo together with Canton were opened to foreign trade, Britons enjoyed extra-territorial privileges. They had their own courts with a British Supreme Court in Shanghai. The British presence in China was so strong that a separate arm of the Foreign Office was created: the China Consular Service.

Little did Fred know then that having leapt out of the bankruptcy frying pan he would, within a couple of decades, leap into a hugely hotter fiery furnace.

Meantime, Fred's journeys 'around the world', as illustrated on the map below, were a continual source of inspiration.

World Traveller

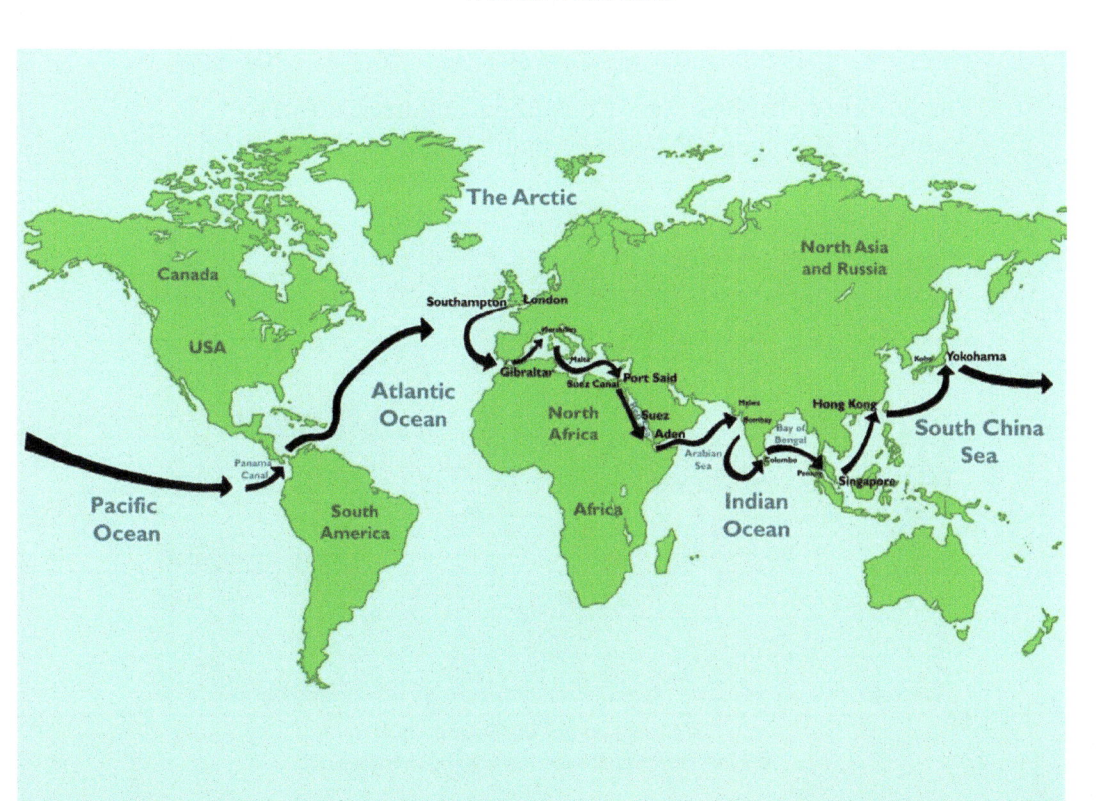

The voyage in 1927 was the start of Fred's world travels. Years later he'd tell local South African farmers that he had travelled around the world three times. Most were incredulous as they had hardly stepped out of their farmer's velskoens, let alone been beyond the borders of their country.

Fred's journeys back to England were primarily to visit his mother. On 14 May 1930 his name appears on the passenger list of the P&O Morea sailing from London to the Far East. The Suez Canal, opened in 1869, particularly gripped him. Sailing through 100miles of desert was one thing, but it was the scale and complexity of the engineering work that exercised his mind.

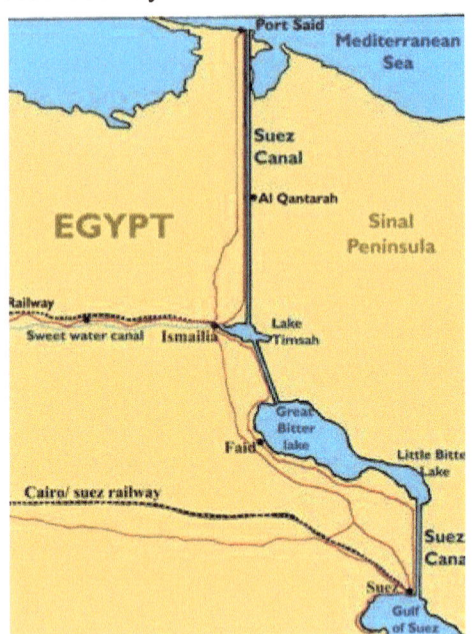

The passenger list had Fred, Consulting Engineer, down to disembark at Singapore. What he did there I do not know.

Morea enters the Suez Canal
© P&O Heritage Collection www.poheritage.com

Suez Canal

> The Suez Canal had a direct impact on world trade due to the speed at which goods were moved around the world. However, ownership and usage problems resulted in conflicts. An international convention in 1888 made the canal available for ships from all nations.
>
> The Suez Canal Authority operates the Canal. It is 101 miles long, starts at Point Said in the Mediterranean Sea, flows through Egypt, and ends at Suez on the Gulf of Suez. Mostly the Suez Canal is not wide enough for two ships to pass side by side but by using the passing bays ships can travel in both directions. Around 11 to 16 hours are needed to pass through the canal. Ships must travel at low speeds to prevent erosion of the canal's banks.
>
> There are no locks on the canal as the Mediterranean and the Gulf of Suez have approximately the same water level.
>
> The Suez Canal supports 8% of the world's shipping traffic and is thus one of the world's most significant waterways. Almost 50 ships pass through there daily. Future plans include widening and deepening the canal to have room for the passage of larger ships.

Fred's journeys from China to England were on liners travelling via the Americas. The voyage was via the Panama Canal. On one or two occasions, Fred disembarked on the west coast of the United States and travelled across country to New York. After a time exploring the city, he'd board a ship bound for England. He often spoke of his journeys across America – backing up his claim to have been around the world three times.

Fred never ceased to marvel at the huge scenic contrasts: the lockless Suez bounded by desert; the Panama wending its way through lush green vegetation.

Panama Canal

The earliest European colonists of South America first saw the potential of creating a canal across the narrow land bridge between South and North America to provide a shipping route between the Pacific and Atlantic Oceans.

It was only when technology was sufficiently advanced that such a scheme was attempted. In 1881 the French began work on the Panama Canal. From the start, major engineering problems hindered its construction. By 1904 the construction of Panama was taken over by the United States. The motivation came from US President Theodore Roosevelt, who was convinced that a U.S.-controlled canal across Central America was of vital strategic importance.

Constructing the Panama Canal turned out to be one of the largest and most difficult engineering projects ever undertaken.

During 1913 the construction of the canal was completed dividing Columbia. Hence the State of Panama was created.

A decade later the canal was officially opened. Today it facilitates commercial and leisure shipping between the Atlantic and Pacific Oceans – a vital link in world shipping.

In 2007 a project began, to double the waterways' capacity. This will have a direct impact on on the global economy. At the time of writing (2016) this project's end is in sight.

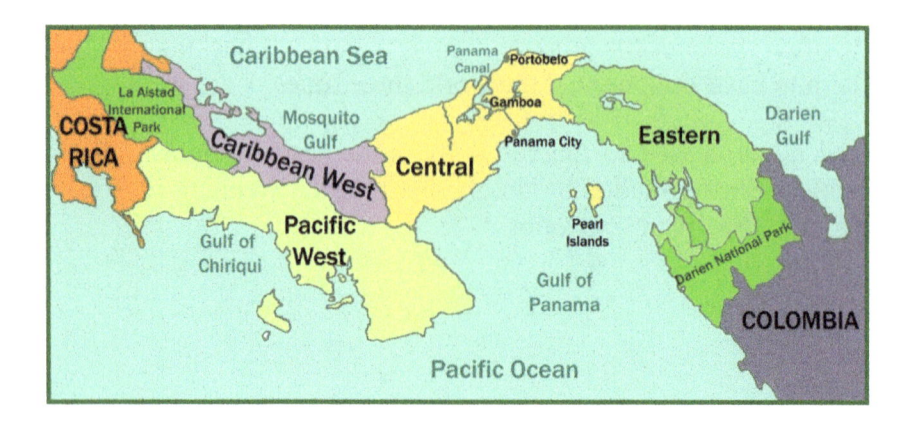

CHINA

Source: University of Texas Libraries   http://www.lib.utexas.edu/maps/faq.html

We cannot achieve what we cannot imagine;
We cannot do what we cannot dream.
Musalaha News, Winter 2015

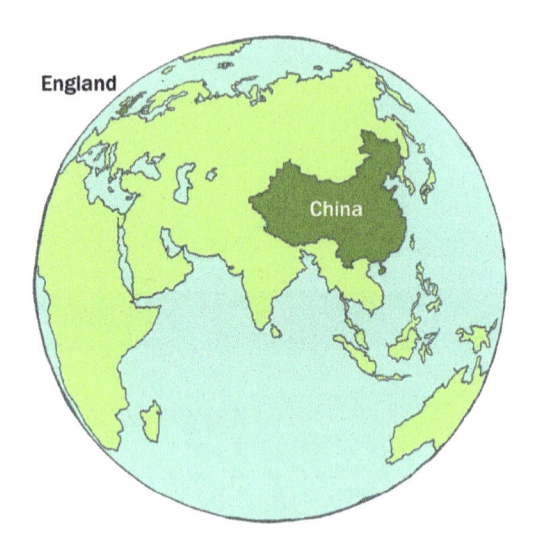

It was March 1927. From the time Fred left London on his first voyage to China, he was alert to his newly-adopted country. He had left behind all that was familiar – Britain, the island of his birth and home for 36 years, family, friends, and his achievements. He, with some three million other Britons in the late twenties and thirties, were leaving the sinking ship of the Depression, hunger marches and rising unemployment, in search of a better life abroad, emigrating to pastures new.

Fred's green and bonny, tiny island was receding on his mental map displaced by the sheer scale of his prospective new country which loomed larger every minute. England with its recorded history back to around 43 AD began to look like a very young country.

Fred was about to connect with China – that vast continental mass of over nine and a half million square kilometers – the fourth largest country in the world after Russia, Canada, and the US. Earliest written records of China date back to 1200 BC under the Shang dynasty – over 3000 years ago.

Chinese literature and philosophy developed further during the Zhou dynasty (1045–256 BC), centuries before any known history of Britain. This was the country with the oldest continuous culture in the world.

Along with fellow Europeans, Fred knew about China through the Silk Road trade (over 4000 miles long). And he had read the famous 13th century Venetian merchant traveller, Marco Polo's *Book of the Marvels of the World.*

Skating over Apects of Chinese History

This segment of the Great Wall is the part we climbed in 2010

73

The Wall was built in stages to keep out invaders like the Mongols. Then, the First Emperor, Qin Shi Huang, decided to extend this to a single giant wall to cover much of the northern border of China as a protection. The resulting 5500 mile long wall includes thousands of lookout towers.

Knowing about a country, and knowing that country, are often two very different 'knows'. At the stage of entering China for the first time, Fred dreamt that this was where he could move on from his broken world of his Windhill Mill woollen episode. He had much to offer China as an Industrial Consultant and Efficiency Engineer.

China was unique. It had developed independently from other world civilisations as it was isolated from much of the rest of the world by, to the North and West, two of the world's largest deserts: the Gobi Desert and the Taklimakan Desert. With the Pacific Ocean on its eastern border and the impassable Himalayan Mountains to the south – the highest mountains in the world – the weak point was the Northern border. Hence the Great Wall was built as a protection.

The two major rivers flowing through China are the Yellow River and the Yangtze, providing fresh water, food, fertile soils and transportation. Today, the Three Gorges Dam on the Yangtze is the world's greatest source of hydroelectricity. The wide and difficult-to-cross Yangtze at 3,988 miles long is the third longest river in the world and forms the boundary between Northern and Southern China. It has played an important role in developing the culture and civilisation of ancient China. The lands along the banks are fertile and the climate is warm, attracting wealth and development throughout history.

> CHINA EXPERIENCE. With the introduction at home of a policy of restriction of production resulting in the breaking up of efficient Plants, of necessity, the writer's consulting activities were transferred to Hong Kong and China. The experience here covered a survey of Chinese industries in Hong Kong, Shanghai, Tientsin, and areas as far north as Harbin. The main experience was in Hong Kong, where, through industrial and commercial interests, contact was made with most of the factories there. During this period the writer prepared industrial reports for a number of China companies, including Jardines and Butterfield & Swire. For a number of years the writer was an Arbitrator for the Hong Kong Chamber of Commerce concerning Textile disputes, (Raw and Semi-raw materials, processes, and finished products are intimate subjects.)

Steaming up the Coast of China
Why didn't I ask when I had the chance?

The P&O liner, Morea, docked briefly at Hong Kong before steaming on its way to Shanghai where Fred was to meet up with those who'd encouraged his emigration. Who were they?

In the section above of Fred's *Outline of Experience* he mentions the firms Jardines and Butterfield & Swire. He also records some of the towns and cities where he'd worked:

> *Consulting activities covered a survey of Chinese industries in Hong Kong, Shanghai, Tientsin, and areas as far north as Harbin.*

SHANGHAI

Just who Fred met up with, which firms he worked for and when, where and for how long he'd lived in Shanghai is guesswork. I do know that he frequently spoke of Shanghai. I often ask myself:

Why didn't I ask when I had the chance?

An educated guess brings me to the supposition that initially Fred's consultancy work was for Jardines who were, in his day, the largest of the foreign trading companies in the Far East. Their activities included shipping, cotton mills, railway construction cold storage companies and packing and brewing. Then in the 1920s and 1930s, in factories on the Shanghai river front, the manufacture and export of powdered eggs was developed. This became an increasingly important factor in China's economy.

The Jardine Engineering Company (JEC) was formed in 1923. This played a large part in providing machinery, equipment and services for the growing infrastructural developments in Hong Kong and China. In 1930, JEC installed the first lift on mainline China in Tientsin, and the first Schindler lift in Hong Kong in 1931. Also, Jardines had a presence in Harbin in the northern reaches of China.

I recall my father talking of how he'd been involved in opening up some aspects of electricity in China. Could this have been through work with Jardines in Tientsin? Was he involved in their new innovations in Shanghai, Harbin and later, Hong Kong and Canton? The other large long established company Fred worked with was Butterfield and Swire. In 1866 John Samuel Swire, with Richard Shackleton Butterfield, formed the Shanghai-based partnership. In 1872, Swire created the China Navigation Company. In 1883 the Hong Kong-based Taikoo Sugar Refinery came into being. Could it be that colleagues within Swire had encouraged Fred to set up his consultancy in China? This suggests that Fred probably started his consultancy in Shanghai for three years, then, on returning from a visit to England, he left from London on the Morea, on 14 May 1930, and moved his base to Hong Kong.

Before moving on to Fred's time in Hong Kong, there is more to understanding something of Shanghai and his connections there.

Shanghai, Past and Present

Around a thousand years ago, Shanghai was a small agricultural village developed where the Suzhou Creek joins the Huangpu River at what is now known as the Northern end of The Bund. During the late Qing dynasty (1644–1911) the village expanded into one of China's principal trading ports. Since the early 1990s, Shanghai has become one of Asia's main financial centers and the world's busiest container port.

Historical Spotlight on the Treaty Ports

In 1832 the British East India Company explored Shanghai and the Yangtze River with the view to trading tea, silk, and opium. When local officials rebuffed the British proposals for this trade Britain waged war with China (the first Opium war) forcing the Chinese to import opium produced in British India.

The war ended in 1842 with the signing of the Treaty of Nanjing (known as the 'unequal treaties' since there were no reciprocal benefits for the Chinese). The Treaty of Nanjing resulted in a major change in foreign trade.

Alongside of Canton (Shameen Island from 1859 until 1943) where Britons were to be allowed to live and trade freely, four additional treaty ports were opened - Shanghai, Ningpo, Fuchow, and Amoy.
In this period the island of Hong Kong was ceded to the United Kingdom.

Britain gained the right to send consuls to the treaty ports, to communicate directly with Chinese officials.

In Shanghai for example were the French Concession and the International Settlement. At the centre of Shanghai city two concession areas develop (areas under foreign sovereignty). The French Concession was a small colony within the city centre. The more complex International Settlement was controlled by the Shanghai Municipality with the majority of the councilors British, some Americans and Japanese. Until 1928 no Chinese could be elected.

Banking and business firms built their headquarters like the Hong Kong and Shanghai Banking Corporation (1846), Butterfield & Swire (1866) along The Bund in Shanghai. Many of these buildings still stand proud along the Bund today – some used for their original purpose while others have been sold on.

The Bund
Between 1927-1937 (Fred's collection)

THE BUND – 2010
Night scene from the Huangpu River

Foreground (Left): The Hong Kong and Shanghai Banking Corporation (HSBC) Building (Centre): The Customs House, (Right): the former Bank of Communications
(Below) – (Centre) the HSBC building

The Bund (Shanghai waterfront) in rain and sunshine

*Nanking
(Nanjing) Road
1930s*
(Fred's collection)

This is the main shopping street of Shanghai, and one of the world's busiest shopping streets. It is named after the city of Nanjing, capital of Jiangsu province which neighbours Shanghai.

*Nanking Road
2010*

81

Man of Wonder

Looking at Fred's life as a whole, it is clear that one of his characteristics was to be 'a man of wonder'. He never ceased to marvel at the world he encountered wherever he was and frequently set about investigating and understanding whatever it was that fascinated him. And so it was in China when he first encountered silk goods in Shanghai. Once he said to me:

These fine-looking fabrics were made by using the delicate strands of silk produced by little silkworms – remarkable!

He studied these creatures so long part of China's history. As part of his investigations he visited Suzhou. When we were in Shanghai in 2010, the natural thing to do was to visit Suzhou and find out about the story of silk.

Frederick Cope finally left China departing from Shanghai in 1942. He took with him just a few suitcases containing practical and valuable items, some of sentimental note.

One case contained an exquisite silk two-piece ladies gown displaying fine embroidery of birds, insects and flowers. I didn't know it then but this beautiful craft had originated in Suzhou.

Read more about this magnificent Chinese gown in the South African section: Secrets of a Leather Suitcase – F.C.3.

If you happen to be in Oxford, England, do visit the Ashmolean Museum where you may find this Chinese gown on display in the Chinese section of the department of Eastern Arts. When not on display you can arrange for a private viewing by contacting The Jameel Centre, Department of Eastern Arts.

For over 70 years, 'Fred's Chinese gown' has been kept as a family treasure wrapped in acid-free tissue paper, in the dark, in the old leather suitcase mentioned above. It is well preserved. The gown is too beautiful to remain hidden. In memory of my father, and for those who will appreciate seeing it, I have donated it to the world's first public university museum. The Ashmolean Museum was originally built in 1678-1683. The museum is free and can be visited at: The Ashmolean Museum, Beaumont Street, Oxford, Oxfordshire, OX1 2PH, England.

Suzhou, where the gown was made, lies on the Grand Canal, the longest canal in the world. It flows 1,776 km from Beijing to Hangzhou on the Yellow River. The oldest parts date back to the 5th century BC.

The Grand Canal (Beijing-Hangzhoul) in Suzhou

A Simplified Story of Silk

A filament of silk is produced by certain insects as part of their life cycle. When fully grown the worm spins a cocoon around itself which protects it as it metamorphoses and emerges as a moth. The best known silk comes from the cocoons of the larvae of mulberry silkworm, *Bombyx mori*, reared in captivity in China. Production of this silk is called sericulture. It is used in weaving silk fabric as developed in ancient China. China is still the main producer of silk.

Commercially silkworms are bred to produce a creamy white silk thread. In order for the thread to unravel unbroken from the cocoon the pupa is not allowed to eat its way out of the cocoon and emerge as a moth. Only moths for breeding live through the complete life cycle. But how was the use of the silk thread discovered?

A Chinese legend
One day Xi Ling-Shi, the empress of Huang Di (2697 to 2598 BC), collected some silkworm cocoons. By mistake while drinking tea, she dropped a cocoon into her tea cup. Quickly a small strand of thread separated from the cocoon. As she wound the thread onto her fingers she realised it could be used for weaving.

Silk is made of a natural protein fiber. Its splendid shimmering appearance is of the silk fiber's triangular prism-like structure that allows cloth to refract incoming light at different angles. Silk is of benefit in all seasons. Because it is absorbent it is comfortable to wear in warm weather. Its low conductivity means it keeps warm air close to the skin during cold weather. It is widely used in clothing, including formal and high fashion wear, lingerie, night wear, furnishings, wall coverings, bedding and wall hangings. Silk has industrial uses, as in making parachutes and bicycle tires.

To produce 1kg of silk takes 104 kg of mulberry leaves to feed 3000 silkworms and some 5000 silkworms to make one pure silk kimono.

The Silk Road
The Silk Road, an ancient network of trade and cultural routes was originally pioneered from 139 BC to 129 BC by Zhang Qian, a Chinese imperial envoy in the Han Dynasty. The route has been expanded many times since and today it extends over 4,000 miles (6,437 kilometres). Though silk was certainly the major trade item from China, many other goods were traded.

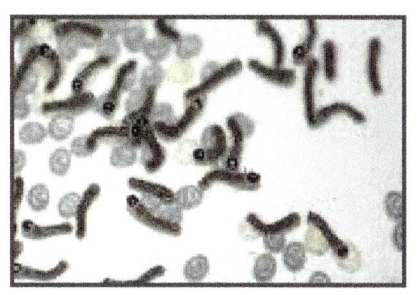

Cycle of Silkworms
Tonia's home-based observation

Silkworm eggs and hatching silkworms

↓

A silkworm climbs seeking a place to spin its cocoon

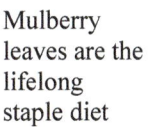

Mulberry leaves are the lifelong staple diet

↓

Spinning starts by making a secure silk hammock and then a cocoon

The worm metamorphoses inside the cocoon into a pupa

Pupa becomes a moth that emerges from cocoon

↓

Moths mate and female lays eggs

Go to top of RH column

SUZHOU

From Shanghai, an easy route to Suzhou is by train. Generally, trains are efficient, run on time and are kept spotless. This train was shortly to leave for Suzhou and no corner, inside or out, escapes the cleansing department.

Suzhou Railway Station, near the city centre, is among the busiest passenger stations in China. Suzhou, dubbed the Venice of the East or the Venice of China, is a major city in Jiangsu Province, Eastern China. Founded in 514 BC its history spans some 2500 years. It is one of the oldest towns in the Yangtze basin, 100 km from Shanghai and one of the fastest growing major cities in the world. Its canals, stone bridges, pagodas, and gardens make it a top tourist attraction. Its classical gardens are a World Heritage Site. Suzhou is an important centre for the silk industry. Throughout China's past, Suzhou silk products have been of high quality. Any Suzhou silk product has tales to tell of its creation, imagination, and beauty.

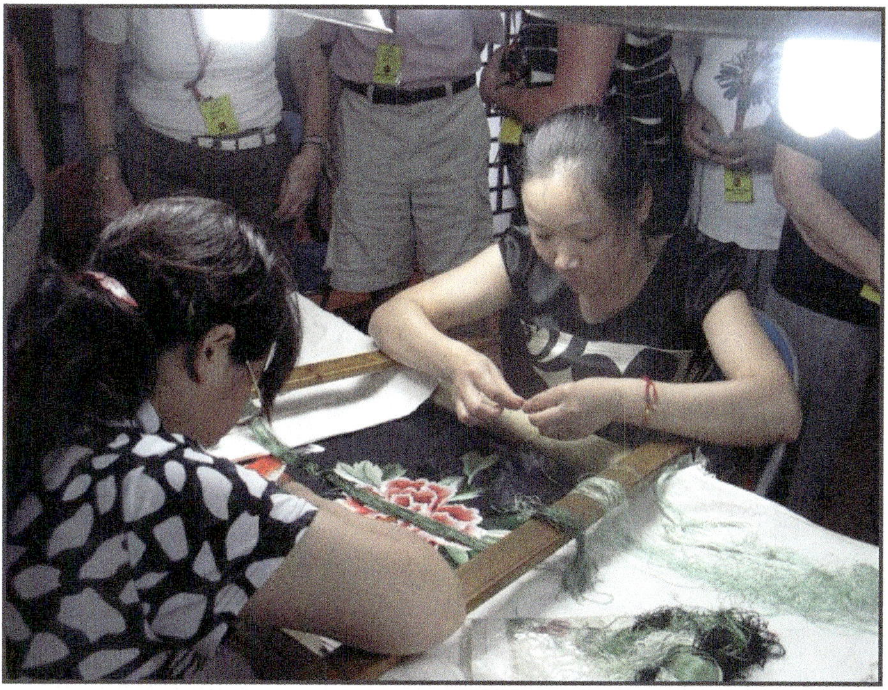

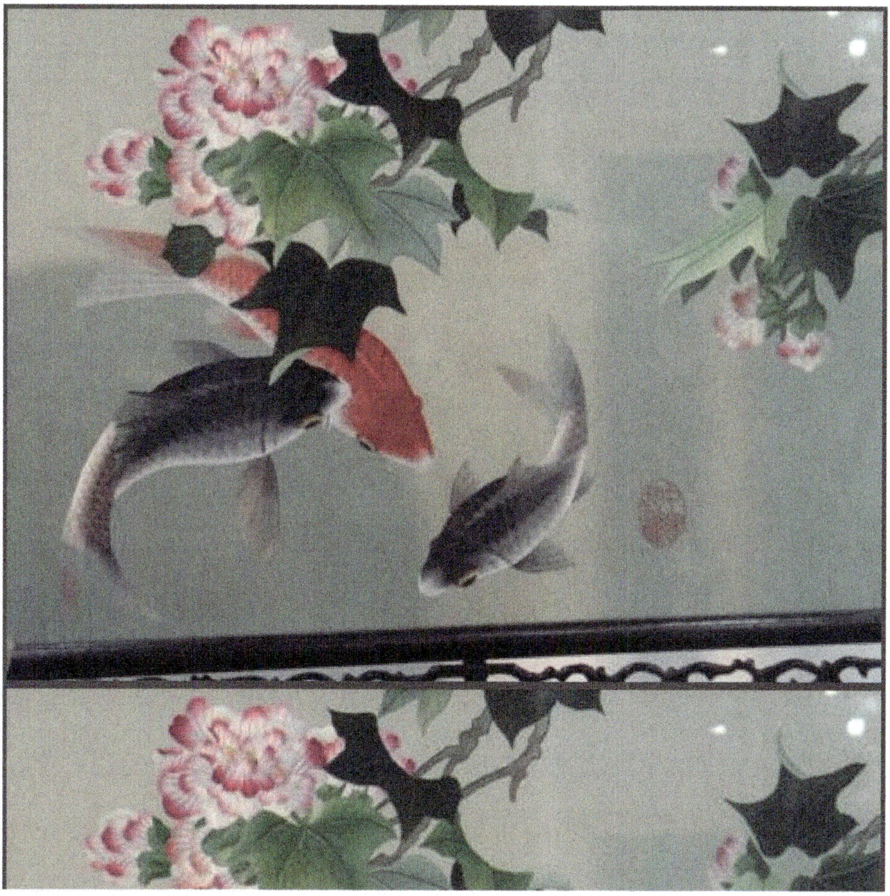

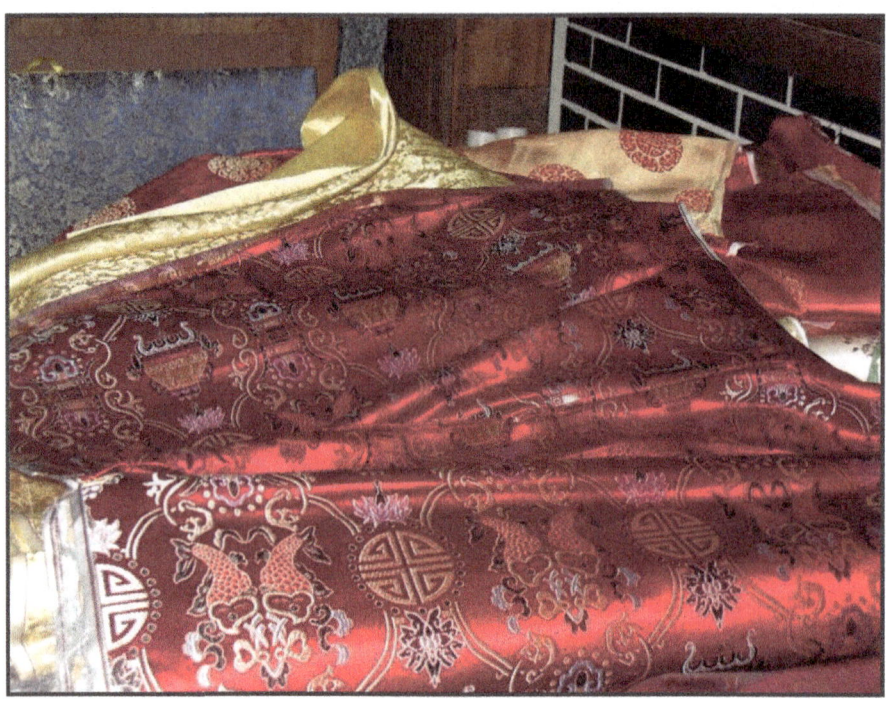

Factory worker producing embossed silk cloth   Photos 2010

Second Passage to China

Early on in 1930, Fred sailed for England via the Americas. It was time, he reasoned, to visit his mother in Scarborough.

Over the three years he'd been in China, Fred observed that conditions in Britain were getting worse. Mass unemployment, especially in the North, was leading to low morale and despair. He needed no convincing that his future lay in China though China too had its problems. Nevertheless he had landed on his feet in Shanghai where he quickly gained interesting work. Political change was afoot. In his first couple of years in China, Chaing Kai-Shek became leader of the Republic of China. The future was uncertain, yet opportunities existed that could only be dreamt of in Britain.

On 14 May 1930, Fred was on the London docks, one of the twenty who embarked on the P&O liner SS Morea bound for Yokohama, Japan. It was to be one of Morea's last voyages as she would be scrapped later that year in Kobe. According to the passenger list, Fred's country of residence was recorded as Singapore and that he would disembark there. I assume this was an error as Fred never spoke of living in Singapore. It is possible he had a short stay there before making his way to Hong Kong where he planned to set up his consultancy.

© P&O Heritage Collection www.poheritage.com

SOUTH CHINA 1930-1942

Hong Kong is an island lying just below the Tropic of Cancer at the mouth of the Pearl River about 90 miles (140 km) from Canton (Guangzhou). Below are images of Hong Kong some seventy years apart – the first in 1937 and the second in 2010.

Hong Kong View, 1937
Photograph by a local amateur (Fred's collection)

Hong Kong Island with Kowloon across the bay
Photo taken from Victoria Mountain in 2010

Hong Kong – Fragrant Harbour

Hong Kong, one of the world's most densely populated areas, is known for its skyline and deep natural Harbour. The name Hong Kong was first recorded in 1842 after the Treaty of Nanking. Archaeologists have found signs of human activity in Hong Kong dating back over 30,000 years.

The origin of the name Hong Kong (or Heung Gong) is 'Fragrant Harbour'. This may have been inspired by the fragrant sweet taste of the harbour's fresh estuarine water from the Pearl River. The original settlement was near the main fishing harbour and port, Aberdeen. Kowloon (Gow Lung), means "Nine Dragons" which originated eight centauries ago in the Sung Dynasty when the boy-emperor, Ping, fled to Hong Kong. He observed eight peaks and named Kowloon area Eight Dragons – one for each peak. As he, the emperor, was considered to be a dragon, it became known as "Nine Dragons" – Ping being the ninth. Hong Kong is also nicknamed *Pearl of the Orient*.

The extent of Hong Kong consists of Hong Kong Island, the Kowloon Peninsular, the New Territories and over 200 offshore islands of which the current 'airport island', Lantau, is the largest. Hong Kong, located just south of the Tropic of Cancer, has a sub-tropical climate with distinct seasons. The two official languages are Cantonese and English – the language of business.

Hong Kong's nearest neighbor, Guangdong (formerly Canton), is to its north on the Chinese Mainland. The capital city, Guangzhou (Canton City), is 135 km from Hong Kong. Transport between Hong Kong and Canton in the 1940s was by rail or boat – links still in use today.

In the early 1800s, Britain and China became trading partners. Britain imported tea and, in exchange, China received watches, clocks, and silver. However, as Britain's imports exceeded her exports she included opium in her exports to China. Opium was legal in Britain and grown in large quantities in colonial India. The Qing state took a strong stand against the opium trade. War broke out – the First Opium War. Then, as a result of new treaties passed in 1842, Hong Kong was ceded to Britain. Many achievements followed like improvements in transportation and the introduction of electricity. However, during the Japanese occupation, December 1941 to August 1945, there was hyper-inflation, starvation, famine and deterioration throughout.

Since 1997, when Britain handed Hong Kong over to China, its full official name became Hong Kong Special Administrative Region of the People's Republic of China. It is still widely known as Hong Kong.

```
CHINA          With the introduction at home of a policy of restric-
EXPERIENCE.    tion of production resulting in the breaking up of
               efficient Plants, of necessity, the writer's consulting
               activities were transferred to Hong Kong and China.
The experience here covered a survey of Chinese industries in Hong Kong,
Shanghai, Tientsin, and areas as far north as Harbin.
The main experience was in Hong Kong, where, through industrial and
commercial interests, contact was made with most of the factories there.
During this period the writer prepared industrial reports for a number
of China companies, including Jardines and Butterfield & Swire.
For a number of years the writer was an Arbitrator for the Hong Kong
Chamber of Commerce concerning Textile disputes, (Raw and Semi-raw
materials, processes, and finished products are intimate subjects.)
```

Industrial Consultant Based in Hong Kong

Frederick Cope A.M.I.E.E. M.A. MIN. E.E.
CHARTERED ELECTRICAL ENGINEER
CONSULTANT

8th Floor,
Pedder Building,
Hong Kong.

EFFICIENCY ENGINEERING.
INDUSTRIAL ECONOMICS.

As Fred spelled out in this section of his *Outline of Experience*, his main practice was in Hong Kong. It was during the early 1930s that he established himself as a consultant based in Hong Kong specialising in Efficiency Engineering and Industrial Economics. His clients, though concentrated in Hong Kong, included factories in cities on mainland China like Canton, Shanghai, Tientsin and as far north as Harbin.

In Hong Kon**g,** through his industrial and commercial interests, he conducted a survey of Chinese industries and made contact with most of the Hong Kong factories. He prepared industrial reports for a number of companies like Jardines, Butterfield and Swire, and the Hong Kong and Canton Refrigeration and Ice Company. For a number of years he was an Arbitrator for the Hong Kong Chamber of Commerce concerning textile disputes. Textiles are a thread that wove throughout Fred's adult life.

During the early 1930s, Fred rented an office for his consultancy on the 8th floor of the now listed Pedder Building, 12 Pedder Street, Central Hong Kong. For much of that period, until 1942, Fred lived at 42 Shameen FC (French Concession), Canton (Guangzhou) on mainland China.

Pedder Building – 12 Pedder Street

Built circa 1924 Pedder Building is dwarfed by skyscrapers - Photos 2010

Pedder Building was opened in 1924 for commercial use in Central Hong Kong. The street was named after the first harbour master, Lieutenant William Pedder.

This is one of the few buildings in Hong Kong which is as it was in the colonial days. My father's office is still there, which is almost unbelievable as most of central Hong Kong has been knocked down and rebuilt once or twice since those days. As land is at a premium, it is surprising that in 1981 the nine-storey Pedder Building was listed as a Grade II Historic Building by the Hong Kong Antiquities and Monuments Office. Pedder Building is the oldest commercial structure in Hong Kong. It survived World War II and, almost a century on, it symbolises the colonial history and is an international symbol of where western and eastern cultures merge. Today, Pedder Building is dwarfed by surrounding skyscrapers. It is well served by public transport: the Mass Transit Railway (MTR – the rapid transit railway system), buses, trams and minibuses.

When we visited Hong Kong in 2010, we were delighted to find Pedder Building still in existence. Stepping inside the entrance led to another world illustrated by the noticeboard of current occupants both local and international.

On our way up to the eighth floor to see where my father's office had been, we came across a door labelled China Tee Club and Restaurant.

China Tee Club and Restaurant

On closer inspection of the poster, I noticed the date it opened – 1932 – almost certainly when Dad had his office there. We just had to go in for a look-see and to sample the fare.

We were definitely in a time warp! Perhaps that slowly moving ceiling fan had been there all along? And what about the magnificent music machine – an original His Master's Voice?

As the Tee Club had been operating since 1932, surely it was frequented by Fred Cope?

Growing Aggression – Japan's Sights on China

The only thing we have to fear, is fear itself.
Franklin D. Roosevelt (from his inaugural address as President of the United States, in reference to the Great Depression)

Through his economist's eye, Fred keenly watched world events. Developments that led up to WWI were still sharp in his mind. In the early 1930s, pots were on the boil. Japanese aggression against China had surfaced. In 1932, the Kwantung Army (Imperial Japanese Army) was fighting Chinese guerrillas in various areas in Manchuria. Back in Europe, Adolf Hitler had become German Chancellor and had, two days later, dissolved Parliament. Freedom of the press was limited. In Britain, Winston Churchill had warned of the dangers of German rearmament. These noises signalled disaster to Fred.

Fred was well known in Hong Kong. It was time, he thought, to voice his views in the press. What followed was a series of articles in the Hong Kong Telegraph. These appeared from 9 June - 25 September 1933 and later reprinted in booklet form by The South China Morning Post with the title *World Crisis: A way out – An analysis of the World Economic Crisis suggesting its Causes and a Cure.* He was much in tune with Emerson's thinking:

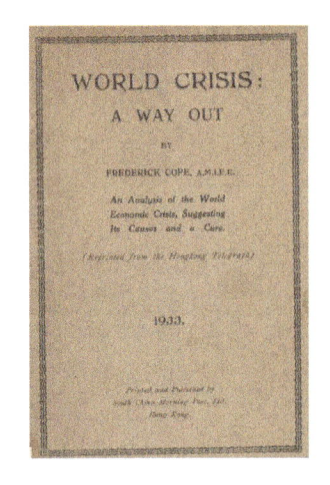

When every man's chief concern is to watch that he does not cheat his neighbour, all will go well.

Fred's articles were based around the up-coming Economic Conference to be held in London from June 12 to July 27, 1933 – a meeting with representatives of 66 nations, at the Geological Museum. A theme of the articles is around the single idea that if there is trouble, the only thing to do is to obtain an accurate measure of the trouble, then find not the superficial cause, but the real cause and remove it. In an early article entitled *How One Dollar Came to Look Like Two,* Fred traces the history of money.

The World in 1933

China
- Diexi earthquake, Mao County, Szechwan, destroyed town of Diexi and close villages, about 9,000 people died
- Defence of the Great Wall – Second Sino-Japanese War

Germany
- Adolf Hitler becomes Chancellor – two days later he dissolves parliament
- President Von Hindenburg limits freedom of the press
- Albert Einstein flees Nazi Germany for the United States
- Nazi Germany withdraws from the League of Nations

Great Britain
- The first modern 'sighting' of the Loch Ness Monster!
- Winston Churchill's first public speech warning of the dangers of German rearmament
- Battersea Power Station, London, first generates electricity
- Harry Beck's London Tube Map introduced – at once popular

Japan
- Announced it will no longer be part of the League of Nations
- The Kwangtung Army captures Shanghai Pass of the Great Wall

Prussia
- Pres von Hindenburg & von Papen ends Prussian Parliament

United States
- Franklin D. Roosevelt became President

World
London Economic Conference (June-July) – 66 nations met in the Geological Museum with the purpose to agree on actions to fight Global depression, revive international trade and stabilise currency exchange rates
- President Roosevelt denounced currency stabilisation
- World Economic Conference failed

The Context

I am no economist but as I have attempted to unravel threads from the World Crisis articles I have come to understand, at least a fraction more, about the whys and wherefores of the world depression and the economic situation in 1933.

I was delighted to find archived articles discussing Fred's papers in The Hong Kong Telegraph. This advert appeared on 25-09-1933 in Hong Kong in The South China Morning Post. What were the similarities referred to between Fred's ideas and those of President Roosevelt in his Recovery Programme?

WORLD CRISIS
A WAY OUT
By FREDERICK COPE, A.M.I.E.E.

Mr. Cope's striking articles on the world economic crisis which were recently published in the *Hongkong Telegraph* are now available in pamphlet form.

One of the features, repaying study, is the close similarity between the plan of reform suggested by this local writer, and certain aspects of the Roosevelt recovery programme. The author's ideas are naturally far too advanced for active promotion at the present time, but they are particularly interesting in view of the fact that President Roosevelt, in striking out on a path of his own, has travelled in the same direction.

The pamphlet is one of forty-four pages and can be obtained from the South China Morning Post at a cost of—

FIFTY CENTS

....

South China Morning Post, Ltd.
Hongkong.

Please send me ...... copies of "World Crisis—A Way Out" for which I enclose $....

Name ....

Address ....

Elements Common to Roosevelt and Cope's Thinking

Clues lie in their mutual concern for the millions of people suffering as a consequence of The Depression:

Fred Wrote on Wanton Destruction:
Never in history have we had such control of physical wealth. Food, which at one time was our chief concern, takes little more than 5% of our efforts today. So plentiful are commodities at the present time, that in order to preserve our present money conditions, they have to be wantonly destroyed. Foodstuffs, raw materials and machinery suffer thus, land is put out of cultivation, and productive plants scrapped, and all this when human desires, and demands for physical wealth, are at their maximum. Unfortunately all this seems to no purpose.

Hundreds of reputable and long established industrial, commercial, and financial firms have passed out of existence. Nations ... have failed in their financial obligations. Men in responsible positions have been driven to dishonourable courses. Peers in goal! There are financiers, industrialists and millionaires committing suicide to escape the heavy burden of adversity. Millions of worthy men are morally broken and without employment.

President Roosevelt – Words in a White House Record
Roosevelt was elected President in November 1932, to the first of four terms. By March 1933 there were 13,000,000 unemployed, and almost every bank was closed. In his first hundred days, he proposed, and Congress enacted, a sweeping program to bring recovery to business and agriculture, relief to the unemployed and to those in danger of losing farms and homes, and reform, especially through the establishment of the Tennessee Valley Authority.

By 1935, through Roosevelt's New Deal Programme which focused on three general goals – relief for the needy, economic recovery, and financial reform' – the United States had achieved a measure of recovery.

Consequences of the Failed Economic Conference

The Conference, which had set about trying to save the world from the Great Depression, gave up six weeks later. Without any major agreements in place, it adjourned amid squabbling and finger-pointing between the world's democracies. The real problem was that despite grand rhetoric about working together, the leaders were not willing to abandon economic policies that they thought were helping them back home.

The US, Britain and France went their separate ways on economic policy and as the economy kept on shrinking aggressor nations such as Japan and Nazi Germany armed for war against them.

World Crisis – Concluding Words

Fred, although not claiming to have all the answers, nor elevating 'boring economics' to that status, ends his booklet with these prophetic words:

> *The Crisis we are facing today is worse than we faced in 1914, except there are no guns – yet.*

Within a few years, guns were out and Fred would become a prisoner of the Japanese.

The Hong Kong Review
If you want to change the world, pick up your pen and write.
Martin Luther

Fred kept busy. In 1937, together with colleagues, he produced a regular news magazine for Hong Kong: **Hong Kong Review.** Fred managed to keep hold of four issues (the images of their covers are on the next page).

I have found no evidence of the magazine continuing in the troubled times of 1938.

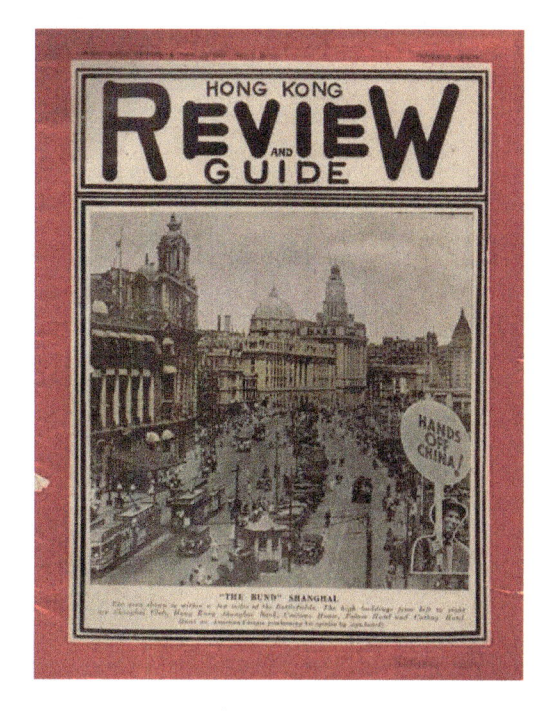

15 October 1937

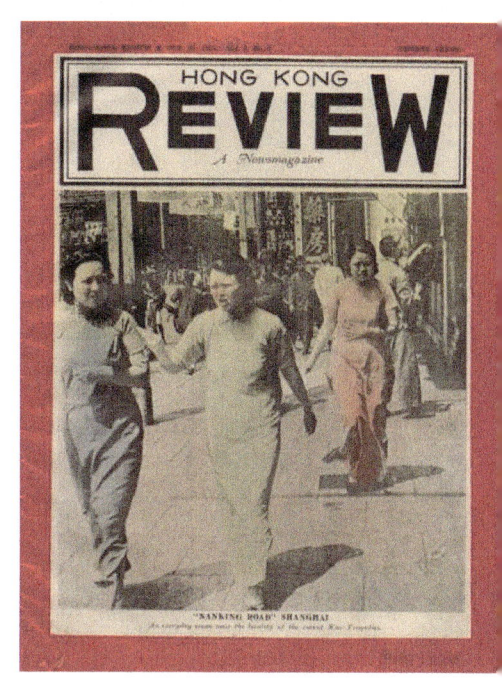

29 October 1937

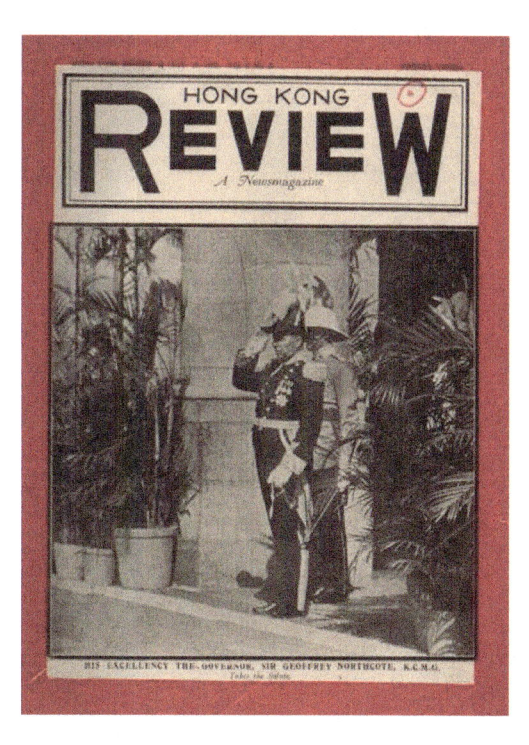

19 November 1937

10 December 1937

15 Oct - Vol 1 No 2
19 Nov - Vol 1 No 4

29 Oct - Vol 1 No 3
10 Dec - Vol 1 No 5

Extracts from The Hong Kong Review

The Hong Kong Review news magazine covered topics like Local Affairs, Foreign Comments, Sport, Religion and Guide to Hong Kong with a peppering of humour. A few extracts:

LOCAL AFFAIRS

Japanese Settle Near Macao

The Japanese have annexed one of the three islands a few miles from Macao and are now busily preparing it as an air base.

Six Japanese warships are concentrated at the island which is at the mouth of the Canton delta. The warships landed marines, who are levelling the ground, and preparing it for aircraft.

The report is of vital interest in view of Japan's seizure of the Pratas, which is also being used as a naval base.

This latest annexation is of high strategic value so far as aerial activities in South China are concerned. It will permit the Japanese to make extended air raids throughout Kwangtung and the provinces north and west. It is also uncomfortably near Hong Kong.

Canton Apprehensive

Japanese aerial activity in Kwangtung seems probable in the near future as a result of the news that the Japanese have landed blue jackets on the islands near Macao and are preparing airfields.

There are persistent rumours in Canton that a large number of Chinese planes from the North are reinforcing the air force there.

A clear warning of Japanese intentions regarding South China is flagged up in this article.

BLOCKADE

Canton River Blocked

The strategic reason for the drastic measure of blocking the channel a few miles above Bocco Tigris, locking up valuable boats in Canton and preventing valuable cargoes reaching Canton, was not quite clear to interested people in Hong Kong.

The small steamer On Lee, normally on the Kongmoon run, successfully negotiated the boom.

Reports from the On Lee's commander, Captain S. H. Laud, indicated that although the Chinese military authorities sank ships in the one remaining channel to the West River and then announced that all shipping was suspended, there still remains a narrow channel through which small ships may pass. This channel is only 14 feet deep at high tide about seven feet at low tide and no more than 50 feet wide. The On Lee being one of the small river steamers, was able to negotiate the channel safely and numerous other steamers on the Canton River runs could, with the care and a favourable tide, also get through despite the boom. Larger vessels, such as the Fatshan and Taishan might just get through.

This did not satisfy the powerful interests affected and collectively they made strong presentations to the Chinese Government. On October 8th the blockaded ships were informed to prepare to move. The morning of October 9th saw 17 ships one behind the other all heading for Hong Kong piloted through a passage which had been prepared.

The Chinese took this step to prevent Japanese naval vessels reaching Canton – an unpopular measure with traders.

Fred often spoke about the Japanese invasion of China. In his view, the majority of people in the south were convinced Japan would not invade South China. However, the Blockade article indicates that those in authority took the possibility seriously. Meanwhile, readers appreciated The Hong Kong Review,

Letters to the Editor

"When I read over the Hong Kong Review and Guide I bought in the street to-day, having been attracted by its 'live' cover, I laid it beside me and marvelled. I couldn't believe for the moment that it actually was produced in sleepy, parasitical Hong Kong.

So refreshing are the views. So kaleidoscopic the survey. So attractive are the pictures."

"The plan to give Hong Kong a 'News Magazine' at a very moderate price is a great one. In these hurried days and rapid happenings, low dollar, and high cost of Home journals, your readers will appreciate your endeavour to give them an intelligent digest at a reasonable price."

Printed by the Hong Kong Daily Press for Frederick Cope. Princes Building, Hong Kong.

Regrettably, the Hong Kong Review was storing up trouble for Fred. The Japanese had an eye on this publication and certainly did not appreciate cartoons like that on the cover of the 15 October 1937 issue. Fred's situation would get worse.

Fred made room for humour in the Review (example below).

"Chuck it, you two. Don't behave like a couple of human beings."—*Glasgow Evening Times*

A Dangerous Publication

Fred, the editor of The *Hong Kong Review*, had allowed a cartoon of the Emperor of Japan to be published in the Nov 19, 1937 issue. This was to prove costly to him at the hands of the Japanese. The following pages are images from this issue minus the cartoon. Fred had kept copies of a selection of the Reviews but once the Japanese had a foot-hold in Southern China he tore out the cartoon of the Japanese Emperor. He knew he could already be in trouble with the Japanese for assorted 'offences', so he figured it would be safer to keep a copy minus the cartoon.

HONG KONG REVIEW, *Nov. 19, 1937.* 13

FOREIGN COMMENTS

JAPAN
The Old Guard

Watching events, in China from the safety of Tokyo, two great families cared little where the war raged, but devoutly hoped it would end in quick victory for Japan, thus preventing an otherwise inevitable economic collapse.

Reports the "News Review." These were the representatives of the Mitsuis and Mitsubishis, who for year have controlled the destinies of the Yellow Empire behind the scenes and have become more powerful than the botanical Son of Heaven himself.

Industrialist Hachiroemon Mitsui.

The Mitsuis were already a wealthy and powerful clan when Commodore Perry anchored in Uraga Harbour and stampeded Japan into hasty Westernisation. Successfully they grafted modern industrialisation on to their feudal family structure.

Originally stewards to the feudal Sasaki lords, the Mitsuis owed their initial rise primarily to the doctrines of the Samurai, the noble and landed gentry who had a profound contempt for money and never allowed any member of their families to touch it. All financial transactions were carried out by hirelings.

17th-Century China Store

Reconciled to being looked upon as "untouchables," the Mitsuis soon found that even in feudal Japan money had advantages.

Japan's Mikado dressed in coronation robes. Subjects cry "Long live our Emperor till the pebbles into rocks grow!"

Almost 300 years ago the founder of the present line, Hachirobe Mitsui, opened a bank and began foreign trade with Dutch sailors. Undeterred when the Mikado banned such business, he rapidly covered his country with Mitsui One Price Chain Stores. This was long before the death of Charles II.

Always the Mitsuis operated as a family unit, and with Japanese industrialisation they pooled their capital to buy properties for their gigantic family trust. To-day when the Mitsuis hold their family council ten branches of the family are represented. At the head of the table sits thin-faced, nervous-looking Baron Hachiroemon Mitsui, 14th of his line, and most powerful man in Japan.

The Mikado—revised version:
The punishment now precedes the "My object all sublime
Has changed in course of time;
crime;
It now precedes the crime!"

Determined to run no risk of having the family fortunes squandered by a play-boy heir they expel from the family any child who reaches the age of 15 without showing promise of commercial ability. After an expulsion a bright youngster, often of poor origin, is adopted into the family and groomed to play his part in building up the Mitsui fortunes.

Nation-Control

The family controls 85 per cent. of Japan's wool exports, 40 per cent. of grain, 57 per cent. of coal, and 40 per cent. of machinery. Under its house flag sails a fleet of 700,000 tons. The octopus MKB (Mitsui Commercial Enterprises) controls factories, banks, sugar refineries, oil companies.

In the United States 90 per cent. of the largest cotton export com-

At such "insu... headquarters, busy... Britons ply yen for yen.

Securely in the pocket of the Mitsuis for more than a generation has been the Japanese Conservative Party. When in office it carefully guards the interests of Harvard-educated Baron Hachiroemon. Because raw materials are essential to the progress of the Mitsuis, Japan's Conservative Governments invariable embark on an expansionist policy and use armed force to obtain fodder for the insatiable Mitsui factories.

Liberal Controllers

Only slightly less powerful than the Mitsuis are the Mitsubishis, who control the Japanese Liberal Party. Interested in finance rather than industry, the Mitsubishis are comparatively peaceful. But they support Mitsui-Conservative sponsored military adventures and finance the development of newly-acquired territory.

Both families are well aware that a stiffened Chinese resistance might prolong the war indefinitely, thus smashing both their houses.

* * *

JAPAN APOLOGISES

The World's best apologists,—

"The Japanese Embassy had been officially informed that Japanese shells killed four British soldiers in Shanghai. Mr. Koki Hirota, Foreign Minister, had communicated Japan's "................for- Government has accepted an apology from the Japanese Government regarding the recent attack on three British Embassy cars in which Britons were travelling from Nanking to Shanghai.

Intervention unnecessary

Within a short time the situation at the front in the Sino-Japanese conflict will be such as to render all Conferences absolutely unnecessary, according to a prediction by General Matsui.

When the Belgian Foreign Office asked the Japanese Embassy if it was proposed to send an observer to to the Nine-power conference. Mr. Saburo Kurusu, the Japanese Ambassador replied that Japan firmly rejects interference by outside Powers. In the meantime she is ready to direct negotiations with China on the conditions that China stops her anti-Japanese propaganda, and secondly stifles communism.

...sh
...r.
...all
...pre-
...inci-
...admin-
......ole, and the
......ent would pro-
...... compensation."

......panese spokesman said that the rice and the junk, which Japanese soldiers took from Chinese as they were unloading cargo in the American Marines' sector of Soochow Creek, is being returned.

Rear-Admiral Denkiti Okoti, Commander of the Japanese naval landing party, called on Brig. Gen. Beaumont this morning and expressed his personal apologies.

"The Japanese Foreign Office has issued a statement that the British

Asked Mr. Kurusu: "Suppose the United States and Mexico were in dispute and Japan, Britain and other Powers met at Brussels to settle it. Would the United States attend?—I think not."

* * *

U. S. A.

Roosevelt

President Roosevelt is dead scared of the China-Japan war. Whichever way he jumps—for diplomatic intervention or for complete neutrality—he is certain to be attacked by his enemies. Faced with this problem he has decided to take the most difficult of the two courses—a rigid "keep out" policy.

He is gambling on other foreign Powers experiencing trouble in Shanghai, which would then enable him to take credit for his far sighted handling of American affairs. Big money and industrial interests would do anything to topple from his throne America's leftwing President. Mr. Roosevelt stood in peril when his newly appointed Supreme Court Judge Senator Black was denounced as a member of the anti-Jewish Knights of the Ku Klux Klan.

To push through his socialistic legislation the President has to rely finally on the Supreme Court, formerly presided over by the famous "Nine Old Men," who wrecked most of his early New Deal plans.

American Institutions

One commentator taking vigorous exception to the overworked phrase "allegiance only to American institutions," says.

"For needless and undeserved poverty in a land of milk and honey is today peculiarly an American Institution. So is the combination of superior resources and wonderful advancement of science in the healing arts, and the 95 per cent of our children of school-age with defective teeth because the remedy, in private hands, is too expensive.

In fact, the whole profit and loss system, called "capitalism," unplanned, chaotic, anarchistic, while not peculiarly an American institution, is now on the way to become one. It has collapsed and has been abandoned wholly or partially in the greater part of the world.

It is certainly making its final stand here in the U. S. A.; and no other world-power is engaging in a conscious endeavor to make it function a while longer by tossing into it billions of the taxpayers' cash every year.

...a long time: Funny, how one can make mistakes. I thought you ...ere someone else. Honourable regrets!

The *Hong Kong Review* (1937) is available in the collection of the Central Preservation Library for Government Publications (Public Records Office, Government Records Service). These may be viewed on site at 13 Tsui Ping Road, Kwun Tong, Kowloon, in the Search Room of the office (call number X2000531).

CANTON (GUANGZHOU)

*Hong Kong and Canton were like twin cities,
120 miles apart by rail and 80 miles by sea and river.*
Hedley P. Bunton: Fourty Years of China

In the 1930s, travel between Hong Kong and Canton (Guangzhou) was by train or steamer. Thousands of Chinese travelled to and fro every day. The journey by boat took five hours skirting the mountainous New Territories coast then up the Pearl River estuary through the 15 to 20 mile wide delta with its maze of channels and islands.

Fred was bowled over by teaming throngs of people jostling for space on the pavements and roads. Fighting to share that space were rickshaws, sedan chairs, bicycles, hand trolleys, private cars, motor trucks and buses. The river was chock-a-block with passenger junks, launches, cargo ships, ferries and sampans. The mass of humanity lived there. Fred made his way to Shameen Island on that steamy tropical summer's day.

旧时沙面水上人家
Shamian climate residents in the old times

30年代的白鹅潭畔
Bai 'e' tan in 1930's

Photos of 1930 pictures in the Guangdong Victory Hotel

CANTON (GUANGZHOU)

Canton's history dates back some 2600 years. One Chinese name for Canton is **Yeung Sheng (City of Rams)** based on a popular creation myth: five celestial beings rode into the city on five rams carrying sheaves of rice which they offered to the people as a symbol of prosperity; once the celestials left, the rams turned to stone. Since then Canton has developed into an affluent and influential city.

By the third century BC an administrative capital city called Panyu existed along the Pearl River. A city wall was built to surround Panyu for defence. Today, Panyu is a district of Guangzhou, the capital of Guangdong. In 1911-1922, except for one section in Yuexiu Park, the ancient city wall was demolished to build new road systems.

Merchants have lived in Canton from around 165AD. In C16 and C17, trade with the West began through the Maritime Silk route. 1715 the authorities decreed Canton to be the only port open to foreign trade and hence China's main link to the outside world. Over the years, Hindus, Muslims, Zen Buddhists and Christians have settled in Canton, a splendid multicultural city. From the end of the 17th century the British and French, Dutch, Danes, Swedes and Americans had a trade presence. All traders heading for Canton had to call at government approved wholesalers known as the Hong Merchants. European purchases, including those of the British East India Company, had to be made through the Hong Guild. No single co-Hong merchant was allowed to provide more than half of any ship's cargo. Today Canton (Guangzhou) is a prosperous and famous trading port, the third largest Chinese city and the largest city in South Central China.

Shameen Island (Shamian or Shamin), European influence in Canton was centred on Shameen Island, an artificial island one third of a square mile in size with three major and five minor streets. Shameen is a reclaimed sandbank in Liwan District of Guangzhou. In 1859 the concessions were given to France and the United Kingdom by the Qing government – 3/5 to the British and 2/5 to the French). Connection to the mainland was by two bridges, which were closed at 10pm. The British arch bridge (the Bridge of England) was built in 1861 to the north. It was guarded by Sikh police officers. The French bridge to the east was guarded by Vietnamese (Cochin China) recruits. Shameen became a strategic point for city defence during the First and Second Opium Wars. Trading companies from Britain, the United States, France, Holland, Italy, Germany, Portugal and Japan built stone mansions on the island, representing Western-plan detached houses. On the centre and south of the island, public gardens were planted together with Banyan trees and shrubs. These thrive today.

It was from diminutive Shameen that 19th century European power grew throughout Southern China and beyond. Although much was unsavoury through this European presence Shameen, today it is regarded with warmth by the Cantonese who value its rich and varied history, its shaded and dreamy streets and its architectural splendour. It is a peaceful backdrop to the vigour and affluence of 21st century life in Guangzhou.

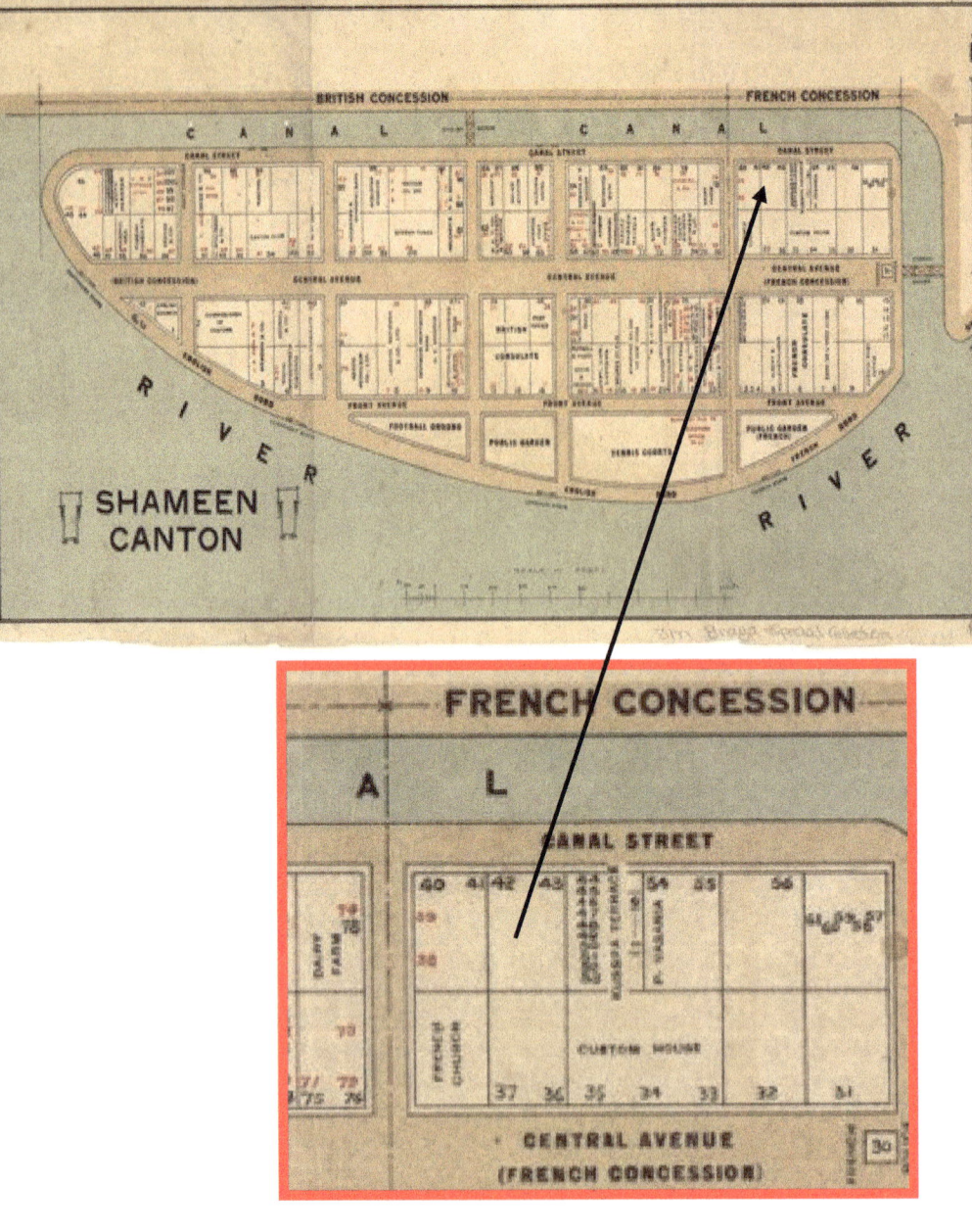

1920s map of "Shameen", showing the location of the British and French concessions and location of Fred's residence – 42 FC

This map shows the French and English Concessions on Shameen that are separated from Canton by a narrow canal. There are many uses of the canal besides boating such as fishing and washing. The new city ring road rides above Shameen. The location of Fred's residence, 42 FC, is indicated.

Shameen is linked to Canton City by the French and English bridges.

The British Bridge
The top photograph (2014) shows this bridge more or less as it was in 1940.

The French Bridge
has been improved. The Ring Road around Canton is seen on the skyline over the French bridge.

The canal has many uses.
Here a trader washes his canvas, open-air, stall roof cover.

Walkway and cycle track on the river side of the island.
View is to the mainland and outer islands like Homan.

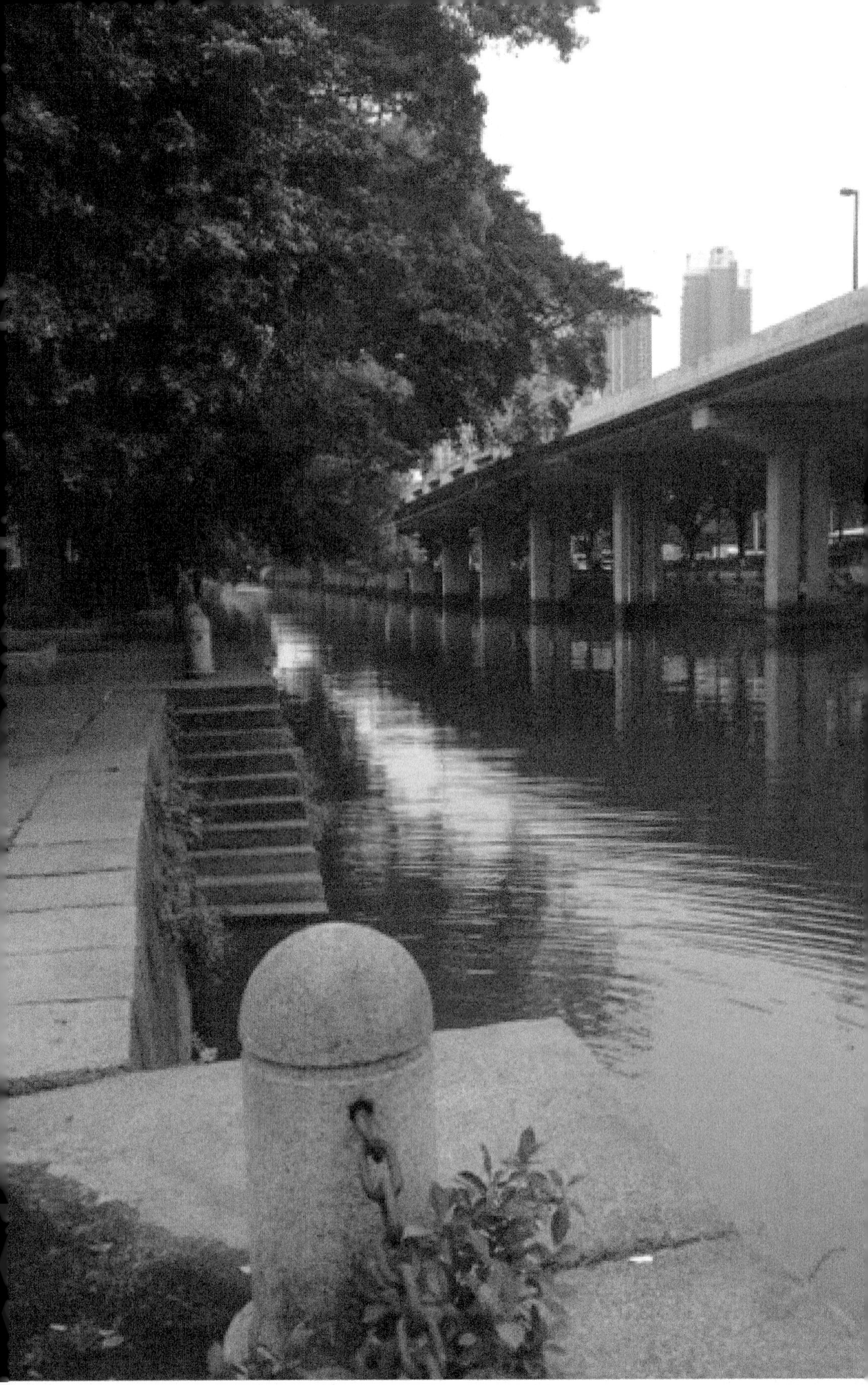

Frederick Cope's residence: 42 FC Shameen Island, Canton, China

Fred lived at 42 FC (French Concession), as it was known in the 1930s. His abode is the section of this building with an open window on the first floor. The building is now listed as an important Historical Monument along with many buildings of similar period on the island. Over the years, house numbers have been rearranged. This plaque is on one section of the building.

沙面北街43号

文物建筑（B）

清末民初建　曾作私人住宅

No.43 North Shamian Street

Gazetted Building(B)

Built during late Qing to Early Republican

Period as the private residence.

广州市文物管理委员会立

2001年6月

Exactly when Fred took up residence in Canton is uncertain. It was probably once his Hong Kong Consultancy was up and running. He chose to live away from his work environment though he probably had alternate lodgings in Hong Kong whilst working there. Shameen was where he relaxed, entertained and thrived. It is where he felt that he'd landed on his feet.

Fred (middle back) with his Chinese Servants

As was the custom, Fred employed Chinese servants to run his household. He always spoke highly of these men.

Fred entertaining at home – 42FC

Across the canal is a Chinese herbal medicine market. (Photos 2014)

For some 5,000 years China was one of the first countries to have a medical culture very different from Western medicine.

Shameen Island, yesterday and today

Magnificent parks from colonial days in the centre of Shameen

A characteristic of Shameen is the extraordinary 258 Banyan trees that flank its streets. These may be 200 to 300 years old so would have been there in Fred's day. Banyan is a fig that starts life as an epiphyte (a plant growing on another plant). Its seeds, spread by fruit-eating birds, may germinate on a tree branch or building when it sends roots down. Older trees are characterised by aerial prop-roots that grow into thick woody trunks and may cover a wide area.

Cantonese – the Local language

Mandarin Chinese is spoken across most of northern and southwestern China. Cantonese is the language of Guangdong Province and some neighbouring areas. It is the majority language of Hong Kong. The written form of Mandarin and Cantonese look almost the same but are pronounced differently.

Learning Cantonese, a tonal language, is demanding for the English. For example, some words may be pronounced in up to six different ways. The tone may be low, high, falling or rising. Together with the context, the meaning of a word is determined. Like most things Fred set his mind on doing, he mastered at least the common usage of Cantonese.

One not-so-respectful term he frequently heard from children in the streets, is calling a foreigner fan kwai (foreign devil). Probably this was derived from Chinese plays where the bad person or demon wears white masks and so white races are equated with devils!

Commodore of Canton Sailing Club

Fred had a passion for the sea and a passion for sailing. As soon as he could afford it, he bought his own ocean-going yacht he named Joan.

In every spare moment, Fred was sailing. He joined the Canton Sailing Club and after a while became the Commodore. At first he sailed on the Pearl River to Hong Kong and local islands.

Above: *Commodore Fred with friend, Henry Coates (of Coates Cotton)*
Below: *Relaxing with sailing friends*

Sailing Joan by day

Sailing solo at night

The Pearl River (Zhu Jiang in Chinese) is so named because of the pearl coloured shells at the bottom of the river as it flows through the city of Canton (Guangzhou). It is China's third longest river and drains most of South Central China. The river's estuary, Bocca Tigris, is regularly dredged to keep it open for ocean vessels.

Below: Sailing friends
Sampans on Pearl River

Once Fred mastered seagoing techniques he'd sail to Hong Kong and then up the Chinese coast and onto the Yangtze River as far as Chungking.

Above: *Scene from Tsim Sha Tsui near Victoria Harbour.*
Photo *F. Cope 1936*
Below: *Stanley waterfront, Hong Kong 2014 by Wong Chi-him, Gary'*

THE YANGTZE RIVER

If you haven't travelled up Chang Jiang, you haven't been anywhere.
An old saying

Fred could never resist a challenge. He had studied the Yangtze River from the time he'd arrived in Shanghai in 1927. Some seven years on, owning his own yacht, he decided to try his hand at navigating the Yangtze from its mouth to Chungking (Chongqing), which he did several times. Fred's final voyage on the Yangtze was most likely in the summer of 1937. Was it before the Marco Polo Bridge incident and the brutal Japanese battles for Shanghai, I wonder?

In any event, I recall him telling us several times that he had taken (illegally according to the Japanese) one or two people as far as Chungking. He would go on to explain how this added fuel to the fire leading later to his incarceration in Canton.

The map includes the Yangtze River Basin and cities where Fred worked and lived: Harbin, Tientsin (Tianjin), Shanghai, Hong Kong and Canton (Guangzhou).

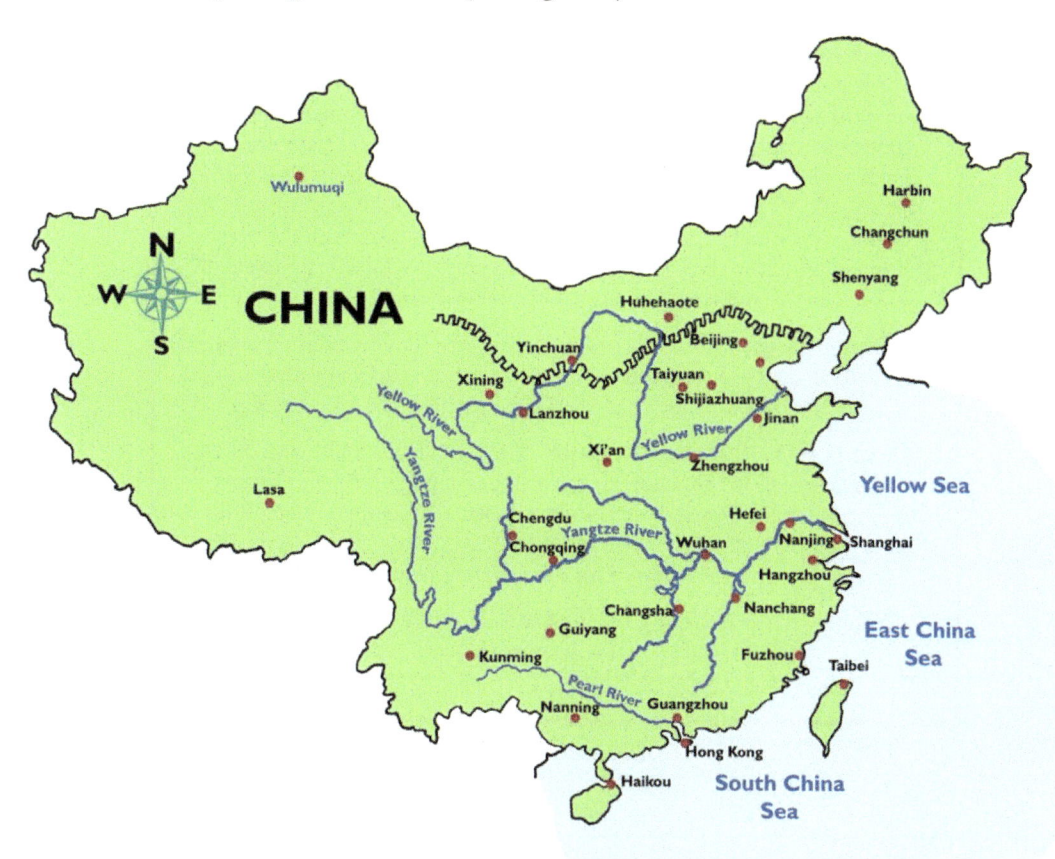

A Short Profile of the Yangtze River Basin

The Yangtze, known in China as the Chang Jiang or the Yangzi, is one of two main rivers in China and the world's third longest river (3,720 miles or 5,263 km). Yangtze means *long river*. Because it was difficult to cross, it became the natural boundary between North and South China. Geologists suggest its origin dates back about 45 million years. The river, fed by several main tributaries and countless smaller lakes and rivers, finally reaches the East China Sea at Shanghai.

Variety on, and from, the Yangtze is a boundless mix of scenic, industrial and ancient sites. Even before the Three Gorges Dam was built, it was navigable for some 1,000 miles (1,600 km) from its mouth by oceangoing vessels. Passing through the spectacular Yangtze Three Gorges, (Qutang Gorge, Wuxia Gorge and Xiling Gorge) the Yangtze was highly hazardous to shipping in this region. To navigate some of the most risky and deadly sections of the three gorges, those on boats and junks engaged trackers to pull ships upriver.

One third of China's population lives in the Yangtze basin, where the river is important for agriculture, industry and inland travel. It is one of the world's busiest waterways with commercial traffic transporting bulk goods like coal, manufactured goods and passengers on river cruises. Prior to the building of the national railway network during the 20th century, the Yangtze was the backbone of China's inland transportation system. The Grand Canal connects the lower Yangtze with the major cities south of the river (Wuxi, Suzhou, Hangzhou) and with those of northern China (Yangzhou to Beijing).

In the rainy season, flooding can be hazardous, like the major Yangtze River floods in 1935, and more disastrous – those of 1954 killed around 30,000 people. Work has been done to make the river safer.

From 1917-1919 Jardine Matheson, Butterfield and Swire and other companies added steamers to the Yangtze navigation – the largest shipping companies in service. Jardines' specially designed fleet, built to meet requirements of the river trade for many years, gave unequalled service gaining a reputation for the efficient handling of shipping.

Yangtze River is greatly honored as being the cradle for Chinese civilisation.

Fred's Yacht

In 2010, we were on a tourist boat on the Yangtze to taste of its splendor and to try to imagine Fred sailing there over seventy years ago. It was hard to imagine how Fred's yacht had coped. Then when we saw a host of small boats that were managing quite well we

129

realised Joan would have coped. The Yangtze is a great facilitator of bulk transport both for commercial and tourists.

Many bridges now safely connect North and South China

At some point, our ship, Victoria Number 3, dropped anchor to allow us to scramble into a small boat that took us to the river's edge to witness a replay of how trackers (usually poor farmers) worked in the Three Gorges before the age of engines.

Trackers

Trackers, wearing no clothes, would rope up, some 50 at a time, each with a bamboo loop slung over his shoulders attached to the towline. They had to pull upstream crawling forward inch by inch until the vessel passed into smooth waters. Some paths, cut on the rocks and cliffs by trackers' ropes, remain. Their life was hard. Some even died without attention from anyone.

Fred told many a tale of his sailing up and down the Yangtze. Yes, he used the trackers. No, he did not like the way they were treated, but tipped them generously. On occasion, he'd notice one of the trackers stumble. The team would not wait and the hapless man simply dropped to his death in the river. Trackers were at the bottom of life's pile.

Writing on the Wall of Three Gorges

As to the meaning of these Chinese words, I consulted a Chinese friend, Chenyu Zhao. This is what she told me:
These words were written by General Yuanliang Sun, a leader of the Kuomintang, who led the army to fight against Japan's invasion at that time. Roughly, these two sentences mean:

Kuimen boasts its incomparable majesty in the world and ships cross there swiftly.

133

CHINA'S WAR WITH JAPAN

In modern times, no foreign power did more harm to China than Japan. In 1931, Japanese troops conquered Northeast China and in 1937 plunged all of China into a war. They reached Canton in 1938, preceded by aerial bombing of neighbouring towns and military points. Japan termed the war The China Incident. It devastated the Chinese economy and cost millions of Chinese lives. Japanese atrocities are still vivid in Chinese memory.

Canton 1933–1937

Canton was a stimulating mix of ancient and modern: department stores with fixed prices and stalls where one could talk prices; medicine shops, mainly herbal; street barbers and professional letter writers (many people were illiterate); shoemakers and repairers who fixed holes in garments so it was almost impossible to see the mend. Tailors' shops abounded. Many Chinese and Westerners had clothes made to order.

Older women still hobbled along on tiny bound feet. The latest Hollywood films were shown in theatres, while on the streets crowds gathered around professional storytellers. There was a wealth of goods and food. Festivals punctuated the year. The most important was New Year, lasting for three days – the only annual holiday for many. Wealth and poverty lived side by side.

The Chinese economy had been at a peak of prosperity prior to the Japanese invasion. Besides the economic disruption, the Japanese stepped up the use of narcotics while Chiang Kai-shek's National Opium Suppression Commission was getting rid of the opium curse.

Plan of the City of Canton in 1910
Shameen Island is seen near bottom left on the Pearl River

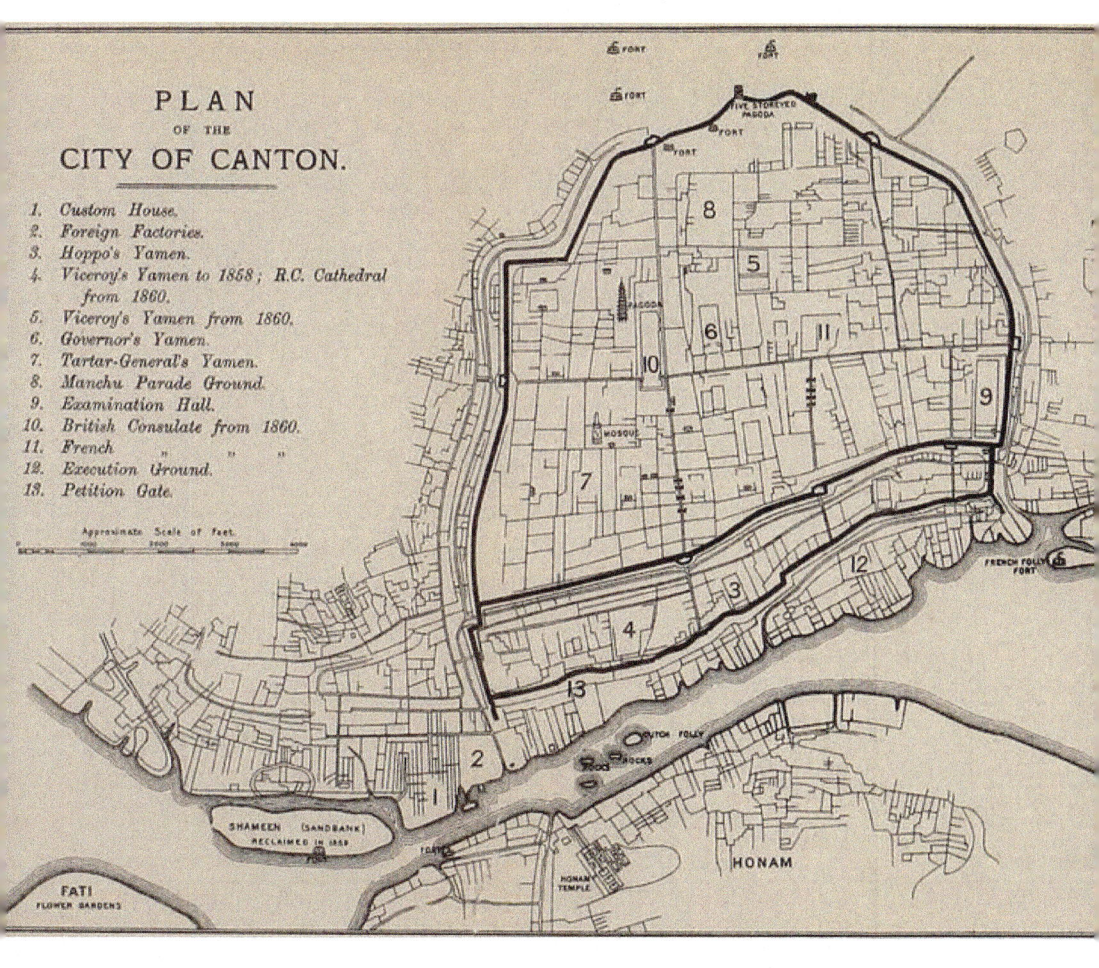

PLAN OF THE CITY OF CANTON.

1. Custom House.
2. Foreign Factories.
3. Hoppo's Yamen.
4. Viceroy's Yamen to 1858; R.C. Cathedral from 1860.
5. Viceroy's Yamen from 1860.
6. Governor's Yamen.
7. Tartar-General's Yamen.
8. Manchu Parade Ground.
9. Examination Hall.
10. British Consulate from 1860.
11. French   "   "   "
12. Execution Ground.
13. Petition Gate.

Aerial photo of Shameen Island British and French Concessions 1935 White ships from left to right are the daily ferry to Hong Kong, a British gunboat and an American gunboat.

Canton 1937–1938

In 1937 the Japanese started bombing the city before capturing Canton. Daily raids were the norm. Businesses closed and tens of thousands of people fled to ancestral villages or Hong Kong for safety, travelling by foot, boat, train, truck and a few by plane to beyond the Japanese reach. Educational institutions transferred to Hong Kong or other centers.

It was not known whether the Japanese intended to wipe out Canton by bombing, or to invade by land and sea and take the city. Bombers flew in from north of Hong Kong at first, concentrating their destruction on military targets and railways like the 100 mile Canton-Kowloon railway. Bombs hit carriages and tracks. Trains ran at night when there was less bombing. All over the city there was spy mania. Anybody doing anything unusual was suspect including Fred.

1938–1941: Japanese Occupation of Canton

Dates and details in this section are extracted from
The diary of H. Staples-Smith, Managing Director of Deacon & Co. Ltd and
Chairman of the Shameen Municipal Council of the British Concession

Early in 1938, there was a heavy raid on Canton. Houses were destroyed, fires raged and many were wounded or killed.

Shameen

On **28 September 1938,** Consul General Blunt called a meeting of the Shameen Council and leading British residents. He warned that the Japanese were planning to march on Canton shortly and advised Shameen to stock necessary food, coal and fuel before it was too late. Three members, Messrs. Farmer, Scotcher and **Cope**, were delegated to organise this and by **1 October 1938** supplies arrived. Coal and fuel were stored in a shed and foodstuffs in the Diary Farm Ice and Cold Storage Company. F. Cope was the manager. There was sufficient to feed all on the island for at least two months. Some days later, twelve English cows were brought on to the island for milk (and slaughter later on, if necessary). Milk was sent to the Dairy Farm for the Food Controller to distribute. Tons of people's goods arrived daily for storage and safe keeping on Shameen.

The work of the Food Controllers was deeply appreciated, as expressed in a letter to Fred. It reads:

Shameen Municipal Council
28 September 1939

Dear Sir,
I am instructed by the Council to express their appreciation of your services to the food control, particularly during the period of winding up, and the establishing and storing of the emergency reserve supply.

Yours faithfully,
[signature]
Secretary.

Japanese army entering Canton
Photograph of a picture in the Guangdong Museum

12 October 1938: Japanese landed at Bias Bay on the East Coast. Locals thought it would be months before they got to Canton, as the river route had been blocked to prevent warships moving upstream. However the Japanese cleared a passage and rapidly took control of Canton.

17 October 1938, huge numbers of Cantonese left the city, as Canton had been subjected to daily air raids for some time.

21 October 1938: The Japanese Army entered the city from the east. Bombs were dropped in the northern parts. The Chinese, determined that the Japanese should occupy a dead city, carried out a scorched earth policy. Fires raged all over the city. Whole streets burned for weeks.

Boy searching a bombed house
Photo of a picture in Guangdong Museum

On Shameen, some witnessed explosions in all directions of the city and on Honam power plants, municipal offices and police stations went up in smoke.

22 October 1938: On Shameen, the food control started to function. Farmer, assisted by Linaker, **Cope**, Reid, Jones and Wahab, was able to feed the community – all the foreigners and Chinese on the island – for at least two months.

23 October 1938: Some fires reached ammunition trucks at the Wong Sha railway terminal resulting in a terrifying explosion which rocked buildings. A second explosion shortly afterwards was worse. It turned out that the two explosions were due to ammunition dumps catching fire. Fred, and others who had been in The Great War, said they had never experienced such deafening explosions. Fred's hearing was damaged – for life.

The Japanese Army seemed well disciplined. Looting was a massive problem. Those caught were shot. With dangerous outbreaks of fires and an unfavourable wind, there was danger of Shameen burning. Everyone, notably the German community, worked as a team to save Shameen. Not many houses escaped damage – doors and windows shattered including the large windows in the Chartered Bank, Hong Kong Bank and the stained glass window over the altar in Christchurch. Apart from minor injuries, no one was killed.

26 October 1938: Japanese officials called on Shameen to deliver permits to residents so they could walk about the city. At that stage, foreigners were under some form of house arrest.

28 October 1938: Medical doctors and missionaries of all denominations and The Red Cross were doing wonderful work in Canton, feeding and rehabilitating people in the six refugee camps where they struggled to provide enough food.

29 October 1938: There seem to be more Japanese troops in the back streets – they were just 'cleaning up'! Foreigners were thorns in the flesh of the Japanese because of their insistence on observing the Treaty Rights. They were able to report to the world the happenings in China up to Pearl Harbour, 7 December 1941. Under the old treaties, gun boats were stationed in various ports and rivers. In Canton, British and American warships went regularly to Hong Kong. They brought mail, medical supplies and official visitors and recruits to help in relief and refugee work. Those needing to go to Hong Kong on business or a rest got free passage with permission of the captains.

24 December 1938: On Christmas Eve, four Chinese nurses looking after the refugees stayed up in the freezing night singing carols like *Joy to the World* in Chinese.

By **February 1939**, conditions had improved enough that people were drifting back from the nearby villages, and the refugee camps were thinning out. When they left for good, each person was given enough rice to last for a week. As the camps closed, there was need for supervising city relief. Twelve churches had set up relief centres for the distribution of food and clothing, which also came from the International Red Cross. Some of them had the equivalent of soup kitchens as well.

Building a Temporary Electricity Supply

Fred's training and experience as an electrical engineer proved invaluable. Conditions in Canton were desperately serious (as in the section of Fred's *Outline of Experience*). During the Japanese destruction of the city, the Canton Power Station was bombed and wrecked cutting off public supply. Maintaining a supply of electricity for the production of ice was vital, not only for the cold storage of emergency food, but for the preservation of vital Red Cross medical supplies.

Fred improvised a temporary electricity supply for cold storage, street lighting and the lighting of public buildings for the foreign community (Shameen) all amid the trials of regular bombings and explosions, fires blazing, and the presence of Japanese soldiers who were none too friendly. He did all this because it was there to be done and he had the skills to do it.

EXPERIENCE UNDER PRESENT WAR CONDITIONS.   Rather more than two years ago the writer undertook to put on its feet, the Refrigeration and Ice production plant in Canton of the Hong Kong & Canton Ice Manufacturing Company.

A preliminary investigation report had been presented, and substantial economies effected, when the Canton War crisis occurred. The seriousness of the position necessitated an immediate suspension of all investigations and required an instant concentration on the problems of maintaining, under crisis conditions, the supply of Ice, the Cold storage of emergency food, and valuable Red Cross medical supplies. This had to be done by means of improvisations midst extreme difficulties The Canton Power Station was bombed and wrecked, and the public power supply ceased. Regular bombings, gun fire, and explosions of munition dumps disturbed machinery. Constant danger of fire from a blazing City without. Staff problems from a fear of explosions within. Lack of repairing facilities and so forth.

During this period the writer improvised a temporary electricity supply for Cold Storage, street lighting and lighting of public buildings for the foreign community.

PRESENT OCCUPATION.   The above phase passed, and under the circumstances the writer remained with the Company managing their interests and those of the Dairy Farm, Ice & Cold Storage Company's food organisation. Now a simple job. During this difficult period of Japanese occupation of Canton the writer gave a good deal of assistance to the Concession Municipal Councils on the various problems in connection with essential services and control.

Always constructive in crisis, his aim was to create conditions that would improve the lot of those around him. It was one of his characteristics.

In March 1941, Fred received this letter of appreciation from the French Consul.

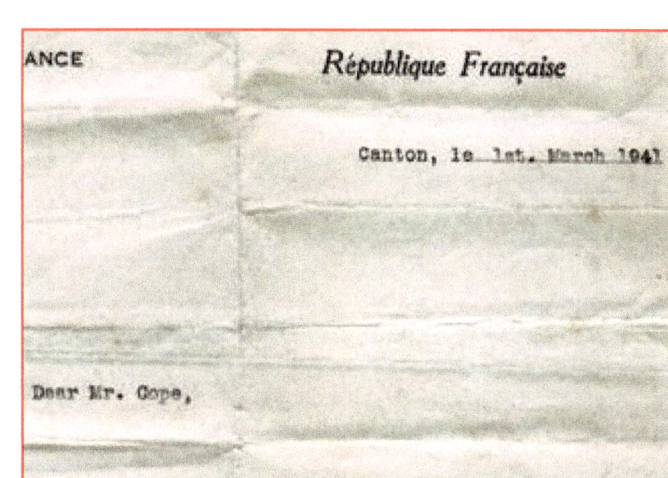

> **République Française**
>
> Canton, le 1st. March 1941
>
> Dear Mr. Cope,
>
> Permit me to take this opportunity of thanking you for your improvisation of an Electric light supply for the public buildings and the street lighting of the French Concession during the Canton Crisis period.
>
> I should also like to congratulate you upon the correctness of your anticipations in this question which enabled you to be in a position to give this valuable service at the critical time.
>
> Yours faithfully,
>
> P. SIMON,
> Consul for France.

CLOSING YEARS IN CHINA

From time to time, my father talked about his China days and would focus on the trials of life once the Japanese had taken control. Looking back over his life I wonder why he spoke relatively freely of atrocities in China but would never say a word about his World War I experiences in the trenches.

Over our years together, a picture emerged of Dad's life under the Japanese. It was grim – very grim – and yet his accounts were always tinged with his sense of humour and resolve to make the most of life regardless of the situation. He had an awareness that those who tortured him were caught up in a system they couldn't escape from.

In Canton on 14 June 1938, Fred was issued with a new passport by the Consul General: Mr F. Cope, C 83909, valid until 14 June 1943. I was delighted to find this amongst his papers as it holds many clues on his remaining years in China and beyond. Of the eleven passport entries from 22 June 1939 to 28 October 1941, most are 3 to 4 months apart. But, between 20 June 1940 and 8 February 1941, the gap was almost eight months. Also, between 15 February 1941 and 20 October 1941, it appears Fred did not travel for 8 months. For over two and a half years Fred had travelled to and from Hong Kong to continue his Consultancy and wind up his affairs.

Most passport entries are stamped by the Hong Kong Police granting permission to disembark. But on 15 February 1941, permission came from the Vice Consul, Canton: valid for departure within 30 days for Hong Kong. CANCELLED was stamped across it. Why? The next is 8 months later, 20 October 1941, issued in Canton. Fred sailed to Hong Kong four days later on the Shirogave Maru and stayed there until 28 October. There are no further passport entries until 1942 – **w**ell after Pearl Harbour (7 December 1941). The remaining entries point beyond China to Fred's third life but more of this later. Meanwhile, Fred's time in China is calling for attention.

> ### *Ron Bridge*
> *To move forwards I must express particular gratitude to Ronald (Ron) Bridge who has added many missing pieces to the puzzle of my father's days in China.*
>
> *Ron was 9 years old and living in the British Concession of Tianjin on the day Fred sailed out of Shanghai leaving China for good. Ron's first-hand experience of living through the Japanese invasion, of having lived in a concentration camp, of having a vast knowledge of China and its history, together with his willingness to spend time pointing an uninformed would-be biographer in the right direction have made a truly invaluable contribution to this book.*

It is worth pausing here to read a true story that typifies how horrendous things were for the Chinese. This first-hand account was told to me by Ami Thomson, a local Chinese friend.

A Grandmother in Hong Kong

My grandmother is 85. She was born in the New Territories, Hong Kong, where she still lives. Grandmother was one of nine children. They lived happily together until the invading Japanese caused havoc. Due to an acute lack of food, everyone in the family died of starvation apart from the youngest boy and Grandmother who was nine at the time. She struggled to look after them both, but she did it. She had lovely long black hair which a neighbour decided it was best to cut short so she'd look like a boy. This gave her more protection in the streets.

Since those days, Grandmother has lived a good life. She is married with eight children and many grandchildren who live all over the world. Their uncle – her brother whom she raised in those crisis days – is her most valued friend.

Suitcase of Secrets

Residents of Shameen and foreign nationals in Canton were aware that they might be interned by the Japanese and would be allowed to keep a suitcase or two. Fred began his preparations. The future was uncertain. Would he be held by the Japanese? What would happen to him? Packing decisions were difficult. The Japanese occupation showed no sign of an early end. There was instability in the wider world so there was no knowing what would happen. He hoped to return to England. Where ever he landed he would need money to tide him over until he found employment.

The Japanese Military Yen was only used in parts of the Far East and was fast losing value. American dollars were valid currency. So, wherever he could, he'd collect American Dollars – piles of them stashed out of sight until he could put his plan into action.

Fred needed a suitcase. He chose one of medium size of strong leather with a tough lining. When there was no fear of interruption, he'd pack it with stuff of value – suitably disguised.

There is a secret story about this case told in the pages of Fred's third life headed: *Secrets of a leather suitcase – FC3*. Here it is enough to know that this was the case he always kept with him – unlocked and packed in such a way that the ordinary Japanese soldier would not care about its contents. In any event, he knew the Japanese were known for their meticulous care of prisoners' property. That case still has a home in my attic.

Civilian Prisoner of the Japanese

After February 1940, there was a general tightening of restrictions in Japanese-occupied territories in the China coastal regions. Many British civilians were interned, but allied subjects were allowed to remain in their homes subject to curfew and under strict guard. As there were no internment camps in Canton it is most likely Fred, for his last two years in China (apart from his traumatic time in solitary confinement) was held under house arrest in Canton as were the consular and business people on Shameen. At a later stage some were transferred to the Victoria Hotel where they were also under guard. The guards took them out for a walk for a few hours each day.

On Sunday, 7th December 1941, there were people of various nationalities worshipping in the little Anglican Church on Shameen. Afterwards, discussion was around the possibility of the Japanese going to war with the USA. Some felt it was inevitable. It was only the next morning that it was announced: a state of war exists between His Imperial Japanese Majesty and the United States of America. The Japanese had taken over the British Concession on Shameen first thing that morning. The soldiers stuck up notices in Japanese indicating this or that property was sealed by the Japanese Army and nothing was to be removed from that spot:

> *His Imperial Japanese Majesty's Military Forces has decided to put all your properties, both private and public, under their control. The occupants, including employees, should remain in their own usual places.*

A Narrow Escape

While Fred was under house arrest on Shameen, an escape plot was afoot. Two or three colleagues had had enough of being cooped up on the island and were planning to escape. They invited Fred to join them. Fred gave this possibility serious thought, but came to the conclusion that his chances of survival were weighted on staying where he was – sitting it out for the time being. On the proposed day of the escape his colleagues disappeared, but within a day Fred learnt they had been caught and shot.

Solitary Confinement

*Everything can be taken from man but one thing:
the last of human freedoms – to choose one's attitude in any given set of
circumstances, to choose one's own way.*
Dr Viktor Frankl

What was the point of my scrutinising my father's passport? It was in an attempt to find answers to when, where, how and why he was held in solitary confinement. Why were the Japanese suspicious of him? Why did they keep him locked up alone under torture and endless questioning? I don't know all the answers, but pose some possibilities.

The Japanese used any pretext to lock someone up for questioning if they were in any way suspicious of him. In Fred's case there were several possibilities. First, the Hong Kong Review published in 1937, long before the Japanese invaded the South. Could they have come across the Review magazine with its anti-Japanese flavour? Possibly! Alternately, had they come across Fred's copies when they raided his house in Shameen? Fortunately, he had torn out the most inflammatory cartoon of the Japanese emperor. Secondly, they must have known of Fred's electrical abilities and his improvisation of an electricity supply in Canton. Had this caused the Japanese to suspect he could sabotage their electric supplies? A third possibility was the incident on the Yangtze when Fred had taken an 'illegal' passenger on board as far as Chungking. The Japanese had cautioned him. Had the local Japanese been informed? Finally, did they know of his involvement in many Chinese companies in Hong Kong, Canton and other cities in the North? Did they think he was a spy?

Strategies for Surviving Solitary Confinement
*Laugh, and the world laughs with you;
Weep, and you weep alone.*
Ella Wheeler Wilcox

Fred steadied himself as the door clanged shut and the sound of heavy boots pounding in unison grew fainter. Where am I? he wondered. He was battered, bruised and dazed. At least there were no bones broken. His brutal removal from his home, where he'd been under house arrest for over a year, had been so sudden – so violent. It happened just when he'd accepted the terms of his house arrest status.

He would have plenty of time to reflect on his life – the question of meaning. First he'd develop a strategy for staying sane in an airless, barren cell with nothing of comfort and nothing to stimulate his mind – not a thing to read! He was exhausted and emotionally spent after the ordeal of the day. He collapsed onto what looked like a sleeping-mat and fell into a sleep shot with nightmares. Locked up alone, most probably in a police station cell, he was beginning to discover the hell of uncertainty.

Fred woke with a start. Two guards were in his cell.

Have they come to kill me? He wondered.

The one standing over him handed him a bowl of soggy rice gruel and murky coloured water that he assumed was tea. The other soldier, bayonet at the ready, guarded the door. As if he could escape? This was the pattern. Fred would fall into a fitful sleep. In the small hours he'd wake with a start. An armed platoon was trying to pile into his tiny cell. He was pulled to his feet helped by random kicking and poking with bayonets as he marched to the bare office where 'big wigs' started questioning him straight away along these lines:

Cope, you will tell us ...
Why you published the Hong Kong Review?

Why you allowed cartoons of Japan?
Why were you saying bad things about the Japanese?
The names of all who worked for this magazine ...

Cope, you will tell us ...

Who you took up the Yangtze in your boat to Chongqing
Who you met there?
Where did you train as an electrician?
Have you ever blown up anything?
Why did you fix up that power supply in Canton?
Who helped you?
Were you planning to destroy Japanese property?

Cope, you will tell us ...

The names of those you worked with in the factories?
What did they make?

Cope, you will tell us ...
Cope, you will tell us ...
Cope, you will tell us ...

On and on went the endless, pointless, wearisome questions. Twice a day unpalatable rice gruel and an excuse for tea arrived. Sometimes Fred pushed it aside preferring hunger. But he knew he had to eat to survive. Is it any surprise then if I tell you that at home on the farm, rice was totally absent – banned!

Fred had time. He partitioned his thoughts to alternate between the past, present and future – between England and China, the rest of the world and himself.

On the complex politics of China he focused on the big leaders of that century. He wished Sun Yat-Sen was still alive. He'd like to have met this man who had overthrown the corrupt regime of Qing and established the Republic of China, ending 2000 years of feudal monarchy in China. There was so much more this man did before he died so early. Then there was Chiang Kai-shek – a close ally of Sun Yat-sen – who took Sun's place as leader of the Kuomintang of China (KMT) when Sun died (1925). Also, Mao Zedong (Mao Tse-tung or Chairman Mao), a Chinese Communist revolutionary who Fred thought was waiting in the wing to take over the leadership of China. (He was the founding father of the People's Republic of China).

Moving on, he'd turn his thoughts to Europe and England. What was Churchill up to and that evil Hitler? What was happening in Yorkshire? … and on and on …

The Flight of a Flea
Two men behind iron bars
One saw mud, the other the stars.
Rev. Frederick Langbridge (1849-1923)

In those long, empty hours interrupted only by the Japanese waking him in the middle of the night and marching him up for meaningless questioning, or those who brought his two 'meals' morning and night of soggy rice water, Fred discovered he had other company in his cell! There were ants and spiders and fleas!

He took seriously his observations. Especially in his study of fleas, he reviewed his life. What did it mean?

So, with nothing to read, and no one to talk to, he studied fleas.

> *How come that little fellow the flea can propel itself so far and so fast? It is over here one moment and on the other side of the cell the next. It must move at least 100 times its own length.*

As Fred reviewed his life, he realised he had always involved himself fully in whatever he was doing. He had been too busy to stop and think about the purpose of his life – why he existed and where he was going. After months of observing the life of a flea, he thought he was getting closer to an answer:

> *These complex little fleas can't 'just happen'.*
> *Someone must have created them.*
> *Where do I fit in the scheme of things?*

The day eventually came when the cell door was flung wide open and the guards ordered him to get up and accompany them. Where were they taking him? To his surprise they marched him out onto the streets and through the front door of the Victoria Hotel into a room crowded with familiar faces. He had no idea of the arrangements between Britain and Japan to exchange prisoners but soon learnt that after Singapore fell (15 February 1942) news had broken that Japan, Britain and America planned to get the diplomats and a large number of civilians back to their home countries through an exchange.

Farewell Canton

In Canton, the Japanese moved all those to be exchanged to Shanghai. They would travel by ship. After many changes the sailing date was finally set for Saturday 9 May 1942.

On Shameen, Fred and about a hundred British and Americans had assembled at the Victoria Hotel and were checked against the Japanese list of names.

When the guards were satisfied, they were taken down river by launch to Whampoa. There their boat, the Sungshan Maru, was waiting to take them on to Shanghai.

The route was familiar to Fred. They passed the Bocca Tigris Ports, through the delta, sailed into the South China Sea, skirting islands and passing south of Hong Kong Island. They continued up the coast to Swatow where a dozen diplomats and English Presbyterian missionaries and children joined. At Amoy, more people came on board. Conditions on the ship were drab, dirty and over-crowded but no one complained. All were prisoners. The tone was raised when someone nicknamed the ship Sunshine Maru. This caught on!

In Shanghai, members of the British Residents' Association (BRA) met the ship and transported everyone in buses to the Shanghai American School. Later, all were transferred to the American Country Club to wait for the exchange ship from Japan.

Those to be repatriated were medically prepared for the journey. According to the certificate issued by the Shanghai Health Department, Frederick Cope was vaccinated against smallpox on 8 May 1942 and inoculated against cholera on 28 July 1942. My guess is that the smallpox vaccination was administered in Canton on behalf of the Shanghai Public Health Department.

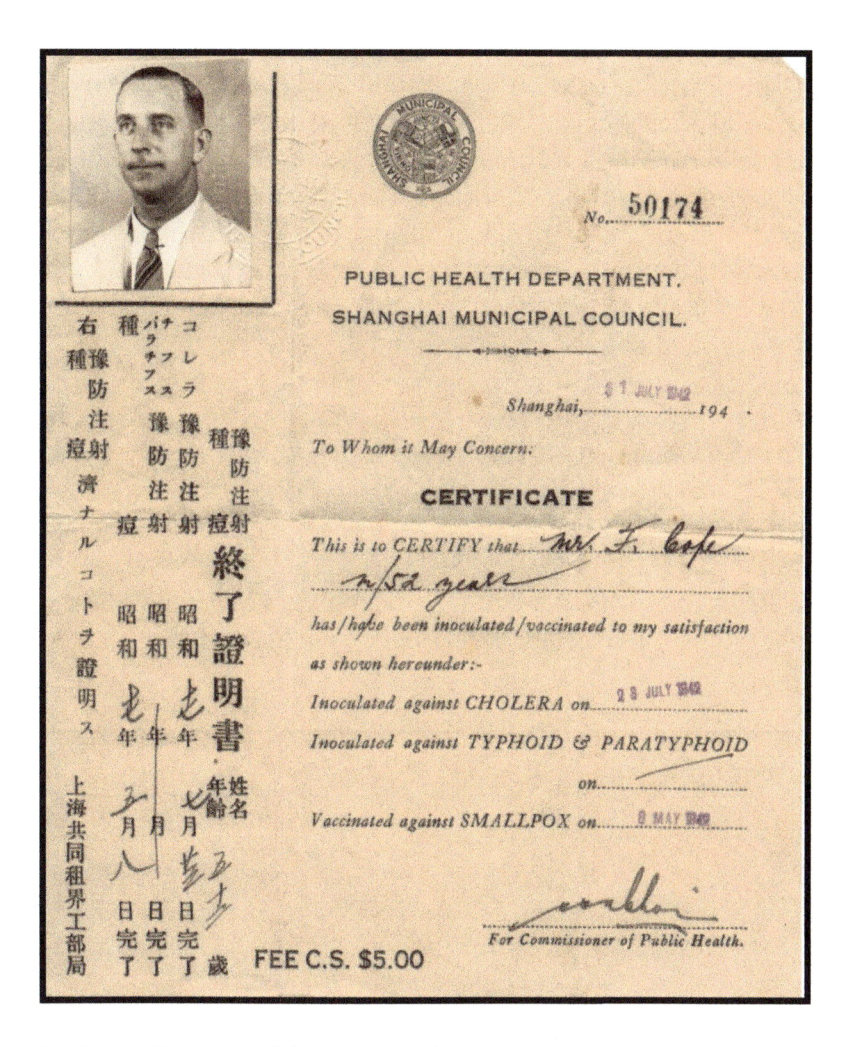

Fred left Canton with other exchange prisoners 9 May 1942 on the Sungshan Maru. The vaccination against smallpox was administered in Canton the day before sailing.

EXCHANGE PRISONER

In 1942, diplomatic correspondence on the repatriation scheme flew back and forth between the Foreign Office in London, the China Association, and the Swiss Consul General in Shanghai acting in British interests. For the first exchange, two Japanese ships – the Tatuta Maru (to leave Shanghai on 5 August, 1942) and the Kamakura Maru (to follow days later) – had been secured to transport the exchange prisoners as far as Lourenco Marques where the exchange would take place. This provided a huge dilemma for the authorities. Hundreds needing passage far exceeded the number of places on the two vessels. A selection system was devised – there were five categories. Only a handful from each could be selected. Fred did not fit any category. Then at the very end of a document I found the answer.

Give priority to those who have been imprisoned by the Japanese.

The dark cloud of his imprisonment had a silver lining after all.

This image below is of a cutting of Kamakura Maru passengers. Those on the Tatuta Maru would have looked similar.

Freedom on the Horizon
There is hope for a tree…
If it is cut down it sprouts again, and grows tender, new branches.
Job 14:7 (The Living Bible)

At last, the day of their departure dawned. On 5 August 1942, hundreds of weary civilians, interned or under Japanese house arrest, crowded the quayside to watch the Japanese exchange vessel, Tatuta Maru, sail into Shanghai harbour and dock.

There was no mistake. Fred's name was on the passenger list of British Nationals from Canton, China, to be exchanged at Lourenco Marques, for the same number of Japanese. He, along with the other named internees, was marshalled onto the ship which departed the same day.

At Saigon and Singapore, additional prisoners embarked bringing the total on board to almost 1000.

```
FROM CHINA

From Canton

Mr. and Mrs. A.T. Ackham and child.
M. Byrne,
Mr. and Mrs. C.A. Cammiade,
A. Cook,
F. Cope,
Mr. and Mrs. A. Darlington,
Mr. and Mrs. W.R. Farmer and two daughters,
Mr. and Mrs. J.H. Ferguson,
C. Forman,
W.S. Fraser,
Mr. and Mrs. M.H. Fulker,
E.B. Gammell,
H. Griffiths,
Mr. and Mrs. H.P. Harris and daughter,
Mr. and Mrs. J. Jones,
R. Longworth,
Mr. and Mrs. K. Lowcock and four children,
Mr. and Mrs. T.J. Macaulay and son,
Mr. and Mrs. D.D. MacGregor and two children,
Mr. and Mrs. J.F. MacLennan and son,
A.J. McGahan,
Mr. and Mrs. A.J. Mandell,
C.E. Molland,
Mr. and Mrs. P.H. Oates,
P.J. O'Brien,
R.B. Peck,
S.J. Sadkowsky,
Mr. and Mrs. P.L. Standley and daughter,
Mr. and Mrs. A.H. Street,
Mr. and Mrs. C.T. Underhill and daughter,
L.B. Wood,
M.W. Wood.
```

155

Life Aboard the Tatuta Maru

4 August 1942 was the twenty-eighth anniversary of the start of the First World War. The NYK liner, the Tatuta Maru (Tatsuta Maru), was on its way to Shanghai to retrieve those caught up in another war. Hundreds of repatriates from Manchuria, Korea and Japan were already on board. Diplomats had the best cabins, women and children the next, and men slept in the hold in lines of specially constructed wooden two-tier bunks.

After months in solitary confinement, Fred found being with hundreds of others in a restricted space almost as unbearable as solitary. Each person claimed their own spot. By the time Fred looked for somewhere to settle not much space was left. Then he smelled something familiar – dried fish! His yearning for privacy was so strong that he chose to settle next to the stinking fish. There was no competition for that spot!

The food was good. The crew treated prisoners well, even showing movies one night. Norwegian, Danish, Dutch, French, Polish, Czech and Indian nationals were on board. A Swiss official ensured all were well treated. White identification marks on the sides of the ship showed that it was nonaggressive. At night it was brilliantly illuminated for safe conduct as in the exchange agreement – no fears of submarine or air attacks. At first, Fred felt revitalized. He was going home. The last couple of years had been a living nightmare but, despite the odds against him, he was alive. He was soon sound asleep – the best sleep he had had for months. There was no fear of being rudely woken in the middle of the night by soldiers marching him up for questioning. Instead he was rocked by motion and the sound of the ship ploughing through the ocean waves and refreshed by the smell of cool ocean air. Fred settled into a sense of cautious freedom. He was still in the hands of the Japanese. He guarded his unlocked suitcase, keeping it within sight or hidden behind the stack of fish. On his movements around the ship, he met his Missionary friends. They had few possessions and seven children, each allowed a case. They carried some of Fred's excess possessions.

Fred's sense of well-being was short lived. Without warning, he began to feel feverish and then very ill. He had severe dysentery, an illness that had spread like wildfire around the ship though he was the only one critically ill. By 27 August 1942, when the Tatuta Maru docked at Lourenco Marques (LM), Fred was declared unfit to travel on the final leg to England lest he die at sea.

S/S "TATUTA MARU" PASSENGERS
TO THE UNITED KINGDOM BY S/S "NARKUNDA".

- 2 -

NO:	ORIGINAL SERIAL NO:	NAME:	AGE:	SEX:
29	95	GAMMIADE, C.A.	48	M
30	96	GAMMIADE, Mrs. C.A.	45	F
31	98	CAMPBELL, V.W.	44	M
32	108	CHAMBERS, C.	36	M
33	109	CHAMBERS, Mrs. C.	30	F
34	111	CHANDLER, F.W.	33	M
35	122	CLARK, J.A.	51	M
36	123	CLARKE, Miss Y.E.	29	F
37	125	CONWAY, J.P.	53	M
~~38~~	~~130~~	~~COPE, F.~~	~~50~~	~~M~~
39	146	CROCKHART, R.S.		F

Prisoner Exchange at Lourenco Marques

*Start from where you are,
not from where you want to be.*
(Anon)

> Note: *In this section there are missing links like how Fred got from Lourenco Marques to South Africa. But drawing on memories of what my father had told us, and on unearthed evidence, I have pieced together a likely scenario.*

Fred stared at the Narkunda passenger list. His name had been crossed off. That British vessel had arrived at Lourenco Marques with Japanese internees for exchange. Soon it would return to England – without him.

Lourenco Marques (Maputo), a Portuguese Colony, was a neutral territory in World War Two. As well as being a 'nest of spies' of all nationalities, it was one of the major centres of prisoner exchange. So when the Tatuta Maru docked, nearly 1,000 interned allied personnel were exchanged for Japanese diplomats – a strained affair with the Japanese embarking at one end of the vessel while the allied civilians disembarked at the other end. The Tatuta Maru returned to Japan with 18 Red Cross parcels meant for allied prisoners of war in Japanese custody. British passengers were transferred to P&O's Narkunda for the voyage to Liverpool. Other nationalities had to wait.

Fred, eager to get back to England, saw that hope burst like a fragile bubble. Weak and weary after his long incarceration in China and the debilitating illness on board, he'd been firmly told by the officer in charge that he was far too weak to travel further.

> *You could die en route to England in your present state.
> Rest up and recover.
> When you are well we'll see you back to England.*

That was that. Fred had no more control over his situation than he had had in the prison cell in Canton. He was used to handling abrupt life changes, but that news plunged him to the pit of despair. He'd come so far on his voyage to freedom but was stopped outside the door. Nevertheless, in his gloom he mustered up every ounce of strength to walk to the quayside to watch the Narkunda inch away from her moorings and slowly edge out of the harbour. For a long time he stood looking at that large liner until she was only a dot on the horizon. His mind raced to and fro across his life, frequently settling on the last turbulent years of cruel torture by the Japanese.

There was that financial disaster he had experienced in England. He reminded himself that he had not only pulled through the Windhill Mill insolvency but, for the next sixteen or so years, he had thrived in China – that is until the Japanese invasion. He had worked hard, very hard, and become a prosperous and respected member of the industrial, local business communities and international consular staff. His work had been interesting, challenging and rewarding with visible outcomes. It had taken him up and down the length of the Chinese coast. For a brief moment Fred was mentally back in his modern splendid Hong Kong office in the prestigious Pedder building. He recalled his spacious and well-appointed home on Shameen Island, Canton. That was all so far away – history! Fortunately, so was the chaos of the past two years.

Then his thinking shifted gear as he moved into positive mode.

> *What is the point in dwelling on the past? I am alive! Many poor buggers died in prison or in attempting to escape. I've lost my home, business, my yacht, friends and colleagues – but I **am** alive! I have written evidence of the work I have done. Life is offering me another chance if only I take it.*

Slowly, Fred wandered back to his 'digs' – a great improvement on his ship bunk next to stinking stacks of dried fish!

It was on 27 August 1942 that he'd arrived at Lourenço Marques. After just two weeks, on 10 September 1942, there are two significant stamps in his passport. The first is by the British Vice Consul (LM) granting him permission to depart within 30 days 'to claim of South Africa'. On the same day, the Consul General for Union of South Africa (LM) writes that Fred is proceeding to the Union of South Africa for Residence. Interesting! On his Passenger Declaration Form it says he was intending to go to South Africa on holiday!

A Link to South Africa

How Fred got from LM to South Africa is a matter of informed guesswork. Two thoughts: The British High Commission would have released the names of those on board about a week before the ship docked. Secondly, Percy Furness, a good friend from Wakefield, was working in Johannesburg. He may have seen Fred's name on the Tatuta Maru's exchange list and, out of concern for his old pal, made his way to LM to meet him.

Imagine Fred's face when Percy turned up! Percy was running the day-to-day management of Escom and was in fact working at the Industrial Development Corporation (IDC) under the esteemed Hendrik van der Bijl. What a stroke of luck!

I assume Fred travelled to Johannesburg with Percy. Because Fred was known to Percy, and the Industrial Development Corporation needed his skills, he was offered an interview. It seemed to go well until Percy said:

> *My dear fellow, you are in no fit state to work at all.*
> *Whatever have they been doing to you in China?*

Fred's face fell.
Was that the end of the interview, and his hopes?

> *Come now old chap, said Percy.*
> *We do need someone with your experience.*
> *But first you must recover.*

You need some fresh mountain air.
When you are well, come back and I'll find you a job.

So Percy arranged for Fred to go to Cathedral Peak Hotel with its spectacular setting in the Natal Drakensberg Mountains.

You'll have plenty of fresh air, scenic walks and good food.
Go, recover and enjoy the serenity of the place.
I'll provide the transport.

SOUTH AFRICA

Approximate location of Oban

Source: University of Texas Libraries http://www.lib.utexas.edu/maps/faq.html

CATHEDRAL PEAK

*Every mountain top is within reach
if you just keep climbing.*
Barry Finlay, Kilimanjaro and beyond

There was a loud banging on the door. Fred woke with a start.

The Japanese guards again?

He murmured as he turned over in bed, trying to delay the moment when he'd be marched up for questioning.

Why do they always come in the middle of the night?

But something didn't quite add up! The bed was soft. The covers warm. The air he breathed was pleasantly cool. He opened his eyes as the banging persisted. There was a crack of light penetrating the floor beneath the lavish curtains. Suddenly, reality dawned.

Oh! I'm free! I'm not there anymore! I'm in South Africa at the Cathedral Peak Hotel. I arrived yesterday evening.

With that, he sprang out of bed, donned his silk dressing gown and got to the door as the banging started up for the third time. He opened it a crack and then fully when he saw a large puzzled Zulu woman holding a tray laden with a teapot and accessories, and what smelt like food hidden under a warming cover.
    Sawubona (literal translation: We see you).
She beamed using the warm Zulu greeting.

*Good morning Sir!
This is your breakfast.
It is a nice sunny day.*

With that, she settled the tray on the table and hurried to the curtains, which she opened with a flourish.

Fred thought he'd landed in heaven.

There, beyond a well laid out colourful garden was the majestic Drakensberg range. And that peak, off to the right, was it, he wondered, the famed Cathedral Peak?

Images taken from 1940s post cards of Cathedral Peak in its early days as a guest house – kindly donated by Cathedral Peak Shop

Instantly, Fred determined that as soon as he was well enough he would bag that peak! But first, breakfast. He lifted the lid gently. A strong smell of bacon wafted up. What a plateful: two fried eggs, several thick-cut rashers of bacon, sausages, mushrooms and some white lumpy stuff he could not identify, plus toast and marmalade. He relished every mouthful but hardly made a dent on the quantity. His stomach had shrunk over the last few years of starving or eating scraps of rice with disgusting so-called weak tea.

Fred pinched himself. No, he wasn't dreaming. He was in a luxury hotel in idyllic surrounds. At first, used to months of solitude in his prison cell, he kept himself to himself. Besides, he'd got a fright when he caught sight of himself in his full-length mirror looking like a resurrected skeleton.

After a few weeks of gradually venturing further and further, enjoying nature – the lush green-girded walks, the indigenous trees, abundant bird life, the unexpected waterfall – his strength steadily returned. And he was putting flesh on his bones!

One evening, as the mountain peaks were haloed by the last rays of the setting sun, and shadows fell across the buildings, Fred ventured onto the hotel terrace.

What better place to watch the sunset? he asked himself.

I think the time has come to break the ice with a gin and tonic. He did!

From that day on, Fred became a regular sunset visitor on the terrace. One by one he met other guests. All were curious about his past as rumours of

Fred, the exchanged prisoner of war from China

had spread. But Fred always avoided that subject. It was all too painful and too recent. Besides he wanted to live his new life, not dwell on that ghastly immediate past. His natural humour was returning so he provided guests with pre-dinner laughs.

Fred always interested in life and his surrounds, eagerly catalogued details of the area in his tidy mind. He was particularly fascinated by the Bushman paintings. He found and devoured a book on their origin – the San people. He consulted a map and found he was 250 km from Durban and 400 km from Johannesburg.

Two months passed pleasantly and Fred was beginning to feel, at least physically, his old self. His walks had grown longer, his appetite stronger, and his zest for life was forcefully returning. The day came when he felt fit enough to attempt to climb the strenuous 3,004 metre high Cathedral Peak with a guide! The exhilaration thrilled him. The ever-changing views refuelled his beaten mind. And he made it to the top after a final thrust up the rusty chain ladder.

167

He was proud of that achievement. It impressed all the guests!

Fred, passionate about world affairs, read every newspaper available from cover to cover. When the weather was good he'd settle under a shady tree, accompanied by his pipe, which, he said, aided his concentration. On one such day, someone who had just arrived was being shown around the hotel grounds. It was Ethel Glaister, on leave from her job as acting matron of Harrismith Hospital. Intrigued by the man sitting under the tree reading his paper, she asked who he was.

> *He is an exchange prisoner of war and a middle-aged bachelor. He was interned by the Japanese when they invaded China. He spent two years imprisoned by the Japanese – nine months were in solitary confinement. He'd lived in China for going on twenty years. But, be warned, he does not like talking about this!*

Ethel's interest moved up a scale. She'd always had a heart for those who had suffered.

It was on 1 December 1942 that Fred and Ethel first met. They hit it off right from the start, despite their twenty year age difference. Clearly they had much in common even with their diverse backgrounds and life experience. Neither had been married before. Fred, a confirmed bachelor of 52, suddenly felt out of control. His heart was beating faster, his stomach felt as though it was tied in a knot, and his usually clear mind became a whirl. What was going on?

Fred knew he might have to return to England at a moment's notice. On the other hand, he might work in Johannesburg for a while. Whatever the immediate future held, he wanted to get back to England as soon as he could to see his elderly mother.

Complications! What 52 year old bachelor Fred had thought impossible had happened. He had fallen head over heels in love with a South African nurse who had turned up at the very point when he was feeling human again. Always decisive, once he had weighed the options, Fred couldn't hold back. So, on 12 December 1942 he popped the question.

Ethel was bowled over by the unexpected proposal. She too had sensed something significant and special between them. She knew the score. Within a few days Fred was due back in Johannesburg where he might take on a job with the Industrial Development Corporation, or he might, very soon, leave for England. Within a few days she was due back at Harrismith hospital. It was 'now or never' she realised – no easy decision. She had to make up her mind fast. So she did!

I just can't say no was her reasoning!

They didn't set out to break the world record but, there at Cathedral Peak eleven days after they'd met, Fred and Ethel became engaged. Things sped up. They were married in Johannesburg nine days later on 21 December 1942.

But wait awhile, as we move on from Cathedral Peak, and before coming to the wedding. We need to discover Ethel, the nurse who'd swept the confirmed bachelor off his 52-year-old feet? What had shaped her? What had she done with her life? What were her interests?

Years later, Ethel, my mother, sent me this cutting with her hand-written note at the top:

Where Dad and I met

170

In the 1980s, Stephen and I visited this idyllic place together with my mother. The pool is the same as that shown in the cutting mother sent with the addition of a smaller 'warm' pool. Then, in February 2015 Stephen and I stayed at the Cathedral Peak Hotel again, with more of an eye on Cope history. We revelled in the ageless grandeur of the Drakensberg – the section seen here in the picture below, from left to right, is Cathedral Peak, the Bell and Inner Horn (including the Outer Horn in the top picture).

CATHEDRAL PEAK – A BRIEF HISTORY

The geological origins of the Drakensberg date back some 180 million years when a massive mantle plume (an upwelling of abnormally hot rock within the Earth's mantle) caused a bulging of the continental crust which much later became Southern Africa. Over time, rift valleys formed on either side of the bulge – the sides forming escarpments surrounding the subcontinent. Subsequent erosion gradually moved the escarpment 150 km inland from the original fault lines.

Today the spectacular towering faces of 'The Berg' give way to valleys, streams and grassy slopes – a hiker's paradise.

The entire Eastern portion and highest part of the Great Escarpment is known as the Drakensberg. It is called uKhahlamba (Barrier of up-pointed spears) by the Zulus and forms the border between Lesotho and KwaZulu-Natal. Cathedral Peak is located in this area where the mountains are rich in plant, bird and animal life. Most of the higher parts on the South African side are now game reserves or wilderness areas.

In 2000, UNESCO declared uKhahlamba / Drakensberg Park as a World Heritage site.

For some 4000 years, dating back to the Stone Age, the hunter-gatherer San people lived in these mountains. Then European colonisation took over and left the San with less and less land. By the end of the 19th century, the San had left the Drakensberg for good. Thousands of their rock paintings remain, depicting humans, animals and objects as a tribute to the San. The oldest known paintings are around 2,400 years old.

Cathedral Peak Hotel had its beginnings in 1936 when Albert van der Riet bought 400 hectares of pristine mountain grassland. Using stone quarried from the site, building was started in 1937. The hotel opened on Christmas Day 1939.

Building the hotel was only part of the challenge. The remote location needed access by road, so construction of the long and curvy road began to link the hotel to Bergville and the wider country.

Today, this much-expanded hotel is one of the best friendly hotels in 'The Berg'. As well as the running of the hotel, social and green issues are supported such as aspects of education for local communities and a range of environmental projects.

The twisty road constructed back in the 1930s remains the route to Cathedral Peak Hotel through the rural areas.

Surprises await you when you get to the hotel, like an early morning walk in the company of wild buck foraging on plants in the hotel gardens.

As we drove away from this magnificent region, in February 2015, I could 'hear' my father, Frederick Cope, quoting, as he'd so often done, from Ella Wheeler Wilcox:

Sing and the hills will answer;
Sigh, it is lost on the air.
The echoes bound to a joyful sound,
But shrink from voicing care.

ETHEL

Prayer of Saint Francis of Assisi

Lord, make me an instrument of your peace.
Where there is hatred, let me sow love;
where there is injury, pardon;
where there is doubt, faith;
where there is despair, hope;
where there is darkness, light;
and where there is sadness, joy.

O Divine Master,
grant that I may not so much seek
to be consoled as to console;
to be understood as to understand;
to be loved as to love.
For it is in giving that we receive;
it is in pardoning that we are pardoned
and it is in dying
that we are born to eternal life.

Amen

This prayer, found in Ethel's Bible, epitomises her life.

Early Years

Ethel was born on a crisp winter's day on 12 July 1910 at or near to Oban Farm, Van Reenen, Orange Free State (Free State). Her father, John Ballantyne Glaister, was of Scottish descent – the son of John William Glaister, the first chemist in Harrismith. His ancestry dates back to 1522. His wife was Margaret Bertram Glaister. Ethel's mother, Anna Antona Glaister, b. 1887 (nee Henrikson), came from the Land of the Midnight Sun, Tromso, North Norway. Her ancestry is traced to 1777.

Anna travelled by ship to Durban, South Africa, in 1904 as companion to her maiden aunt, Inga. For a few years she lived with her legal guardian, Oden Nilsen Sunde, and family on the farm, Uitzicht, in the district of Harrismith. Anna met and married John Glaister in Harrismith.

John Ballantyne Glaister, b.1884, was the eldest of the five children – John, Douglas, Rowland, David and Ethel. They were orphaned after their father died in 1899, aged 39, followed in 1901 by the death of their mother aged 41. The eldest boys, John and Douglas, were old enough to fend for themselves and remained in Harrismith while Rowland, David and Ethel were sent to relatives in Scotland to continue their education.

John and Anna's first child, Mabel, was born in 1908. Their next child, a boy, was short lived. Then, Ethel arrived in 1910 followed by Margaret, Joyce and Grace. Much later, a brother, Johnny, was born.

Mabel was Ethel's greatest friend. They were always together enjoying life on the farm. Their earliest formal education was from governesses. As soon as they were old enough, they walked the mile to and from school on the neighbouring farm of Oaklands. Always laughing and joking, they were sometimes accompanied by a pet lamb or two – at least until they reached the boundary fence.

The Glaister family: (brother, Johnny, was not yet born).
From left: Anna, Grace, Margaret, Ethel (centre), Mabel, Joyce, John

Photo from Ethel's collection – around 1920

Oban Farm

Dunbar, a very large farm in the district of Harrismith, was divided into 9 smaller farms and put up for sale. Around the time John and Anna were married, the brothers, John and Douglas, jointly purchased, for £950, one of these newly-created farms at the top of Van Reenen's Pass. According to Margaret Daff, Ethel's sister, John and Douglas could not agree on a name for the farm. Time was running out. A name had to be submitted for registration of the property. So their Harrismith lawyer (also a Scotsman) made the decision for them. Oban, after Oban in Scotland, became the registered name.

Doug was the main agriculturalist. He became known for his progressive agriculture, stock farming and thoroughbred horses. But there came a major interruption on his farming efforts.

1914

The rumblings of war that were to affect people globally reached South Africa. In 1914, Douglas volunteered to join General Smuts' men on their mission to oust the Germans. It is probable that through a war wound, he lost one eye.

John Glaister kept Oban farm going with the assistance of Ryan Dillon, a young man from a local farm, Waterfall. (To this day, Waterfall is in the hands of Old Man Dillon's descendants.)

1914: Douglas Glaister, 3rd from the left, boarded the train in Harrismith to join General Smuts' men on their way to South West Africa to oust the Germans (Photo from Ethel's album)

> **World War I**
>
> By 1914 the world was a boiling pot. On 28 July 1914 the pot boiled over and kept on boiling over until November 1918, the end of **World War I.** It was a tragic global war with all the world's great powers involved. One of the long-term causes of the war was the imperialistic foreign policies of Europe, including the German Empire. German South West Africa had been their colony from 1884. But, as part of the British Empire, the Union of South Africa, with General Smuts as Prime Minister, wanted the Germans out of South West Africa.

When Doug returned from active service he and John continued working the farm together. But times were hard and something had to be done to make ends meet.

Mabel
On top of that, in 1920, tragedy struck. At the age of eleven, Mabel fell on concrete. Her wound would not heal and resulted in bone cancer. After a long struggle and several operations, she died in Johannesburg. Her body was embalmed for a hundred years and brought back to Oban by train for burial on the farm.

The farm handyman, Jim, was gloomy after Mabel died. For weeks after her burial, he was nowhere to be found. Ethel recalled hearing hammering in the rocks above the graveyard day after day. One day, Jim appeared at the kitchen door and beckoned Anna and Ethel to go with him. He led them to Mabel's grave.

There, on the grave stood a perfect cross carved out of sandstone from the hillside. Around the grave was a skilfully fitted border. So, that is why Jim had been absent.

Mabel's grave on Oban
The remains of the cross are gathered as fragments
Photo by Tonia, 2012

Mabel's death affected Anna deeply. She continued to grieve for months. Ethel recalled her washing their clothes in the large tub in the kitchen day after day, tears streaming into the water.

As for Ethel, she was without her friend and playmate and quite at a loss. Overnight she had become the oldest child in the household and had inherited a more responsible role. She realised how much her grieving mother needed support so, while coping with her own loss, she helped in every way.

Oban Guest Farm
In the tough economic climate, it was urgent that another source of income be found alongside farming. So it was that 1922 saw the beginnings of Oban Farm boarding-house. Over the following years, with much banging and building, the boarding-house gave way to the popular Oban Guest Farm – the main buildings still stand today.

THE HOMESTEAD, "OBAN" FARM GUEST HOUSE, VAN REENEN, NATAL.

Anna Glaister

While John and Doug continued farming, providing meat, fruit, and vegetables for the table, Anna managed her children and the guest house – the bookings, the guests, the kitchen and dining room, laundry and dairy where the popular homemade butter pats and butter balls were made daily. And, she trained the cooks – some, she decided, were naturals.

Morning and afternoon teas had guests running to the veranda even before they heard the gong, so as not to miss out on the scrumptious homemade crumpets, scones and the like – all, of course, served with the option of fresh farm butter, homemade jam and cream.

Anna's pride and joy was her garden. People visited from far and wide to see her garden design and plantings of such variety: cacti, the rockery, shrubs and trees, and every kind of flowering perennial mixed in with a few annuals.

Her hollyhocks always seemed taller and brighter than those of her neighbours!

Inside, on a veranda, was an exotic fern house crammed full of an unbelievable variety of both delicate and more robust ferns.

The Privy
At the bottom of the garden stood well-camouflaged 'long-drops' (pit toilets) covered with creepers – one for the men and one for the ladies. A necessary visit there could be challenging, even frightening at times. Spiders could suddenly land on the occupant and all sorts of creepy crawlies and flying things might appear. On occasions an inquisitive grass snake would slither in and, worst of all, a highly-poisonous Rinkhals in search of a rat! Screams would penetrate the peace of the garden, with the hapless victim rushing out in an attempt to escape the danger. Rapidly, a gardener or handyman would capture and exterminate the offending snake and string it up for all to see.

Uncle Doug
Nothing was mechanised on Oban farm. Cultivation was done using oxen to pull ploughs, harrows etc. Tractors had been on the scene elsewhere for some years, but they were expensive. In Doug's opinion, these were not as reliable as his oxen.

1935 – Span of Oxen pulling a covered 'guests' wagon at Oban (From Ethel's album)

Rear of passenger wagon
(Photo from old Outspan, Weekly)

On occasion, a team of oxen hitched to a covered wagon would take the family and guests to Van Reenen and sometimes for a picnic day out. This was considered great fun by the guests who lived in cities like Durban and Johannesburg. The covered wagon, drawn by a strong team of healthy oxen, would arrive at the guest house soon after breakfast. A loud gong would be struck to announce its arrival. Guests would rapidly scramble for seats with the best view. The discomfort of being bounced around on the rough dirt roads didn't seem to faze anyone.

Uncle Doug, a confirmed bachelor, was a friend to everyone and loved by all. He was easy-going and had a great sense of humour. Wherever he was, there was laughter. One day, as he and John were leaving to go shopping in Harrismith, Doug pulled out his glass eye and put it on a post. This will be watching you, he told the farm workers, so you'd better work hard. Evidently they did!

Another tale is told of the mischief Uncle Doug got up to with the guests. A shy honeymoon couple arrived at Oban and kept themselves very much to themselves. One afternoon, when Doug knew the couple were out walking he caught his prize rooster spun it round and round until it was dead giddy. That was the end of his involvement as he handed over the comatose rooster, head tucked under its wing, to some pranksters who slipped into the honeymoon suite and popped the bird far under the bed. The pranksters revelled nearby all night. An hour or so before dawn they heard a loud cock-a-doodle-do followed by shrieks and screams as the honeymooners rushed from their room.

Oban bowls team setting out for a match in Harrismith circa 1933
Uncle Doug is second from left

Doug was a great sportsman. Bowls was one of his favourite times for relaxing and leaving the farming matters behind him.

An Abrupt End
On a mid-summer's day, Sunday, 6 January 1935, Uncle Doug took a party of visitors fishing. At lunch time they sat on the river bank tucking into their picnic and listening to Doug telling yarns. Mid sentence, there was an unusual silence. Wondering why Doug had stopped talking, a guest discovered him lying flat on his back. He was dead. At 47, he had had a massive heart attack.

Everyone who knew Uncle Doug was stunned. Ethel, nursing at Johannesburg General Hospital, hurried home for her beloved uncle's funeral and to be with the family. Countless people came from far and near, including the African farm staff and others in the district.

Uncle Doug's Will
Doug left his half share in Oban to his four siblings. This was a complication for John and Anna. In order to continue on Oban with the guest house and the farm, they raised a mortgage and bought out the other three: Aunt Ethel, living in Johannesburg, and Rowland and David Glaister in Canada.

Ethel returned to Johannesburg aching for her parents. She longed to be nearer to them and decided that once she'd finished her training she would try for a job at Harrismith Hospital.

A Rescue Mission
1938 brought with it an unusually heavy and prolonged snowfall. Ethel happened to be at home on leave. Most of the animals at Oban 'disappeared', buried under the deep white blanket. This was bad news indeed for the farmers and for the animals.

At daybreak the family, labourers and guests donned gum boots and warm clothing and went in search of the sheep. At first, not one was to be seen – not even in the camp where the sheep had been grazing. Eventually, they found them, one by one, due to their breathing holes in the snow. Most were dug out, fed and kept under shelter until the thaw set in.

Ethel 1938

Ethel is Sent to Boarding School

Ethel, an intelligent child, had always dreamt of becoming a nurse. With no further education available in Van Reenen area, she was sent as a boarder to Dundee High School in Natal to complete her schooling. Her favourite teacher was R.O. Pearce, later headmaster at Estcourt High School. He was a great lover of nature and spent every free moment exploring the Natal Drakensberg. In 1990 he published *Barrier of Spears: Drama of the Drakensberg*. This is still in print and well worth reading.

The Guest Farm

None of Ethel's sisters went to boarding school. They were needed to entertain guests. All three – Margaret, Joyce and Grace – became fine tennis players and loved all the outdoor life. After a few years, each found a husband and moved on!

The Glaister girls, popular Oban Guest Farm entertainers,
From left: Grace, Margaret, Joyce in the Cosmos fields
Nelsonskop and some of the Seven Sisters in the background

COSMOS have naturalised on the South African Highveld. In autumn they form waves of pink colour along roadsides, hillsides and on ploughed lands. They are indigenous in countries like Mexico, Florida, Arizona, Central and South America.

Oban was becoming very popular. The good food, fun, the farm life, cool mountain air and the welcome they always got kept many returning for their annual holiday. Ethel was no exception. Every chance she had she spent at Oban where she too helped to keep the guests happy. John and Anna were generous in the extreme. At the end of their holiday, visitors left laden with (free) farm produce, especially fruit and vegetables.

Recreational facilities were fabulous, providing variety and opportunity to do fun things. Guests, especially those from town, thought they were in heaven! They could enjoy the likes of bowls, tennis, quoits, table tennis, mountain climbs, visits to Van Reenen and Harrismith, walks to the Bushman paintings in the local Kloof, and horse riding. Evening entertainment included beetle drives, bingo, fancy-dress competitions, an occasional quiz, concerts and dances. For the children there were swings and roundabouts, feeding the chickens, ducks and pigs and bottle feeding the lambs. There were chances to ride ponies and even horses under supervision. For rainy days there were indoor games galore – even snakes and ladders!

There was the sheep shearing competition. The first man to finish was the winner – almost always an expert staff member. To ensure a water supply for the homestead, John and Douglas dammed a stream. It was also used for boating, swimming, diving, fishing, walks along a path around the dam and picnics.

THE SWIMMING POOL, "OBAN" FARM GUEST HOUSE, VAN REENEN, NATAL.

There were trips to the falls on the Wilge River, a tributary of the Orange River, located on Dillon's farm, Waterfall. Transport was by ox wagon, horseback or on foot.

When Ethel was home she'd take guests out riding. An outing to Nelsonskop meant a long ride there, a climb up the mountain via the red rocks, and a picnic on top while taking in the breathtaking views. After a scramble down they had a rather weary ride back to Oban. There a delicious tea with homemade cakes and scones awaited them.

Ethel's favourite long rides were to Nelsonskop, de Beer's Pass and Van Reenen's Pass. Only the fittest did the long rides.

Ethel (right) with Oban guests at Pitcher's Rest near to de Beers Pass in the 1930s

De Beer's Pass

De Beer's Pass is located on a minor road between Ladysmith and Harrismith. At the time of writing there is a proposal to create an alternative route via De Beer's Pass to the nearby N3 national road via Van Reenen's Pass. This second alternate route would shorten the route between Durban and Johannesburg and would provide a gentler gradient than that over the existing, somewhat dangerous, Van Reenen's Pass.

Strong opposition to this second route is based on evidence that its construction would destroy some of the important wetlands.

Ingula – The pumped-storage hydroelectricity plant on the escarpment of the Little Drakensberg range straddling the border of the Free State and KwaZulu-Natal, close to De Beer's Pass, is under construction by Eskom, the Ingula Pumped Storage Scheme. It consists of an upper dam (Bedford Dam) and a lower dam (Bramhoek Dam) 4.6 km apart connected by tunnels. The underground powerhouse will house 4 x 333MW reversible pump-turbines. The plant will be used to generate electricity during peak demands during the day. At night, excess power on the grid generated by conventional coal and nuclear plants will be used to pump water to the upper reservoir.

The name Ingula is associated with the cream on top of milk.

Road to Nelsonskop. The crevice in the centre is on the route

Reaching the Red Rocks

Starting out

Battling the bush  *Beauty along the way*

Breathtaking views from the top of Nelsonskop.
Once at the top there is no desire to descend!
Below: Stephen enjoys a well earned lunch

Ethel's son-in-law, Stephen Bowley, admires the views from the top of Nelsonskop, 1981

The exotic climb up Nelsonskop is no doddle. In spring and summer, climbers are rewarded by the beauty of the indigenous plants, the sound and sight of baboons on the rocks and vultures flying overhead. The odd grass snake or Rinkhals may be seen sunning itself on the path.

Stephen and I climbed Nelsonskop via the Red Rock Route as described by my mother, Ethel.

Men encountered at the bottom of the climb

The Kloof (rocky valley)

The Kloof, barely half a mile from Oban Guest House, is an exciting place, especially for children.

Dassies (South African rock rabbits) are most often seen sunning themselves on large rocks. Always on duty is the lookout Dassie. The moment there is the threat of danger, like a human, the lookout lets out a high-pitched cry that sends all the Dassies fleeing for cover. Also to be seen are: birds, beetles, rocks, rock pools and mini waterfalls.

Lizards dart along the rocks and, on rare occasions, a lucky person may see a semi-aquatic leguaan slip into the water and disappear under a rock. The occasional buck may be about, and the spiky black and white collectable quills of the seldom-seen porcupines are evidence of their presence.

Butterflies, bees and flowers, like the natural arum lilies, add to the interest. A visitor may be startled by the noisy cry of a hadedah as it takes flight.

Bushman Paintings

The biggest pull to The Kloof is undoubtedly the Bushman paintings, known also as rock art. These can be hard to find without a guide who knows their whereabouts.

Unfortunately, over the years, guests, keen to see these historic works of art, have slapped water on the paintings to enhance them. In the long term, repeated application of water only destroys them. The Bushmen knew this and painted their 'messages' on rocks protected from the weather. Worse still, some have etched their own rock art – sometimes on top of the existing Bushman painting.

Most destructive of all, during the war years, young men with rifles would sit on one side of The Kloof and use the Bushman paintings opposite for target practice. Fortunately, not all is lost.

A few of the best-preserved Bushman paintings on Oban are hard to find and remain in good shape.

Here I point to one of the well-hidden Bushman paintings on Oban. One interpretation is that this represents some kind of enclosure. Another possibility is that it represents a snake!

Oban's Bushman paintings are only a small part of a vast collection in the Drakensberg.

Bushman art in the South African Drakensberg

The Drakensberg has between 35,000 and 40,000 Bushman works of art – the largest collection in the world. These paintings are difficult to date, but anthropological evidence indicates that the Bushmen people existed in the Drakensberg at least 40,000 years ago and possibly over 100,000 years ago. The oldest rock painting in the Drakensberg dates back about 2,400 years.

The Drakensberg (meaning 'Dragon Mountain' in Afrikaans; and 'Barrier of Spears' in Zulu) is the highest mountain range in Southern Africa – 3,482 meters (11,424 ft) at its highest. It extends over the Eastern Cape, KwaZulu Natal, Lesotho, Swaziland, Mpumalanga and ends in Limpopo Province.

Van Reenen's Pass

Photograph from Ethel's album: 1920 -1935 A young man leads a span of 8 pairs of yoked oxen, pulling a heavy load up Van Reenen's Pass

Van Reenen's Pass
Van Reenen's Pass, renowned for its precarious roads, particularly in the frequent misty conditions, passes through stunning scenery. The new 'old road', as seen in the photograph, was opened in 1925. It followed much the same route as did the old transport riders and, before the advent of the motor car, was used for trekking animals between Natal and the Free State each spring and autumn. Wending its way through the Drakensberg Mountains, it forms part of the road between Johannesburg and Durban. Van Reenen is a village at the summit of the Pass between Harrismith in the Free State, and Ladysmith in KwaZulu-Natal. Van Reenen's history is steeped in the Anglo-Boer War.

Farm Workers

Most farm workers at Oban were Zulus or from Basutoland (Lesotho). They lived in mud huts similar to those above.

Ethel spoke fluent Zulu and some Sesotho from a young age. Sometimes at breakfast she'd join the women who worked in the bedrooms. This was eaten under the great gum trees, sitting around a large-legged cast iron cooking pot, fuelled by a fire. The meal was always the same – phutu with amasi (Zulu words) and sugar, washed down with tea. Phutu is made from maize meal and water. It is stiff and crumbly. Amasi is soured milk. A handful of phutu was squashed into a sausage shape, and dipped in sugar! Delicious! Sometimes it was dipped in amasi.

Ethel liked to play with the African kids. It bothered her that they did not have warm clothing in the freezing winters, so she collected second-hand clothes to give to them.

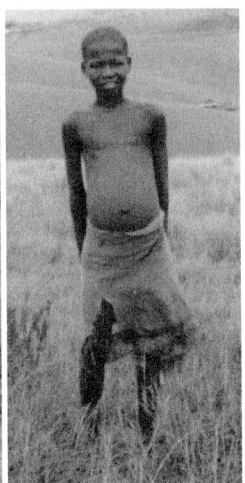

Ethel, the Nurse

Ethel started her nurse training at the Johannesburg General Hospital. She was a natural. After her general training, she went on to specialise in midwifery, fever, and theatre in various hospitals. She had a special soft spot for babies. She was a natural leader so in due time became a sister. Her final job at Harrismith was acting matron.

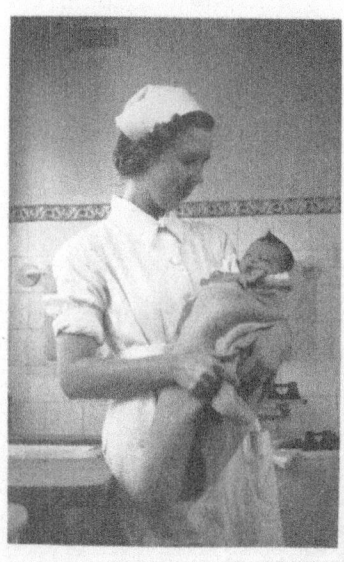

East Africa – Trip of a Lifetime

One of the main points about travelling is to develop in us a feeling of solidarity, of that oneness without which no better world is possible.
Ella Mallart

Ethel's East African family
Right: Uncle Oden; Centre: Ethel

It was 1938. After months of saving and planning, and brim full of anticipation, Ethel boarded a ship in Durban at the start of her dream voyage to East Africa. It was her first step out of South Africa – the only Glaister girl to be so adventurous.

Always a lover of geography, this was Ethel's chance to see new places first-hand, and to meet her mother's Norwegian relations in East Africa. She disembarked in Dar-es-Salaam, Tanganyika (Tanzania), ready for her adventures in Uganda, Kenya and Tanganyika.

Elgon homestead.

At last she arrived at Elgon on the Kenya-Uganda border. What a wonderful world. Every day brought new surprises. She was as free as a bird and revelling in every opportunity. Elgon was so like Oban in its rural beauty, peace, and warm welcome.

It wasn't long before Ethel was shown the coffee plantation, their main source of income. Next, she had to dress up like a Norwegian in full national dress. Perhaps, for the first time, she truly identified with her Norwegian roots.

Life in Uganda was a long adventure. Ethel enjoyed wandering alone or walking with a dog. She borrowed a bike and explored further afield. There were day and weekend outings too. An excursion Ethel found particularly fascinating was to the famed Budongo Forest in the Masindi district of Western Uganda – the largest forest in Uganda. The variety of animal and plant species had to be seen to be believed. For example, there were 24 recorded species of small mammals, 465 species of trees and 359 species of birds

Speke discovered this source of the Nile on 28 July 1862

A highlight was seeing the source of the Nile – the longest river in Africa. At 6,650 km (4,130 miles) long, it is the longest river in the world. The plaque reads:

Explorer, John Hanning Speke (1827–1864), assumed this to be the source of the Nile. David Livingstone doubted this was the real source and devoted his life to finding it, but he died before he did. About 100 years later, satellite photography revealed the source is high up in the mountains of Burundi.

The Nile

The Nile runs through ten countries: Sudan, South Sudan, Burundi, Rwanda, Democratic Republic of the Congo, Tanzania, Kenya, Ethiopia, Uganda and Egypt.
Two major tributaries are the White Nile and the Blue Nile. **The White Nile** rises in the Great Lakes region of central Africa. **The Blue Nile** begins at Lake Tana in Ethiopia and flows into Sudan.
The two rivers meet near the Sudanese capital of Khartoum. The northern section of the river flows almost entirely through desert, from Sudan into Egypt, whose civilisation has depended on the river since ancient times.

All too soon Ethel's adventure came to an end. She had no idea what the future held for her. But, in the not-too-distant future, her life was to change dramatically in more ways than one. She decided to apply for a nursing job at Harrismith Hospital.

Nursing Days at Harrismith (Thebe Hospital)

A 2012 view of the location of Harrismith Hospital (Thebe Hospital)

Ethel got the job as a Sister. She liked the work and was able to go to Oban for her days off. She soon made friends, especially with Mary, the matron. On their days off, they enjoyed Harrismith and sometimes visited each other's home farms.

After some time, Mary married Marnie Wessels. Ethel was bridesmaid. She became acting matron, taking over Mary's responsibilities. It was hard work but Ethel had learnt the value of a good break. So, as soon as was practical, she booked a holiday at Cathedral Peak. Little did she realise what lay in store.

Harrismith hospital staff, early 1940s
Front row: Ethel second from right; Mary (Wessels), the matron, centre

Harrismith

Harrismith, an attractive town in the Eastern Free State, a few miles from the Kwa Zulu/Natal border, snuggles close to Platberg, the mountain, rising from an almost level plain. Geologically it is called an inselberg.

Harrismith, established in 1850, is packed with history and associations. Named after the British Governor Sir Harry Smith, the town is on the Wilge River and on the N3 highway, midway between Johannesburg and Durban. It is nicknamed The Halfway House by travelers. During the diamond rush at Kimberley the town was a staging post on the Natal transport route. Ladysmith, in Kwa-Zulu/Natal, was named after Sir Harry Smith's wife. During the Anglo-Boer War, Harrismith was a major British army base. The blockhouses and a military cemetery are evidence of this. Harrismith is an important centre for the farming community who raise mainly sheep (for wool production) and cattle. For many years Harrismith was renowned for its factory making woollen blankets.

The Platberg National Reserve, home to herds of Eland, Black Wildebeest, Blesbok, Mountain Reedbuck and introduced species, covers the western slopes and summit of the mountain. It is said that prior to 1850 lions roamed on Platberg. Various trails, and the Donkey Pass road, lead to the summit. Aqueducts, from the Gibson Dam on top, were built to supply water for the town and British troops stationed there. A sandstone blockhouse was built to guard the water supply. Near the base of the Donkey Pass is a grove of oak trees that provided a picnic site for the British Royal Family, including Princess Elizabeth who became Queen Elizabeth II, during their Royal Tour in 1947. As a shy little farm girl, I well remember this visit – the crowds, the flags and that small tub of ice-cream – the first I'd ever tasted!!

The Harrismith Town Hall, built in 1907, a national monument, is a graceful sandstone and brick building. This, the lovely wide streets (suitable for Ox wagons!), the Wildflower Gardens, together with many attractions within easy reach, make Harrismith well worth a visit.

Embedded in my memory, and still a going concern, is The Harrismith Butchery, famous for its Boerewors and Biltong as in Ethel's youth. Boerewors is derived from two Afrikaans words: boere (farmers) and wors (sausage). The main ingredients are mincemeat and spek (beef or pork fat finely cubed) and spices. For cooking, sausages are made in strings or rounds or as dried meat – Droe Wors.

Biltong is made from dried raw fillets of meat – game, ostrich or beef – rubbed with a mix of herbs, salts and spices and hung to dry. It has evolved from the wagon-travelling Voortrekkers who needed durable food as they migrated north from the Cape (away from British rule) during the Great Trek.

FRED AND ETHEL ARE WED

Having discovered something about Ethel, it is time to return to the days following the momentous moment at Cathedral Peak, 12 December 1942 when Fred and Ethel became engaged.

Below, I have tried to embroider the threads of the whirlwind days following their decision to marry. Maybe not every detail is accurate, but it is based on my parents' recollections and details extracted from papers they left to me.

On 13 December 1942, the day after their engagement, both were resolute. Given their circumstances, they wanted to tie the knot as soon as possible. Fred sprang into action. Phone lines buzzed between Cathedral Peak and Johannesburg where they planned to marry. First on Fred's list was Percy Furness. Fred wanted him to be a witness.

Ethel was sure of the way ahead. She had broken off an engagement a few years earlier. This had helped refine her thoughts on the kind of man she might marry. Fred arrived on her scene. He was unlike anyone she had ever known. He was interesting, well travelled, broad minded and had a great sense of humour. He had had a tough time – lost his job, home and his treasured possessions. His imprisonment by the Japanese included nine months solitary confinement when he had been brutally treated. At times he had wondered whether he would survive. On top of that, he had been desperately ill on the Tatuta Maru Exchange ship. The authorities decided not to take him beyond Lourenco Marques – the port of exchange – for fear that he could die en route to England. In spite of all this, there was no hint of self-pity in Fred. He was in a new country. He was ready to begin a new life. He wanted Ethel to be a part of it.

Fred had never met anyone like Ethel – an attractive, intelligent woman with wide interests and great compassion. Instinctively, she seemed to understand him and his history. She was the first person, in his fifty-two years, who had caused him to think that marriage would be a good thing. Fred was convinced they would be an excellent match. This marriage idea was no rash emotional decision but, on the other hand, his circumstances meant there was need for haste.

Already, at Cathedral Peak, tongues were wagging, accompanied by quizzical looks. Ethel knew this was just the start of what she would have to endure. How would her parents and siblings react? What about the nurses at Harrismith Hospital? And what would her friend Mary think? But she had made her decision. Raised eyebrows had to be ignored.

Ethel got on the phone to Oban. Her mother answered. Fumblingly, Ethel tried to tell her about Fred and their decision to marry. She could detect the anxiety in her mother's voice.

Wait till you meet Fred, Ethel soothed.
I am coming home tomorrow and he will be with me.

As Ethel arrived at Oban with Fred, they were immediately encircled by big warm smiles and excited greetings in Zulu. They were delighted Ethel was to be married. After all, she was the oldest child. Her three younger sisters were already married. Ethel's parents were more reserved, if a little concerned, but they trusted Ethel and her judgement. She was not given to making rash decisions. They instantly liked Fred with his indomitable humour, but found it a bit strange that he was only a few years younger than Ethel's father! Fred's stay was brief. He sped away to Johannesburg to make plans for the wedding. Also, there was the big question to answer: how long would he work with the Industrial Development Corporation before he sailed to England? The possibility of their eldest daughter disappearing to England, Anna and Johnny found disturbing.

Ethel had a few short days in which to adjust her leave period at Harrismith hospital and hand in her notice. She was met with the surprise she expected.

Whilst at Oban, dozens of local farming families turned up to wish her well. The news had spread like wild fire!

In a few days, Ethel was on her way to Johannesburg to her friend and confidante, 'Mom' Martin, who was delighted to witness the marriage.

The next port of call was Aunty Ethel (her father's sister) and Dr Alex Smith who agreed to be at the wedding and represent the family as it was impossible for her parents to attend.

'Mom' and Ethel had fun shopping for their wedding outfits.

'Mom' Martin in 1979

Meanwhile, Percy Furness agreed to be their witness. The magistrate was booked and a small reception room reserved in the Carlton Hotel for both ceremony and wedding reception.

The wedding

Honeymoon

*Fred and Ethel Cope on honeymoon
in Johannesburg*

The Telegram that Caused Consternation

The day after the wedding, Fred sent a telegram home to his mother in England telling her of this momentous event. It read:
Married Ethel Glaister in Johannesburg yesterday – Frederick Cope

Unbeknown to Fred, his nephew, Dick, was aboard a military vessel in S. African waters. Harry, Fred's brother, had named his boy after his younger brother, Fred. To avoid confusion in the family, his boy was called Dick except on official documents when the name on his birth certificate was Frederick Cope. The arrival of the telegram in England caused consternation. They assumed that young Dick was the one just married ... so out of character. It took a little while to unravel the truth.

Extravagant Presents

Fred and Ethel stayed on at the Carlton Hotel – their first home. The Carlton, built in the centre of downtown Johannesburg in 1906, was South Africa's first luxury hotel. It became the social centre of Johannesburg and the meeting place of financiers, diplomats and business executives. Fred, with his background in such circles, felt comfortable.. On the other hand, Ethel was quite unused to such luxury. For her, it was a huge adjustment.

Fred in the flush of newly-married life took Ethel shopping. He had a taste for good-quality merchandise. Despite Ethel's protests against the extravagance, Fred bought her two magnificent pieces:: a large cameo broach, and an exquisite butterfly broach. That piece, with its bejewelled wings and pearl-covered abdomen was their favourite. In persuading Ethel to accept his wedding gifts, he had said:

Ethel, you'd better have these now.
They could be the last big presents you'll get from me.

His forecast was accurate!

Back to Work

Early in 1943, Ethel returned to Harrismith to work her notice. Fred began work with the Industrial Development Corporation (IDC) under Percy Furness. The founder, Dr Hendrik van der Bijl, had established the IDC in 1940 to promote economic growth and industrial development in South Africa.

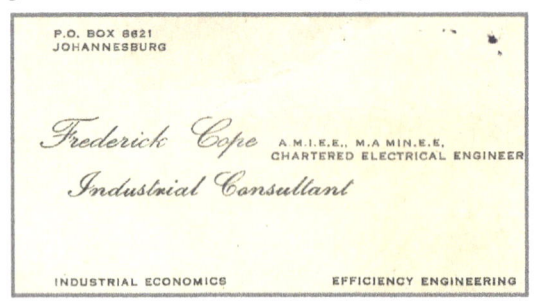

Today, the IDC flourishes as a self-financing, national Development Finance Institution (DFC).

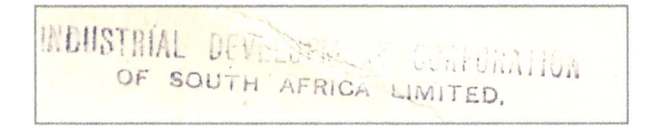

212

Fred often spoke of his time working under van der Bijl – his broad-thinking role model.

Dr Hendrik J van der Bijl   1887-1948

Dr Hendrik van der Bijl was the eighth generation of the van der Bijl line to be born in South Africa. After his early education he studied in Germany before moving to New York, where, amongst other avenues, his work had a direct impact on the first successful transmission of speech by radio in 1915. By 1917, he had made significant contributions to the development of the photo-electric cell and hence to television.

By 1920, van der Bijl's fame had spread and at the persuasion of General J C Smuts, Prime Minister of South Africa, he accepted the role of Scientific Adviser to the Cabinet. In 1923, the Electricity Supply Commission (Escom) was founded with van der Bijl as Chairman and went from strength to strength. In 1927, he was President of the South African Institute of Electrical Engineers (SAIEE). He established the Iron and Steel Corporation of South Africa (ISCOR), and was its chairman for many years. The city of Vanderbijlpark where ISCOR's major steel works were built and still operate was named after him.

In 1940, he founded the Industrial Development Corporation to promote economic growth and industrial development in South Africa.

During WW11, while he ran the supplies directorate, he appointed George Harding and Percy Furness to handle much of the day-to-day management of Escom.

Van der Bijl was one of the first truly great South African scientists. He had been responsible for the founding of Escom, Iscor, Amcor and Vecor, the development of Vanderbijlpark, and the rapid advance of progress and prosperity. He was Chancellor of the University of Pretoria from 1934-1948.

Hendrik van der Bijl's philosophy can be summarised in his words:

It is not the Government's function to do everything for its people, but that it is its duty to create conditions that will encourage enterprise, not the type of enterprise that results in the unfair enrichment of some at the expense of others but enterprise that results in equitable distribution of all the benefits.

The Right Place at the Right Time

Ethel had hardly got back into the swing of Harrismith Hospital when her beloved father, John Ballantyne Glaister, was rushed into the hospital.

John had been ill since mid-winter, but seemed to be making a good recovery when he had a sudden relapse. When a blood transfusion was deemed necessary no less than a dozen young men, guests at the farm, offered their blood. But it was Jonny's time to die. Ethel nursed her father through his last days and was with him when he died. It was a huge shock for the family.

Jonny Glaister, 58, born in Harrismith, was a well-known and popular proprietor of Ethel's childhood home, Oban Guest Farm, Van Reenen. Although a mere youth at the time, he served during the South African War and later in the 1914 Rebellion. He was a good shot, keen huntsman and an all-round sportsman. Jonny was a generous man. Half of the £400 he collected for war funds went to swell the funds of Van Reenen's Women's War Work Party.

The funeral took place in the private cemetery amidst the towering gum trees on Oban Guest farm. Many mourners attended from far and wide. Sadly, Fred could not be there.

John Ballantyne Glaister's grave at Oban. Photo 2012

Early Married Years

Fred was soon engrossed in his work for the IDC. His rapidly increasing knowledge of the development needs of South Africa fired him up. One of his first projects was to investigate, and make a proposal for The Nationalised Production of Road Passenger Transport Buses in the Union. The confidential report was ready by 31 August 1943

Selected Aspects of the Proposal

BMS bus in Durban

BMS bus in Pretoria

There were a number of small companies in the Union of South Africa working on the manufacture of bus bodies. The recommendation in the proposal was to form a national body to manufacture complete buses – the bus bodies and chassis (chassis were at that time imported).

Home manufacture would be profitable for the country and specifications meant buses would cope with the various local conditions. At the time, there was a deteriorating situation of road passenger transport.

The report stated that to overcome this situation, the business objective was to construct buses of varying types – single deck, double deck and electric trolley buses – using materials mostly produced in the Union. This would provide new and permanent employment, directly or

215

indirectly, for 3,000 persons. The business could attract sound investment. B.M.S. Limited, probably the largest and most experienced company involved in bus body building, should become part of the business.

For reasons unknown to me, the recommendations of this meticulously presented proposal were never followed through. Today 'black taxies' have largely superseded the use of buses.

The Carlton Hotel

We are better and stronger than we think we are ...
Love can bring you back from the darkest place.
   Eric Lomax (The Railway Man)

Ethel returned to Johannesburg to join her husband. Living in a posh hotel in the middle of Johannesburg was no easy adjustment for an independent, nature-loving country girl. For Fred, the aftermath of imprisonment by the Japanese was part of his psyche. Personal consequences, invisible to the rest of the world, were all too evident to Ethel. Daily, she sought to understand and support Fred in every way. I doubt whether she realised just how important her role was to healing the depths of his painful and prolonged torture by the Japanese.

Nightmares

In those early days, nightmares visited Fred frequently. Often at night, Ethel would wake with a start as Fred suddenly sprang into apparent wakefulness thrashing about shouting in Cantonese. To avoid injury, Ethel had to leap out of bed and keep a safe distance until Fred cast off his nightmare and calmed down. Then they talked. Ethel realised there were incidents in Fred's time in China that were just too horrible for him to revisit. Each time they talked after one of his nightmares, Ethel's insight into the man she had married deepened. He was a strong, deep thinking, determined character who'd been, as it were, to hell and back.

All Change

After a few months, Ethel was pregnant. Fred was overjoyed, realising life was about to take a big turn. He was to be a father at 53 – something beyond his dreams.

Much soul-searching went on about where their baby should be born. The high life in a hotel in the middle of a busy city was no place for a newborn baby, they decided. So, when Ethel was almost due, she moved back to Oban. Her baby was born in her old place of work – Harrismith Hospital.

It's a Girl

Fred learnt of this arrival by telegram. In return, he wired:
Name her Esmerene.
Ethel was not happy with this name and, together with her mother, modified Fred's suggestion. On the birth certificate was written: Esmerene Tonia Cope.
Right from the start I was called Tonia.

Ethel was torn between the peace of the farm and bustle of Johannesburg, but decided she must be with Fred. When she arrived in Johannesburg, she found Fred very frustrated. The Afrikaans language used in his working environment was beyond his comprehension. Despite having mastered Cantonese in China, he was older and had a severe hearing handicap – a consequence of munitions dumps exploding during the Japanese invasion of Canton. He had no hope of learning Afrikaans. Fortunately, a new way was opening up. Jonny Glaister had left everything to his wife, Anna. Some time later, Anna chose to share the proceeds between her five children provided they agreed to provide her with an income for the rest of her life.

Ethel opted to take her share in land – one-fifth of Oban farm. The others opted to continue running the guest house. That is how the Copes came to be landowners. Rosedale was chosen as the name of the farm, after Rosedale in Fred's beloved Yorkshire. It was in 1944 or 1945 that Fred and Ethel finally waved goodbye to Johannesburg and moved to Oban where they helped Anna in the guesthouse business. Ethel was thrilled to have her daughter enjoy the freedom of country life on her childhood farm.

I was a healthy and happy little girl – the apple of Fred's eye.

The Ostrich Feather Factory

Fred and Ethel knew this was their chance. Everything Fred undertook was with engineering precision. After much thought and research, he decided on the Ostrich Feather Factory.

The site of the stone used in building the factory. Photo 2012

He surveyed every inch of their new estate. The natural sandstone was ideal building material and some farm-hands were already skilled in basic stone masonry. Thus, an area ideal for cutting out building material was suddenly filled with sounds of blasts and chisels.

The factory was sited on a hill with a grand view. Fred found a natural spring on the opposite hillside and piped the fresh water to the factory. Local material was used in building including roofing thatch. The large centre room of the main building was the working area. On either side, small rooms provided sleeping quarters and a kitchen. In the background, separate from the main building, was the bathroom with water tank on the roof.

Tonia, 1947, in front of the new Ostrich Feather Factory.

While works were underway, Fred and Ethel remained at Oban helping with the guesthouse until one of Ethel's sisters and her husband stepped in. Fred, Ethel and Tonia moved to Rosedale, living in the building together with the factory.

Once, as Ethel went to take a bath, she heard an alarmingly loud hiss. A Rinkhals (a highly poisonous snake) slithered, forked tongue flicking, from under the bath. She made a rapid exit. With the help of a labourer, the situation was made safe. Such was the beginning of life at Rosedale!

Ethel, fluent in Zulu and in Sotho, was Fred's interpreter. The local Africans spoke little English. Fred did not understand a word beyond the Zulu greeting 'Sawubona'. Without Ethel, he would have got nowhere fast! Ethel, the nurse, also became the Florence Nightingale of Van Reenen as her skills were sought by all and sundry. Towards the end of the building phase, Solly, the main builder was securing the roof beams when his large hammer slipped and landed on Fred's head knocking him clean out. Fred came round to the only English he'd ever heard Solly speak:

Oh my God! Oh my God!

Fred survived.

Research and Experimentation

All the while, Fred had been doing his homework on ostriches and their feathers – where they were farmed, where to purchase the best raw material, how to process the feathers, what dyes to use, the state of the markets, what merchandise could be made, and where his products could be sold. Ethel, with her creative talents, designed the products. She had an expert eye for colour and before long created a folder of ideas and patterns for their proposed feather samples, dusters, hats, handbags and coats. It was a busy period for both Fred and Ethel. They worked hard day and night to get to the stage where production and sales were up and running.

Fred could see the risks. It was still war time and markets for luxury goods were unstable. But he needed something creative to get stuck into and he needed an income to support his family. He was just not the kind to bury his head in the sand!

Ostriches

The Cape was the place to start where ostrich farming was a long-established industry. They produced large flocks of fine birds. So he placed orders for black feathers, and white feathers, dyes, glues and more.

That is where the fun began! Fred was able to draw on his experience with colour in his student days in Leeds and at Windhill Mill, the Yorkshire woollen factory he'd part-owned and where he'd invented the new wool, *Esmerene*. Also, he'd done work regarding textiles in China.

At last a consignment of raw ostrich feathers arrived – both black and white. Excitement was mixed with trepidation. But overnight, theories evolved into practice. And I soon developed the art of dodging Daddy's tickles as repeatedly he chased me round the table long feather in hand.

221

At this point in writing this story, I retrieved the Chinese leather suitcase labeled F.C.3 from our loft. It houses samples of my parents' ostrich feather work – evidence of their joint creativity.

Evening bag

Feather duster

Hat

Colour-mix test samples

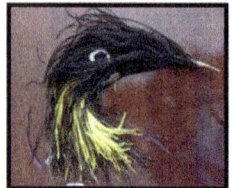

Ostriches – Some Facts

The ostrich is the world's heaviest bird weighing between 100 and 160 kilograms. In spite of a wingspan of approximately 2 metres it is unable to fly because of its weight. Ostriches live mainly in semi-arid savannahs of Africa in mixed groups of up to 50. Occasionally, one may live alone. They feed on grass, roots, leaves and flowers and occasionally on small invertebrates like lizards. An ostrich does not usually bury its head in the sand!

An ostrich has a small head connected to its huge body by a long bare neck. Their large eyes are the largest of any land animal. This flightless bird is built to run. Its feet have only two toes, which are adapted for running. Its long, thick, powerful legs can cover great distances. It has the longest legs of any bird and can reach up to 70km/hr in a sprint and keep up a steady speed of 50 km/hr. A stride can be 3 to 5 meters long.

Unlike feathers on most birds that hook together, ostrich feathers are loose, soft and smooth. This gives them their dishevelled look. Rain soaks their feathers since they do not have special glands like many birds to waterproof their feathers while preening. The adult males display the striking black-and-white plumage while adult females and immature birds have grayish brown feathers. One striking thing about ostrich feathers is they are always alive. For example, this *Fascinator,* made at Rosedale around 1946, has been kept in a case for around 70 years. This photograph was taken as it came out of its dark hiding place – magnificent!

Ostrich feather goods were the height of fashion. This was the main indicator to Fred that creating ostrich feather goods would be a profitable enterprise. Initially, the venture paid off with hats and coats, their best sellers especially on the Johannesburg markets. Then, the post-WWII market slump hit. Luxury goods no longer sold. It was a sad day when the factory was dismantled and packed up, but it had to be done.

Potatoes

Immediately, Fred moved on to his next scheme to keep the family finances afloat – potatoes! Oxen, ploughs and other essential equipment were bought. Soon an entire hillside was under potatoes. The bank balance improved!

Evenings were times to enjoy as a family. There was nothing Fred liked better than to walk about his farm. Often, it was the Kloof they walked to. They would sit quietly and watch the rock rabbits while hadedahs broke the silence with their earsplitting squawking. Lizards darted about and sometimes there would be a snake.

A favourite stop was at the rock pool where a leguaan lived. Very occasionally it appeared from beneath the rocks. That was always a cause of great excitement.

225

Running Oban

Just at the point when the potatoes were reaped, Fred and Ethel had an urgent request to lend a helping hand at Oban as there was no one else available to work with Anna Glaister. So, with the ostrich feather factory put to bed and nothing else on the go, they packed up and moved to Oban full-time.

Fred immediately examined the books. He was horrified! Financially, Oban was in a bad way. So he set about comprehensively planning how to stabilise Oban's dwindling income. WWII was over, but the recession was biting hard. Guests expected higher standards. Oban needed upgrading – the accommodation, the facilities, the farming, the orchard, better staff training and so on.

Unpopular as this would prove, certain practices had to cease. Throughout the lifetime of Oban, guests had left to return home laden with free produce – fruit, vegetables, eggs and more. This had become custom through the generosity of Ethel's father, Jonny Glaister. Rates had to be increased – equally unpopular, not least with some family members who failed to see the financial disaster writing on the wall.

Ethel was more than fully occupied organising the restoration of bedrooms and function rooms, supervising the kitchen and grounds staff, organising the catering, taking bookings, seeing to the never-ending needs of the guests and keeping them happy.

Then there was their little daughter to look after. Ethel employed a nanny to help out on that score.

Bonzo's Double

Something was missing! Fred, reflecting on his Yorkshire Bonzo, concluded it was time to find a new companion. He sourced a Bull Terrier breeder and soon Bonzo (II) arrived making all the difference to Fred's disposition.

Improvements at Oban included better quality vegetables grown for the guests' table. Horse riding, tennis, swimming and walking remained popular.

Fred's pride and joy was his creation of a quality double bowling green – the best in the district. And as bowls was a major sporting attraction, Oban saw an increase in the number of guests.

FARMING AT ROSEDALE

Fred and Ethel had put huge energy into improving Oban, but it was time to move on. Some of the family wanted to sell, but others were not ready to part with their childhood home. The guesthouse was to be let.

About 1952, Fred and Ethel moved back to Rosedale determined to make a go of farming. The first thing Fred did was erect large stone gate posts, painted white, to mark the entrance to Rosedale on the main district road. The house was improved and painted white and a wattle and daub store outhouse built. Fred planted an avenue of trees along the boundary as a potential windbreak.

Meanwhile, Ethel worked on the gardens – growing vegetables and flowers. Within a few years it was one of the best in the neighbourhood.

Home was a happy place. Fred often extolled it as one of the best locations he'd seen in the world!

Ethel's Gardens

Over the years, every last bare patch was planted up. In the evenings, Fred and Ethel would sit on a garden bench and discuss the day and their plans for the next.

Money was always tight. But treats were important. Every three months, a small barrel of Cape wine was delivered. A glass each was drunk each evening – never more.

Fred was the most disciplined man I have yet known.

It was indeed a home with an incredible view – Nelsonskop the centre piece is the largest mountain of the Seven Sisters range.

Animals

Many animals found their home on Rosedale. Bonzo remained Fred's constant companion and a terrific guard dog fearlessly tackling intruders – jackals, porcupines and snakes. Years later, a Rinkhals got the better of him. Fred found him dead in long grass below the house – a sad day indeed.

Pets included dogs, cats, ducks, geese, chickens, injured birds, a tortoise, orphaned lambs and calves – never a dull moment.

Dad was not happy about the number of cats-in-residence and the frequency of new kitten arrivals. From the locals he learnt of their method of control. Soon after a batch of kittens as born the little innocents would be located, moved into a sack, and drowned, much to the consternation of the mother cat.

Saving Kittens

One day when Dad was on a mission to find and exterminate the latest litter, I was ahead of the game. I loved kittens and Mamma-Puss was my favourite cat. I kept my eye on my father's movements. This is my account of the great rescue':

> *Dad disappeared into the storeroom, sack in hand.*
>   *Where has Mamma-Puss hidden her kittens?*
> *Furious, and yet with an air of triumph, I crept in behind him. He's not going to find them this time and drown the litter. I've made sure of that. He'll never think of looking up in the beams.*
> *Dad shone his torch around the room. No kittens!*
>   *Where in the dickens are they hiding? They must be in here somewhere. Mamma-Puss always has her litters here.*
> *At that moment there was a tiny squeak! I held my breath. Maybe my deaf daddy hadn't heard. He hadn't and soon gave up his search.*

But truth will out and weeks later, when he saw this scene, he knew he had been tricked. I was not popular!

Bee Keeping

Time moved on. The trees Dad had planted became strong and thick forming a substantial windbreak. That was when he took up a hobby that had long interested him – bee keeping, one of mankind's oldest pursuits dating back to antiquity in Egypt.

He did his homework. He needed to acquire beehives and bees, protective clothing and equipment.

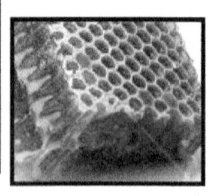

Soon, he and Ethel were donning protective gear in order to extract honey from their hives. There was no shortage of honey! Delicious! For some years all went well until Fred was stung one too many times and developed an allergy to bee stings. Sadly, the bees had to go.

232

The Farm Labourers

Most farm labourers working at Rosedale lived on the property together with their extended families in homes like those in the photograph below. In the evenings, they'd gather round while the women cooked the meal in pots standing on legs poised over an open fire. Tales of the day, and of old, would be told. Sometimes singing and dancing started up with the accompaniment of drums and penny whistles. Their merriment carried in the wind, so we enjoyed it too. Children seemed to appear around every corner.

In the 1940s and 1950s, it was unheard of for an African to own a car – financially out of their reach! The rare man owned a much-prized bicycle. For most, the mode of transport was their feet. Rosedale, four miles from Van Reenen village, is a half day's walk away. Every load – firewood or produce – was carried on the head as was the tradition.

Headman Paqua

Fred was on the lookout for talented helpers. Before long it emerged that although Paqua was young, and had had no formal education, he was as bright as a button. He soon grasped Fred's Yorkshire drawl and they engaged in some form of dialogue. Paqua was exceptionally good with machinery, including cars. Fred would explain a problem then Paqua would sort it out often suggesting an alternate method that worked.

Paqua became Fred's indispensable right-hand man and friend. There was mutual respect. Paqua was reliable and gradually took charge of managing the farm workers – 'boys' (as these grown men were called by the whites in those apartheid days). But Fred would have none of that. He had employed men in Yorkshire and China and always respected them.

Paqua was married and regularly, every year, a new baby was added to the family. His pleasant and efficient wife, Maria, was Ethel's main helper in the house and garden.

This arrangement of husband and wife working for Fred and Ethel continued until Rosedale was sold in 1963 – going on 20 years.

It was a sad day indeed when they parted ways. Some years later, Fred learnt of a terrible incident. It was a Saturday night. Drink was flowing. Paqua got involved in a drunken brawl and in his stupor killed a man. He was held in prison for many years charged with manslaughter. There was not much Fred and Ethel could do but from time to time they sent Paqua a food parcel. Whether he received these, they did not know.

Years later, in 1997, I took my own family to visit my childhood patch. There we learnt that Paqua had long since been released and was living with family members near to Swinburne, on the top of a windswept hill.

We set out to find Paqua, guided by his son Molweni. And find him we did.

Never before or since have had I witnessed such incredulous delight as on our arrival and reunion.

It did not take long for their kids and ours to engage.

Farewell, Paqua!
It was the last time I'd see him.

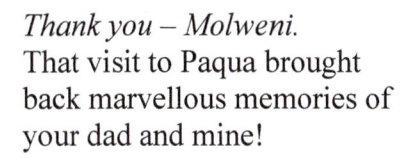

Thank you – Molweni.
That visit to Paqua brought back marvellous memories of your dad and mine!

It was the last time I was to see Molweni – the boy who seemed as bright as his father.

When, in 2006, I was back in the area and hoping for a repeat visit, I learnt that young Molweni had died the year before of the scourge of Africa – HIV AIDS.

Chicken Farming

Life is a grindstone. Whether it grinds you down or polishes you up depends on what you are made of.
Anonymous

Chicken farming for egg production was one of Dad's attempts to secure the family finances. When all was ready, he ordered batches of day-old chicks. I would get up early to meet the train with him Van Reenen. Boxes of chirping fluffy chicks arrived.

At home the chicks abandoned crowded boxes and scratched around for joy in their new spot! When it was cold, they huddled around a hurricane lantern in the middle of the pen.

Day-old chicks grow rapidly into laying hens. The first batches were raised on the deep litter system in sheds that Fred built on the Cape Dutch style. At Christmas time, each family was given a few chickens for their celebrations. This lad has his chicken 'bansela' (gift) to take home in a bag!

Before long, a problem arose – the number of hens sporadically and mysteriously diminished. Theft? As people living on local farms were poor, a cooped-up hen, secured in the dead of night, was an easy source of dinner!

One dark moonless night, Ethel woke with a start to the sound of ferocious barking. Blackie, the long-haired Australian Blue Kerry who slept outside, sounded the alarm. Short-haired Bull Terrier, Bonzo, slept inside near the back door. By the time Ethel reached the door, revolver in hand, Bonzo was attempting to break the door down and shot out vanishing into night with the speed of the (blank) bullet warning Ethel fired into the air. Sounds of feet running for life across the field, dogs in hot pursuit, reached her satisfied ears!

Just when she questioned why the dogs were taking so long to return, Bonzo sped round the corner bearing a large ragged patch in his mouth which he proudly dropped at Ethel's feet. Ethel felt relieved that it was just a patch and without accompanying flesh!

Such were the adventures of living in a remote region of South Africa.

Fred's shed, built in mid 1950s – first used for housing battery hens. Later, sheep shearing took place within.

Besides the deep litter system, Fred tried out keeping the hens in batteries. He built a shed for the purpose and in fact was one of the first in South Arica to use the battery system.

Egg collecting was a daily routine. Easy pickings came from the battery hens. What proved more adventurous was looking for eggs laid in the deep litter system. Yes, there were laying boxes that most civilised hens used, but there were always the wilful, delinquent hens who laid just where they pleased.

Crates of eggs were dispatched from Van Reenen railway station to markets in Durban and Johannesburg – an expensive operation. When Fred found he was exchanging just twenty shillings for a pound, giving him no profit at all, he realised they lived too far from the markets. Fred was made of tough stuff. Chicken farming had to go.

Sheep Farming

*If at first you don't succeed,
Try, try and try again*
William Edward Hickson (1803–1870) popularised this proverb

Sounds of bleating lambs filled the air. The size of Fred's flock had steadily increased. Lambs skipped and leapt. With his knowledge of sheep from his Yorkshire days, Fred was in his element. The Corriedale, bred largely for meat, was the favoured in the Eastern Orange Free State but it was Merinos he'd opted for. Fred was interested in the fine wool of the Merinos.

I took care of the orphans.

241

Fred with his prize Merino ram

Merino Sheep

The Phoenicians (1500-300BC) introduced sheep from Asia Minor into North Africa. *Merino* sheep reared nowadays came originally from Turkey and Central Spain. Wool was highly valued in the Middle Ages.

Merino is one of the softest wools available. Today it is widely used in the manufacture of textiles as it is especially suitable for clothing worn next to the skin. It is commonly used in high-end athletic wear such as that made for running, skiing, climbing, cycling and aerobics and is far superior to modern synthetic fabrics providing warmth without over-heating the wearer. It draws sweat away from the skin. Like most wools, it contains lanolin which has anti-bacterial properties.

Merino sheep are reared in many parts of the world including the United States, Australia and South Africa. In 1932, the South African Meat Merino (SAMM) was bred from the German-imported *Merinos* for wool and meat. It is a hardy dual-purpose sheep which from 1971 has been recognised as a separate breed.

There are two main types of *Merino* sheep – those without horns, or just stubs, and rams that have curved horns close to the head.

Farm workers hand-shearing sheep

Sheep farming proved profitable. If only Fred had had more land, it would have put to bed his financial worries. It was just as well the future was hidden. What was to happen within the next years was to prove Fred's biggest farming challenge.

Climate

Rosedale enjoyed an ideal climate. Warm summers were followed by dry and cold winters with freezing cold nights. Some years heavy snowfalls were experienced.

Sheep sometimes got buried under the snow and had to be dug out. Summers were warm, with about 750 mm rain per year, which usually came in the form of summer thunderstorms.

Fred worked outside whatever the weather – always with his walking stick. Mother and I would share a private joke, laughing every time we saw dad in the fields with a visitor. He'd be wildly waving his stick, drawing attention to something.

Dad could talk the hind leg off a donkey! More than once he'd said to me:

> *I talk so I don't have to listen. Ever since the earsplitting explosions when Japanese bombs hit munitions dumps in Canton, I have struggled to hear. This is why I left my well-paid job in Johannesburg. I couldn't hear well enough. I could not speak Afrikaans. You may wonder why I did not learn that local language when in China I'd learnt Cantonese – a difficult tonal language to learn. Then, my hearing was good and I was a younger man. Think about it! You need good hearing to learn a new language.*

I understood.

Cattle and Dairy Farming

Fred had watched the Harrismith milk lorry many an early morning as it clattered along the dirt road a mile from our house. There must be money in milk production, Fred mused.

There were several dairy farmers in the district. Mick Dillon (M. J. Dillon) on Waterfall farm, a near neighbour, was a prime example. He encouraged Fred to move into milk production. So, Fred started dairy farming – yet another experimental enterprise which he hoped would satisfy the bank manager further down the line. He soon swung into learning about this new business.

Ethel was always alongside of him as interpreter. He fenced off areas suitable for grazing, built a milking pen, and purchased a few cows and oxen.

Fred's oxen were healthy and hardworking beasts. Before long, cart loads of hay piled up forming sizeable hay stacks ready to feed the animals through the winter months. Bonzo and I were determined to join in the fun with the farm workers!

Daily Routine on the Farm

Fred and Ethel rose at 4.30 am to 5.00 am daily. After a cup of tea, they were out tending to animals. Labourers arrived by 6.30 am and worked till breakfast at 8.00 am. The staff gathered in one of the outbuildings and settled into phutu and maas with generous helpings of sugar and hot milky tea. Occasionally, when a beast had been slaughtered, meat was added to this diet. Fred, Ethel and I (when at home from boarding school) and any visitors indulged in a breakfast of bacon, eggs, wild mushrooms (in season gathered on the farm) cooked on the wood-burning stove in the tiny kitchen. The meal ended with toast, Ethel's homemade marmalade or Msoba jam and strong tea. By 9.00 am everyone was up and out attending to the tasks of that day.

Msoba berries are berries that grow wild on low ground plants on the South African Highveld. These are deep purple to black when ripe in mid-summer. The African women used to pick berries by the basin-full and sell them to Ethel for her jam making.

245

Work continued until 1.00 pm when the main meal was served. A well-deserved rest followed until 3.00 pm. After milking, around 5.00 pm, the staff left. The day's work was done.

End of Day – a Time to Relax and Read

After a homemade soup supper, we would settle down to read, play games or sew. Our lounge was a welcoming room, sparsely furnished with second-hand furnishings. In one corner lived a large tea chest containing 'the library' artistically disguised by a draped antique croqueted cloth. Periodically, Mother would 'undress' the box and exchange the books lodging on the top for a selection of those inside. Of course these included A.A. Milne's Pooh books, Alice in Wonderland and so on.

The Florence Nightingale of Van Reenen

My mother was not just a good wife, mother, creative gardener and dressmaker but a compassionate, caring and much-loved lady. People of all shapes, colour and creed sought out her aid in matters medical. This, she regarded as a contribution she could make to the local community. The nearest hospital was some 25 miles away. The dirt roads were a challenge to negotiate. We had no telephone. Urgent repairs needed to be dealt with immediately lest the 'patient' die. As a young and wide-eyed watcher I would, on occasions, witness mother work on difficult repairs. I recall a particularly gruesome and messy challenge that she met with calm efficiency.

A local African had been injured in a man-to-man drunken brawl. His skull was visible through the large slash on his head. Ethel got straight to work cleaning the wound and stitching it and him together again with needle and soothing words in Zulu. That wound healed without further intervention.

Only recently, through the research of my good friend, Gillis van Schalkwyk, I learnt my mother's nick-name was:

The Florence Nightingale of Van Reenen

Sex & Drugs & Rock & Roll
*Song title – 1977 single by Ian Dury
that became part of the English language*

What, you may legitimately ask, has a song released as a single in 1977 got to do with Fred? Good question! By 1977, Fred was 86/7 and, as his hearing had diminished and he was never into modern music, I doubt he would have been familiar with the music or the lyrics. However, using my author's prerogative, I have chosen to use this nowadays well-known song as a peg on which to hang the following bit of my father's story.

In our no-holds-barred sex-focused society, some seem to think that nothing on earth is more important than sex. Well? Without sex our species would become extinct. No doubt about it, sex is the vital and pleasurable function of our survival. However, in my parents' day, open discussion on such a delicate and fundamental subject was virtually taboo. Intimacy in marriage was a closely-guarded private matter.

My main sex education was secured by observing the birds and the bees and the shenanigans of the farm animals. Mother introduced me discreetly to women's issues. Generally, Dad was tight-lipped on the subject, bar one memorable occasion. I recall him telling me that *it* was exhilarating on the first few unions, but when the novelty wore off so did the excitement. I did not question nor pursue that conversation. Plentiful evidence for me was my parents' deep affection for each other.

Drugs were a scary issue. When I was ten, a friend's father was murdered by cannabis-growers in the Drakensberg foothills. He'd been on a police raid seeking to eliminate the weed. From that moment, drugs were a no-no. Rock n roll hardly featured in my life. Dad had strict control of our only radio powered by a car battery. Once every few days he'd tune into the BBC news. Regularly, on a Saturday afternoon, he would be glued to that radio, hearing aid turned to whining full blast, listening to sports commentators. This meant that when I returned to boarding school after the holidays, I felt like a left out ignorant nobody as I could not join in discussions on the latest hits!

Cracks in the Marriage
Broken worlds are not uncommon; they can happen to any of us.
Gordon MacDonald

My father had always been in control. Even in solitary confinement, when a prisoner of the Japanese, he at least managed his own thought processes and responses to his torturers. But after the seemingly endless setbacks on the farm, and having to depend on my mother, as his interpreter, cracks began to appear in his self-control. His mood became edgy as he placed unreasonable demands on my mother, speaking to her in derogatory tones. It seemed to me that he thought she was just there for his benefit, and in my opinion did not treat her with the respect and kindness she deserved. I thought that in his mind he was back in China ordering his servants about, only this time Ethel was the servant.

I was touching my teens and no longer stood by in silence watching the mirror of my home and security shatter. Whenever I judged that my father's demand on my mother was unreasonable, I'd climb in with comments but only succeeded in multiplying the mounting tension.

No marriage is perfect. However well-matched, a couple need to work hard to make it glue and stay glued. For many, if not most couples, there come times when things need serious sorting out. Cracks need repair before grave damage is done.

The day came when my mother had just had enough. I was in the kitchen when I overheard them arguing back and forth. Then the bombshell – my mother's broken voice:

Freddie, I've had enough!
You can get on and manage on your own.
I'm leaving for good.

That was more than I wanted to hear. I grabbed our dogs and ran off into the warm afternoon sunshine until I reached our orchard. I wrapped myself around an apple tree trunk and sobbed my heart out with the two dogs licking and nuzzling me in curious compassion.

If my parents split up, who will I live with?
I love them both deeply in different ways.
Agony! This just can't happen.
Please God help!

I have no idea how the two of them plastered over the cracks and sorted out their problems and how their marriage was in fact strengthened. But slowly and surely, harmony took over. And for the rest of their lives they grew closer.

VAN REENEN DISTRICT AND VILLAGE

Van Reenen (VR) is a unique little village nestling at the top of the steep and scenic Drakensberg pass – Van Reenen's Pass. It straddles the border of the Orange Free State (OFS) and Natal (KwaZulu-Natal). It is one of South Africa's little-known gems.

In Fred's farming days, VR was one of South Africa's most multi-racial villages. It included a variety of people whose origin was English, Afrikaans, Zulu, Sotho and Indian. In 1881 the OFS, at that time an independent Boer Republic, passed a statute prohibiting Indians from residing in that province. Thus, Indian families lived in the Natal section of the village. They owned most of the village stores. Apartheid legislation, passed in the 1950s, disadvantaged the Indians further. However, Percy, the Indian barman at the Green Lantern pub, and Fred became firm friends.

Important things happened in Van Reenen, like the livestock auction. Animals were driven to and from the auction from miles around. Auction day was a social occasion when farmers got together to catch up on latest farming news. It also provided for their families – teas and delicious homemade cakes – and acted as a source of entertainment for visitors in the area.

There was also the Saturday afternoon Tennis Club which met on courts opposite the Green Lantern. I joined in as often as I could when home on holiday and whenever there was a lift on offer or Mother could take me. The contingent from Swinburne made up a vital part – especially the Abe Sparks family of six attractive children, some around my age! We all shared in taking treats for half-time teas. One day, when I was chosen to contribute, the occasion proved to me that my mother was a great (and confidential) sport. In fact, so was my dad.

We had spent the morning baking. I had tried my hand at butter-icing and decorating the large chocolate cake. It looked professionally splendid – that is until, in my eagerness to get a move on, the cake landed on our kitchen floor top-side down. Disaster! Dad, who had just returned from Van Reenen, witnessed the scene. He burst into laughter. I struggled to hold back my tears. Mother, in her usual unflappable manner, said:

Don't be upset, Ton, we can repair the damage!

With that, she carefully scooped up the cake, removed the top most layer of icing and fluffed up what was left on top with swirls of a fork. She placed the cake in my shaking hands.

Nobody will ever know you dropped it!

Both parents kept their secret and all at the club said it won the prize for the best chocolate cake of the year!

Van Reenen's Early History

From the earliest days of White farming in the area, the Pass provided migratory routes for cattle and sheep which spent the summer months grazing at the top of the Berg and the winters on the warmer Natal side.

The pass was named after Frans Van Reenen who farmed at the base of the Pass. In the mid 1800s he assisted the transport riders to lay out the original wagon track (pass) enabling the transport of supplies to the gold mines. In the late 1800s, a daring engineering feat was undertaken to construct a railway up the steep inclines of the Pass. A series of tunnels and reversing stations were built to negotiate the terrain. The railway line, opened in 1891, gave birth to the village of Van Reenen as services for the railway were centred there.

Thick fogs frequently enveloped Van Reenen's Pass making travelling dangerous and tediously slow. Travellers were always delighted to see a green lantern at the top of the pass signifying the summit.

From 6 a.m. to 6 p.m. there was a manned border post in Van Reenen and no movement across the border was allowed outside of these hours. In 1892, The Van Reenen Hotel opened, but by 1899, during the Siege of Ladysmith, it was commandeered by the British as their headquarters. Troops stationed on nearby Gun Hill had a commanding view of the Orange Free State and Natal. In the years that followed, Van Reenen became a popular holiday destination. Five guest houses / hotels sprang up in the area: Cairngorm Hotel and Van Reenen Hotel in the village; Oban Guest farm, Mountain View and Oaklands Park within a radius of 6 miles. Guests arrived by train and enjoyed activities like walking, tennis, bowls, cricket, horse riding and swimming.

In 1948 the Van Reenen Hotel was renamed the Green Lantern Inn.

There are four miles of district dirt road between Rosedale and Van Reenen which were graded from time to time. In between gradings, the road became rutted as heavy lorries churned it up in the wet weather. In dry weather, clouds of dust enveloped vehicles travelling along it.

As the Cope family car-cum-farm transport – the Nash – grew old, Fred found travel to and from the village increasingly tricky. Getting to Van Reenen was manageable as it was mostly downhill, but the return journey sometimes proved impossible.

In the photograph below, the road wends its way from the mid-right and ascends towards the top left. This section is known as Wessels Hill after the farmer Wessel Wessels whose house was amongst the trees. The house has long since gone, but the family graveyard stands as a memorial.

Oxen Power

No matter how hard Fred worked, he could not raise enough capital to buy a newer car. Through the skill and workmanship of Paqua and Fred's ability to locate spare parts, the Nash kept going long after its pensionable age! In its last years, Fred treated the aged vehicle with great respect and care. When he had to go to Van Reenen, he would load the car and then Paqua would give it a vigorous crank while he operated the accelerator. As the car sprang into life, Paqua rapidly withdrew the crank and Fred took off at the speed that a dirt road allowed!

Ethel was briefed on how long Fred expected to be gone and what time she should organise for the oxen to be in spanned and sent to the bottom of Wessels Hill to await his return.

Wessels Hill

This was also the case on Saturday when, at midday, Fred went to the Green Lantern Inn Pub – a strictly male domain – for his weekly recharge. Usually he'd meet up with his farming friend Abe Sparks and they'd put the world to rights! Fred was always punctual leaving the pub so that he would be at the bottom of Wessels Hill in time to meet up with his oxen. The oxen would then be hitched up to the car, and, with all their strength they pulled! The Nash and Fred got home in style! A sight to behold!

The Green Lantern Inn

It is hard to miss The Green Lantern Inn. It dominates the main street which in those days was on the main road from Johannesburg to Durban (now the N3) right in front of the Green Lantern. In 1965, the route changed by passing the main village. The pub is where it always was opening onto the street. Today, it is still one of the main meeting points for locals – women included!

Fred and Abe Sparks

This was where Fred Cope and Abe Sparks regularly met. Abe, astute business man, was always doing deals. The day came when he did a deal much in Fred's favour to help out his struggling friend. Fred's Nash really was on its last legs. He would have been stuck without it. At a good price, he bought Abe's old Pontiac thus saving his farm enterprise for years ahead.

Fred

Abe

254

Local farmers often congregated at the pub. On one occasion, a heated controversy arose between the Afrikaans farmers. As Fred did not understand Afrikaans he asked Abe to explain.

> *They do not approve of the long hair worn by some of the younger men. What should they do?* Abe translated.

Fred, with a wink, plunged his hand into his pocket and pulled out a pound note. It displayed Jan van Riebeeck with his flowing locks – an Afrikaner hero. Fred slyly slipped this onto the counter for all to see! The controversy died.

South Africa in the 1940s and 1950s was like a pot ready to boil over. Fred was not one to remain silent in the face of injustice. After every pub visit, he'd tell Ethel what had taken place. Ethel was anxious for Fred's safety as people were imprisoned for no obvious reason. She feared that Fred could face prison again as in China. The South African Government could be as cruel.

Like every other time when Fred reached the top of Wessels Hill on his way home and saw this view of The Seven Sisters (as the locals called this scenic range), he would say:

> *Now we are on top of the world.*

Aspects of the Early History of South Africa

Today, long after the Mandela era put a stop to apartheid legislation, the name South Africa evokes images of unfairness and inhumanity. When, where and how did apartheid come into being? The Afrikaner nationalists of the 1950s and 1960s did not invent it. Although it had its origins in earlier centuries, it was when D F Malan and Dr H F Verwoerd and the rulers of the time legalised the divisive and controlling laws that draconian apartheid was fully born.

Segregation along class and race lines took root back in 1652 when the first Dutch settlers, under the command of Jan Van Riebeck, established themselves in the Cape and imported slaves. By the time British troops occupied the Cape in 1795, the slave population of 17,000 outnumbered the whites who owned most of the land way beyond Cape Town. At that time, the majority of non-whites was unskilled and under Dutch rule. Segregation became entrenched. It was rare to marry across the colour line. Whites grew to believe they were the superior race.

In the late 1830s and 1840s the Boers, unable to come to terms with the British colonial policy, left the Cape in search of land of their own – The Great Trek. There was to be no integration with blacks. Eventually, they reached the Orange Free State and the Transvaal – theirs by right of conquest. In the years following The Great Trek, stronger details of apartheid were laid. The mineral discoveries of the Northern Cape in the 1870s, marked the beginning of South Africa's industrial era of gold and diamond mining was reliant on cheap black labour.

The start of 19th century saw the beginnings of a raft of legislation demeaning non-whites – stating where they could live and work, how they could travel, sit, stand, queue and so on. Marriage across the race bar was strictly illegal. Forced removals multiplied – areas occupied by non-whites for generations were stripped from them and they were moved to unsuitable areas further from employment opportunities.

Opposition by the Blacks mounted, peacefully at first, but their protests fell on the deaf ears of those who aimed for White, and in particular Afrikaner, supremacy, inflicting suffering and indignity at every turn. Clashes became violent, jails overflowed. In 1952, the African National Congress (ANC) organised a nationwide defiance campaign against the unjust laws. In 1958, when Dr H. F. Verwoerd became prime minister he turned on the screws – apartheid was in full cry. By 1964, Nelson Mandela (ANC), Robert Sobukwe (Pan African Congress) and others were incarcerated on Robben Island.

The Tea Room (former Methodist Church) and its view over Van Reenen Pass valleys

Llandaff Oratory *(Photos 2012)*

Van Reenen hosts the Llandaff Oratory, the smallest church in the southern hemisphere. It was built by Maynard Mathew as a memorial to his son, Llandaff Mathew, who was killed in a rock fall at a coal mine near Dundee, Natal, while saving eight trapped miners. The privately-owned Oratory was originally a Catholic Church. Today, it is more widely used across denominations for services, weddings and renewal of wedding vows. It seats eight.

The Oratory is visited by thousands each year. It was declared a National Heritage Site on 8 October 1983 and has become a spiritual centre point for many on their travels.

Van Reenen shoppers 2012

The Inferno
How quickly things can change

The morning began bright and crisp – one of those typically pleasant winter days on the South African Highveld. It was during the mid to late 1950s that things on the farm were the best they'd been for quite a while, the bank manager was not knocking at the door and life looked good. Ethel discarded her coat as quite suddenly she was sweating.

Oh! A Berg wind must be on its way,
she said, recognising the familiar symptoms.

Berg Winds

> **Berg** winds, (the South African name for katabatic winds, get their name from the Afrikaans word *'berg'* meaning 'mountain' and 'wind'). In South Africa, these hot dry winds occur mainly in winter, blowing from the mountainous interior to the coast.
> *Berg* winds usually result when there is a strong high pressure south or south-east of the country with a high pressure also positioned over the country and accompanied by coastal lows.
> The first indication that a *Berg* wind is imminent is a rise in temperature which, on occasions, can be very rapid.
> This is in part due to the air in a high pressure warming up the air as it descends.
> The speed of a *Berg* wind can vary from a mild 10 km / hour to gusts up to 100 km / hour which, at that speed, invariably causes damage to property and trees.
> The first indication of the arrival of a *Berg* wind is a rise in temperature that can be rapid.

The day that had begun so well felt hot and unpleasant. The wind was quickly gaining strength. Ethel was in the vegetable garden when she noticed an ominous, rapidly-rising black cloud on the western horizon. Before she had chance to look again, she saw a bakkies (South African word for 'truck') roaring down the hill towards the house. The truck, overloaded with farm workers, was driven by Mick Dillon. He shouted:

*Ethel – a veldt fire is heading for Rosedale.
Where is Fred? We've come to fight the fire.
First, we must move your animals out of the way.*

Fred appeared round the corner of the house visibly disturbed. Mick sent some men to round up the cattle and sheep and drive them towards his farm. By then, flames leaping high were speeding towards the house. Drivers leapt into their vehicles, Fred included, racing them to safety.

Men were sent over the neighbour's fence to try and divert the blaze with their fire-fighting equipment. There was already a wide fire-break in place. Maybe that would stop the fire? But no! Soon the men had to retreat to protect themselves from the inferno. The wind was so strong that it carried live sparks right across the fire-break and into the fir trees lining the fence. In no time, the sheds were ablaze. But where was Ethel?

As was her habit, Ethel cried silently to God for help. Immediately, she knew what she had to do. Quickly she found a small Umfaan (young black boy) to help her, a long stepladder and the garden hose. They stationed themselves with a clear view of the homestead's thatched roof. As soon as a spark landed on the thatch they quelled it with the hose. This went on until there was no danger of the fire starting up again close to the house. Meanwhile, there was not a lot for Fred to do other than wearily watch his sheds, hay, animals and machinery burn.

*The aftermath of a fire that burnt Rosedale out in August 2007
Photo by Bruce Nel, current owner of Rosedale*

Years of hard work went up in smoke. The worst part was the sound of agonised bleating by sheep caught by the fire. Having devastated Rosedale, except for the homestead, the fire raced on way beyond Rosedale hungry to devour everything in its path. It had started 34 miles away in the Harrismith direction. A man had been ploughing a large field. With only a small grass section left unploughed, he decided it was safe to burn the remaining rectangle of grass in the middle. Barely had he put a match to it when, to his horror, he saw a round of dry cow dung alight, caught by the wind and reaching the field beyond. Wild fire! The fire spread so rapidly that all he could do was alert the local police.

It was a terrible day indeed, but the help from Mick Dillon (see photo), neighbours and local staff was spectacular. At the end of the day, out of compassion and need, the burnt sheep were slaughtered and given to the African helpers.

Mickey Dillon and Ethel
Rosedale cattle and the sheep they'd managed to rescue

Goodwill Follows Tragedy

Fred and Ethel had barely got going the next day when the first of the goodwill gifts arrived – a meal for that day, a load of hay to feed the remaining animals and so on it went. In the days that followed, help was at hand. People turned up to fix fences and sheds. Letters arrived with anonymous Postal Orders. I was at boarding school, arriving home weeks later when the worst of the evidence had been cleared away. Most importantly was fresh evidence of my parents' indomitable spirits, illustrating the words of South Africa's most famous son:

> *The greatest glory of living lies not in never falling,*
> *but in rising every time you fall.*
> Nelson Rolihlahla Mandela

Perhaps now is the time to mention something of Fred's philosophy.

FRED'S PHILOSOPHY AND VALUES
TOTT
– Think On These Things –

Finally, brethren,
whatsoever things are true,
whatsoever things are honest, whatsoever things are just,
whatsoever things are pure, whatsoever things are lovely,
whatsoever things are of good report;
if there be any virtue, and if there be any praise,
Think On These Things.
Philippians 4:8 – King James Version

The Living Bible puts it this way:
Fix your thoughts on what is good and true and right.

I don't know when my father first encountered this bit of Paul's letter to the Christians at Philippi:

Think On These Things.

Undoubtedly this was imprinted on his mind as TOTT, and as far back as I can remember it was part of his life philosophy. He was positive, always seeking solutions. Nothing got him down for long. He was never meanly critical of anyone, but gave people a chance. What is more, TOTT is what he encouraged my mother and me to practice – always.

Perhaps TOTT is one of Fred's life-threads that helped him through those dark times when under house arrest and most testing of all, nine months in solitary confinement by the Japanese in their war on China. Perhaps TOTT helped him to see his captors as human beings trapped in a ruthless system from which they could not escape rather than as cruel captors in their own right. Certainly TOTT had helped to release Fred from bitterness, vindictiveness and hatred of those who did such terrible things to him.

This life-habit of Fred left no mental room for wallowing in self-pity. Instead, it propelled him on to a solution and the next thing. He was a great one for planning ahead.

Around this time on the farm, I was aware of my father focusing rather more on his past. Below is an example.

Secrets of a Leather Suitcase – F.C.3

Daddy seemed far away – somewhere else. He was staring at the sturdy brown leather suitcase on his bed. His initials, F.C., followed by 3, were painted near the handle. I had often noticed this suitcase stowed on planks under his bed and wondered what it contained. That day, Dad had pulled it out and was staring intently at it, oblivious of my presence.

> *Daddy, would you like a cup of tea?*

Startled by the unexpected intrusion into his private thoughts and space, he spun round. His face relaxed as he saw me.

> *What a good idea, Ton. Let's have a cup of tea together. I'll tell you about the secrets this case is keeping. You might even like to see some of the treasures it's hiding.*

And so began one of those long sessions that started with a history lesson on China. I recall a bit about Confucius, a Chinese philosopher from around 500 BC who had a major influence on Chinese culture. Dad pointed out that some of his sayings are still in use today like:

Do not do to others what you do not want done to yourself.

This is the Golden Rule. Dad went on and on about Chinese Dynasties, the Great Wall of China and various invaders and wars. I was nodding off when I heard the words 'silk worms'! That did interest me as we had a mulberry tree at my first school and every summer old shoe boxes housing silk worms grazing on mulberry leaves would appear and provide for major competitions like whose silk worms would start spinning first!

I'll show you something really special,

Dad said in a secretive tone as he removed a package from the leather suitcase.

It was a garment carefully wrapped in tissue paper and cellophane. As the wrapping fell off, I gasped. I had never seen such perfect, beautiful needlework. It was almost too good to be real. To top it, the garment was in my favourite colours!

I've recently learnt that this gracefully-crafted gown was, in all probability, made during 1900-1920 – the late Qing Dynasty. Most likely it belonged to a lady high official. It is beautifully made with silk embroidery on silk, a fine example of delicate work done at the famous Suzhou embroidery workshops.

The Suzhou workshops and the Chinese silk industry were discussed earlier in this book – in the section on Fred's 'second' life. Take a look at the photographs of the two-piece gown – jacket and skirt – and some of the details.

The embroidered jacket and skirt panel

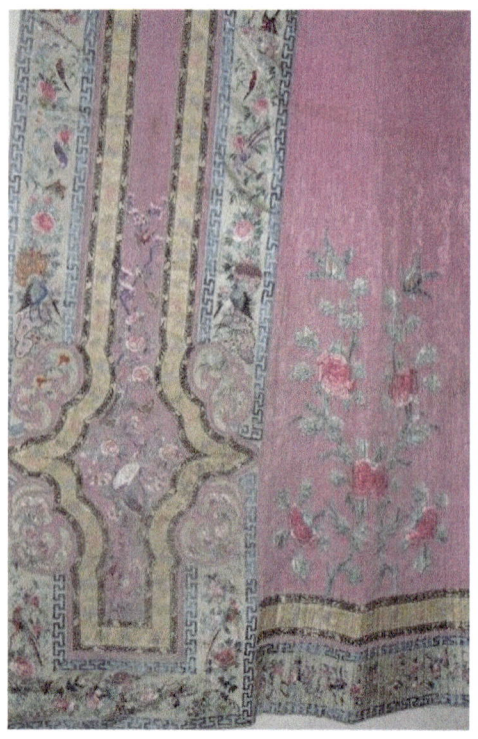

The longer I stared at the jacket and pleated skirt, the more amazed I became. There was such a variety of birds, insects and flowers – each embroidered in such delicate detail.

I noticed that Dad was carefully unwrapping a tiny object.

Take a look at this little treasure, Ton.

He passed me a small porcelain pot on a wooden stand.

Do you know what it is?

I shook my head. Dad continued:

It is a seal paste box. It was intricately decorated using extremely fine brush strokes. Look at the mark underneath. This particular mark was first used by artists in the Qianlong period (1736-1795) though people continued to use this seal into the late 19th or early 20th century. This makes me unsure of its age.

A seal is used as a signature in artworks and usually reveals the artist's name and where it was made. Seal paste is kept in this type of little porcelain pot, or 'boxes' as they are called, like this one. The seal stone is dipped in the paint then transferred to the artwork. A good friend gave me this one as a gift some years before I left China.

My curiosity had woken up. I wanted to hear more!

Daddy, why did you leave China? Was this the suitcase that carried your treasures?

Dad seemed pleased at my interest.

Yes indeed! This was my special suitcase. And, by Jove, I was forced to leave China as a prisoner of the Japanese – and how fortunate that was!

The Japanese allowed each civilian prisoner to take out a certain number of cases. I knew this ahead of time. I chose this case to carry my secrets. I always kept it nearby, but never locked it so as not to arouse suspicion.

As well as being an electrical engineer and industrial consultant, Dad was an economist. He kept a keen eye on what was happening in China, the Japanese invasion, and the world stage. He explained that Japan invaded China primarily for economic reasons. They wanted to control China's mineral resources and agricultural production. In 1931, Japan invaded Manchuria. Then Japan moved south and seized control of most of Eastern China including Shanghai. It was clear to Fred that the Japanese would aim to control Canton.

At the time, the local currency was rapidly falling in value so Dad hatched a plan. Whenever he could, he accumulated American dollars. Carefully, he lifted the lining of F.C.3 and inserted several layers of his American dollars. Equally carefully, he stuck the lining back into place.

He also got tins of tobacco which he cut open and emptied. Then he weighed the tobacco and carefully inserted the same weight of dollars and replaced the label wrapper. Clever! His secrets were never discovered. When he was disembarked from the Tatuta Maru in Lourenco Marques he owned a few thousand American dollars – a great help, he said, in getting started on his 'third' life.

Having his farm, and consequently his livelihood, burnt to a cinder was not only a huge shock but for a while it numbed his brain – not a permanent state of affairs.

Tomatoes

Never, ever, ever, ever, ever, ever, ever, give up.
Never give up. Never give up. Never give up.
Winston Churchill (in his talk to students at his old school, Harrow)

After a month or two of winter hibernation, when they mentally regrouped, Fred came up with a range of ideas. First, he would plant hundreds of tomato plants – a quick cash crop. In the same season, he would plant Russian Comfrey to use as a cattle feed and to propagate it for sale. Once this was underway, he would grow and sell Brussels sprouts which were new to South Africa.

Fred planned, the oxen ploughed, the staff planted, and interpreter Ethel was close at hand. Within three months, the tomato plants were weighed down and ready for picking. Fred had prepared the boxes for packing and dispatching of tomatoes. Expectation rose high – at last the bank manager would be satisfied. And then… on the eve before picking was to begin, the sky darkened and a frightful storm blew up. In just 10 minutes, tomato-sized hailstones decimated the entire crop

Russian Comfrey

An optimist is 't chap who knows when his boots wear out
'e'll be back on his feet.
Yorkshire proverb

The tomato loss was a difficult pill to swallow. Staff still had to be paid and the Copes had to live. However, Fred moved on positively. His next try – Russian Comfrey – was underway.

The livestock thrived on the wilted leaves, compost improved and the roots of the first set of plants were divided and sold on.

Something was working in Fred's favour at last. His adverts in the *Farmer's Weekly* and elsewhere brought in a steady stream of orders. This continued for some years then sales dropped off due to a saturated market. Russian Comfrey had provided the means to keep the bank manager at bay! The time had come to put Fred's third idea into action – growing Brussels sprouts.

> Russian Comfrey, a member of the borage family, is a high-yielding leafy perennial herb. The leaves are long and hairy; the black roots turnip-like; the small bell-like flowers often cream or purple in colour.
>
> It is used as a livestock food and tonic, in herbal medicine, organic fertilizer and more. Originating in the Caucasus Mountains of Russia, it is drought tolerant and can survive temperatures way below zero and intense heat. It includes vitamins such as A, B and C, calcium, potassium, iron and iodine. Its yield is prolific.

Brussels Sprouts

This was a vegetable Fred had always enjoyed, especially in winter with roast beef and Yorkshire pudding! He had done a thorough search on how to grow Brussels sprouts and concluded that Rosedale had the ideal climate for this enterprise. Also, Brussels sprouts were not well known in South Africa, so he would be breaking new ground.

Although I have not unearthed hard evidence to back this up, today, locals in Van Reenen who knew my father when they were children are convinced he was the person who introduced the vegetable into South Africa.

When the first crop was ready to reap, I was roped in to help prepare the little plastic bags to make them suitable for display and sale. Each had to have several holes punched through for ventilation, using an office punch, then packed, weighed and closed. When the car was fully loaded with bags of Brussels sprouts, Fred set off to market these in Durban or Johannesburg. Brussels sprouts became a novel and desirable addition to the menu in some classy hotels. All in all this was a successful, if labour-intensive venture.

A brief History of Brussels Sprouts

> The first sprouts were cultivated in large quantities in 1587 in Brussels. As a member of the cabbage family, Brussels sprouts are a cool weather crop that improves in flavour after a frost. Numerous small sprouts appear along a single, upwards stem. They are a storehouse of healthy nutrients and vitamins and an excellent source of antioxidant vitamins such as vitamin C, A and E.

Fred was proud to be promoting this healthy food in South Africa.

The Night Sky

*When I look at the night sky and see the work of your fingers
the moon and the stars you set in place
what are mere mortals that you should think about them,
human beings that you should care for them?
A Psalm of David: Psalm 8 v 3, 4   New Living Translation*

Before settling in for the night, Fred would stroll outside to savour the crisp evening air and gaze on the stars. When I was lucky he would invite me to accompany him. Then he would begin his lesson on the stars. He would remind me how fortunate we were to live at Rosedale where there was no light (or noise) pollution. The stars always looked so bright.

The Milky Way, one of many galaxies, he explained, is the galaxy of our own solar system. Individual stars cannot be seen with the naked eye, but together they produce a 'milky' appearance. Astronomers tell us that the Milky Way may contain as many as one trillion stars and probably one hundred billion planets. These facts blew my mind! Fred's attention would then turn to The Southern Cross (Crux) and can only be seen in the Southern hemisphere. It is the best known constellation.

So, how important is man? Dad would ask.

Is There Anybody There?

Empty space is like a kingdom, and earth and sky are no more than a single individual person in that kingdom. Upon one tree are many fruits, and in one kingdom there are many people. How unreasonable it would be to suppose that, besides the earth and the sky which we can see, there are no other skies and no other earths.
Teng Mu, Chinese scholar Sung Dynasty 960-1280 A.D.

Since the dawn of recorded history, men have sought to find the answer to the question:

Do intelligent beings exist somewhere beyond our planet?

Almost every civilisation or major culture has speculated on this – in mythology, religion, science or in philosophy. Gradually, as man has learned to realise the vast scale of the universe, the idea of life in the cosmos has become accepted as likely. The question today is not:

Is there life out there? But: When will we find it?

Fred would go on to muse about the possibility of life beyond our own planet. He'd say:

Orion is my favourite constellation. Wherever I have been in the world (and remember, I have been round the world three times), Orion was there with me – a good companion.

Many myths have been connected with Orion – named after a hunter in Greek mythology. The three stars in the middle are known as Orion's belt. Orion was seen as a gigantic, supernaturally strong hunter of ancient times.

Constellation of Orion

You can read about Orion in books like Homer's *The Odyssey*.

THE WRITING IS ON THE WALL
Book of Daniel

It was 1963. Fred was 73. He couldn't sleep. In his mind's eye, he was a young man back in Yorkshire wrestling with fear of failure but with the hope and schemes to keep Windhill Mill afloat. In the end it had been a case of relinquishing his hopes and going for voluntary liquidation.

What was to become of Rosedale, their home for twenty years? How would he provide for Ethel and me if Rosedale had to go? Yes, Brussels sprouts were profitable but the scale of the crop was just too small to provide a living and pay the interest on his Land Bank loan. Was it better to go for voluntary liquidation again rather than wait until the Land Bank seized his land? He was no spring chicken. How long could he keep working at this pace? Round and round, his mind raced.

It was 6.00 am when Ethel appeared with a cup of tea. She too had been mulling over the future. At 53, she figured she could return to nursing and keep them financially afloat. So a decision was made. They would sell up and move to the coast near to a hospital. Ethel soon secured a post at Port Shepstone hospital on the coast south of Durban.

Ironically, as they prepared for the sale, Fred received an official letter from a large canning factory in Johannesburg offering to buy his entire Brussels sprouts crop the following year provided he could supply 50 tons - a feather in Fred's cap but too little too late. It would have meant ploughing up all useable land on Rosedale and require energy and equipment he did not have. The day of the sale came and went. Fred and Ethel emerged with a small nest egg with which to start their new life. With heavy hearts and their remaining little dog, Pepe, they climbed into the old Pontiac loaded to the roof and, not looking back, they drove away.

PORT SHEPSTONE

For reasons of economics, Fred and Ethel could only live under the same roof when Ethel was off duty at Port Shepstone hospital where she lived in the nurses' quarters. For Fred they'd found a delightful little guest house in Umtemtweni to the north of the Mzimkulu River, the largest river on the south coast. Port Shepstone is situated on the mouth of the Mzimkulu River 120 kilometres (75 miles) south of Durban. It is the administrative, educational and commercial centre for Southern Natal.

Fred lived in a rondavel which gave him the privacy he was used to. What is more, the owners were happy for him to keep their dog – little Pepe.

Fred lived a few minutes walk from the sea where he'd walk along the shore on most days with Pepe energetically exploring. For a while, all went well. But then, one day, Pepe ate something poisonous on the beach and that was the end of Pepe.

Body, Mind and Spirit
Fred's Search for Truth

Since 1943, when as a newly-married man Fred had started work with the IDC in Johannesburg, his life had been jam-packed with challenging obligations. The most recent, his farming career was over. He had time to reflect, read and write and methodically catalogue his modest library and cuttings.

I have often pondered on how my father managed to rise so positively above the multitude of bleak life situations that beleaguered him. After an initial shock, he'd always emerged with cheeriness and a plan for his next venture.

It has taken me until this point, to begin to understand the essence of the secrets behind his thriving optimism.

In the process of completing the third draft of this book, I turned to review the materials he'd left. Staring me in the face were two items I'd missed – a tatty old file and a faded brown envelope of cuttings covering a wide range of topics including articles from the *Reader's Digest* and *Time Magazine* (1965–1974). Here I draw attention to just three from the collection.

1. **The Man Nobody Knows**
   Abridged from the book by Bruce Barton first published in 1925, illustrated with drawings by Rembrandt
   Reader's Digest Book of the Month, December 1965.

Below are a few samples of the sentences highlighted by Fred:

- *Introduction: A modern masterpiece ... appeared in translations all over the world. It portrays an unorthodox, but compelling portrait of Jesus: as a buoyant, laughing, virile man, a leader of extraordinary magnetism.*

- *An episode: It was very late in the afternoon in Galilee. The dozen men who had walked all day over the dusty roads were hot and tired ... Their leader ... sent two members of the party ahead to arrange for accommodation ... the messengers returned ... their voices angry. The people in the village had given them blunt notice to seek shelter elsewhere. The backwoods village had refused to entertain their Master.*

Lord, these people are insufferable... Let us call down fire from heaven and consume them. ...

There are times when nothing a man can say is more powerful as saying nothing. The lips of Jesus tightened. ...

Would they never catch a true vision of what He was about? He had come to save mankind and they wanted him to gratify His personal resentment by burning up a village! ... He knew that pettiness brings its own punishment. ...

He forgot the incident immediately. He had work to do.

This book helped me understand why my father had for so long avoided the institutional church with its trappings, rules and judgments. He was a free spirit. He was a seeker after Truth. He avoided places where he thought man had muddied the waters.

2. **Prayer is Power**
    Simplified and condensed
    from R*eader's Digest*   November 1963 Page 57

A selection of the 24 point summary is in Fred's handwriting.

1. PRAYER is worship (fervent esteem, adoration, highest respect).
...
3. PRAYER is the most powerful form of energy that man can generate.
...
9. PRAYER is not a refuge for weaklings or a childish petition for material things.
...
16 PRAYER to be effective must become a habit. Any place, any time, any posture will do.
...
21. PRAYER is the basic exercise of the Spirit.

Fred ends this summary with these words:

Know God by the sight of the wonders of earth

And one of Ethel's favorites:

The most perfect prayer is a single thankful thought towards heaven.

Often, my father had gazed at the stars, marvelled over nature and the complexities of the human body, the discoveries of science, and exclaimed:

There must be a mind behind these marvels.
Things like this don't just happen without a designer.

I don't recall him talking about prayer though I remember him remarking on people's lack of reverence for the Almighty.

3.   **The Game of Life** – *TIME:* January 21, 1974

Computer time is a precious commodity to scientists and engineers; the speed and capacious memory of the giant electronic brains are vital to operations as varied as space navigation and supermarket inventory control.

It was 1993. I'd lived in Tromsø, Norway, well within the Arctic Circle – The Land of the Midnight Sun – for over a year. Anna Glaister (nee Hendrickson), my Norwegian grandmother, had died a few years before. She'd left her 'small change' to us nine grandchildren. Probate was granted as I was planning my sabbatical year (a year's leave without pay from the Natal Education Department) to spend in England (1992-1993). My share was just enough to pay for a return passage from England to Norway – the best way of spending my inheritance from Granny, I decided. I would meet up with some of her vast extended family for three weeks and then return to England.

Tromsø

*There is a divinity that shapes our ends,
rough-hew them how we will.*
Shakespeare

Once in Tromsø staying with Mother's first cousin, Gunhild Nyvold, my plan was revised. Gunhild persuaded me to stay on.

Norway was where I'd learnt the elements of computer programming on a semester course at the University of the North. I recall it being the first year of that department – Data behandling. At 70 degrees north, the university is the world's northernmost university.

Although I'd learnt to speak Norwegian, my language ability was below the standard required in the professions. So, in 1993

I moved to England in search of a programming job. Two were potentially on offer in Oxford – teaching programming at Oxford University or programming for British Leyland. I phoned home to consult. I expected my father, an industrialist, to come down on the side of British Leyland. But no, he was of the firm opinion that the university job would suit me best. My father was a wise advisor.

How right he was. How well he knew his daughter. For the next twenty-eight years, Oxford University was my place of creative work. My roles involved teaching then, during the latter half of my time there, using computers as a research tool.

The Electro Magnetic Spectrum (EMS)

Keeping to the scientific theme, I recollect my father attempting to explain scientific advances made by using information beyond the visible in the EMS. Only years later, when managing Oxford University's Imaging Processing Centre (1988 – 1995), did I grasp what he'd tried to explain.

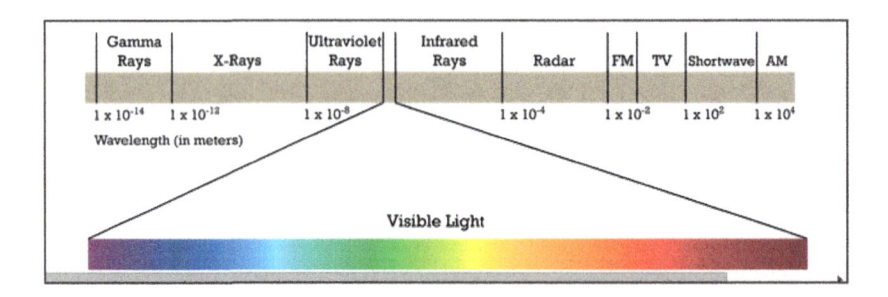

Gamma Rays	X-Rays	Ultraviolet Rays	Infrared Rays	Radar	FM	TV	Shortwave	AM
1×10^{-14}	1×10^{-12}	1×10^{-8}		1×10^{-4}	1×10^{-2}		1×10^{2}	1×10^{4}

Wavelength (in meters)

Visible Light

What we see is only a minute fraction of what is there. Much more is hidden from the naked eye. And that is one reason why we struggle to get to grips with the spiritual side of things. We focus on what can be seen with our eyes and neglect the spirit.

Ethel's Crisis

Ethel's health became a critical problem. When she'd left nursing in 1943 there was no penicillin. By the 1960s though, it had become standard in treating a wide range of bacterial infections. The irritating itch that alerted Ethel to something wrong, developed within weeks into Anaphylaxis, a serious allergic reaction that is rapid in onset and may even cause death. It got so bad that even after time off she only had to be in the same room as a nurse administering a penicillin injection for her body to start swelling. Once, on visiting my parents, I could not recognise my mother so swollen was her face that her eyes were just pencil slits. Doctors were gravely concerned and told my mother that if she wanted to live she would have to give up nursing. This worried them both as Ethel's job was their only source of survival. Meanwhile, the doctors arranged for Ethel to work in Maternity where, on the whole, she could avoid coming into contact with this life-threatening antibiotic.

The tide turned. At that stage (1964), I was a student at Natal University, Pietermaritzburg. I had previously met the Sister of the Women's Sanatorium. One morning, on my way to breakfast, we bumped into each other. She told me she would be leaving within months. Immediately I phoned my mother who applied for the job and got it. She was to start early the following year, 1965, by which time I would be studying at the University of Cape Town.

PIETERMARITZBURG

The city of Pietermaritzburg, founded in 1838, is in the midlands of Natal (KwaZulu-Natal / KZN), an hour's drive from Durban and two hours from the Drakensberg Mountains. It is the birthplace of Natal University College (1910-1949), forerunner of the University of Natal (NU), (1949-2003) and University of KwaZulu-Natal (2004-). By 1912, the Old Main Building was completed and stands today as the oldest of the university buildings. The campus offers a broad range of academic degrees, including agriculture, theology and fine arts.

The University Old Main Building

Pietermaritzburg, also known as Maritzburg or PMB, is the capital city of KwaZulu-Natal. Its Zulu name, derived from the phrase meaning the place of the elephant, is umGungundlovu.

In 1964, Ethel moved to this academic institution as matron of the Women's Sanatorium (The San). The university did not cater for a live-in husband. Fred stayed on in Port Shepstone and they met for one weekend a month. Living so far apart was most unsatisfactory, so Ethel put out feelers for other jobs.

When her boss, Mrs (Ma) Kirwood, learnt that she may lose her admirable nurse she at once arranged for alterations to be made to the San to suit a married couple.

Fred was delighted to join his wife. And, as I was by then teaching mathematics at Russell High School in the city, we could be together again at weekends.

Ethel, Fred and Tonia
Photo 1966 NU, PMB

Living in Pietermaritzburg

The San

Those were happy years.

Fred settled into a routine. He had signed up for a short story writing course, hopeful of earning. He was uncomfortable as a passenger and aimed to supplement Ethel's income. Each morning was dedicated to writing and cataloguing his books and papers. Ethel thought he was writing on his China days, but no, he was trying his hand at writing romantic novels. None sold. A Victorian's writing did not hit the target readership!

After lunch, Fred took to walking and exploring his surrounds. He was a keen follower of sport, so when there was a match – be it rugby or cricket – he would be there supporting a side. At the time, I was sharing accommodation with friends. Meg, from Rhodesia (Zimbabwe), was studying at Natal University so often bumped into my father and stopped for a chat. Recently she wrote to me including her memories of my father.

Meg's Memories

I used to walk to university each day and would often meet your father going for what he called 'his constitutional'. He always stopped for a chat, and was a true gentleman of the old school and beautifully turned out even on the warmest of days, wearing his signature bow tie, which if memory serves me correctly was blue with white spots.

Even more memorable was the fact that he always had a twinkle in his eyes as if he was enjoying a private joke or had an amusing tale to tell. This is all the more remarkable when you reflect on what he had been through in China and on the farm.

First Holiday in Twenty Years

'Holiday' was not in Fred's vocabulary at Rosedale where, for twenty years, he and Ethel never went away. But when Ethel was working they had the luxury of spare cash, and time to get away during varsity vacations. Their first holiday was with Ethel's sister Margaret Daff and Eric her husband living at Skoenmakerskop, (Skoenies), a seaside village 24 miles west of Port Elizabeth. On the south side it is bound by the sea. Dense coastal scrub covers dunes.

When the invitation came for Fred and Ethel to join them and their extended family for a summer holiday, excitement ran high. Fred had not swum since his China days.

The Daffs lived close to a cove safe for bathing and most days saw them swimming there. For those with goggles, the plentiful marine life provided extra attraction.

285

The Last Move

After ten years working for the university, it was time for Ethel to retire. They found a suitable flat in the city not too far from the sports grounds!

Once they had settled in, they launched into planning a visit to England. It was over forty years since Fred's last visit 'home'. He longed to see his green and pleasant land again. Ethel had never travelled beyond Africa, so for her it was a dream coming true. Besides, this would be an ideal opportunity to see me in Oxford where I was employed by Oxford University to teach computer programming – a brand new subject in those days.

England after 50 Years

It was 1976. Fred (86) and Ethel (66) landed in England for 3 months. One aspect was disappointing for Fred. The 'green' England he'd remembered was as dry and brown as Rosedale farm in the dead of winter. Severe drought had hit Britain.

Yorkshire was high on the list of 'must-visits'. I drove them north, spending most time in Scarborough and on the coast. (Read more about this visit in the section on England / Scarborough.) My parents enjoyed every minute of their time in England. In Oxford, they shared my rooms in Southmoor Road, close to the Oxford Canal. We explored Port Meadow, the River Thames and riverside pubs. The house belonged to Miss Pollack, a charming, petite old lady, who had escaped Hitler and the extermination camps. Sadly she had to leave parents behind. As Jews they were predictably 'punished' by the Nazi regime. Fred and Ethel were delighted to meet her.

The last family photograph – Oxford 1976

CLOSING YEARS

Old age is like owt else
To make a success of it, thou's got to start young.
(The Little Book of Yorkshire Proverbs)

Between a Rock and a Hard Place

Even in painful old age, Dad seldom lost his sense of humour. All my life, I'd known a father who was positive and resourceful, no matter what happened. Even when his brainchild, The *Ostrich Feather Factory*, had to close in the post WWII recession, even when hail decimated the entire tomato crop he'd planted in hopes of restoring a positive bank balance; even when the farm burnt out, animals and all, he remained resourceful. In such dire circumstances he'd retreat for a day or so in his den and emerge with a joke or two and, what is more, his next solution. But during my visit over Christmas 1977, I'd noticed an ominous change in Dad. He was in a state of bewilderment – between a rock and a hard place. To quote him:

> *I am afraid of dying, but living is too ruddy agonizing.*
> *Oh the pain, the pain. Nothing relieves it any more.*

It was hard seeing Dad so dejected, in low spirits and apparently defeated. Death was a challenge to which he had no solution. Not even quoting TOTT worked. I returned to England dragging my heart in my boots. In a sense, all that year I lived with Dad every day. News from Mother indicated decline.

The Last Christmas

Joy to the World, the Lord has come ... (the) wonders of his love ...
A Christmas carol – based on the Psalm 98: written in 1719 by Isaac Watts

As planned, I returned to see my parents in December 1978. Shock! Just before my arrival, Dad was rushed into hospital with a strangulated hernia. The doctor told Mother:

Fred will die if we don't operate, but may die if we do.

We waited in tension.
The phone rang …
The doctor's voice:

Something most unusual has happened. The hernia has reduced itself. Perhaps moving him about assisted this. We are sending your husband home by ambulance.

Dad, though frail, was overjoyed to be home again and delighted to have escaped the surgeon's knife! As we settled into the days before Christmas, my old friend Michael – more like a brother – told me of his own father's last days and death three months earlier. Mr Cassidy Senior too had been naturally anxious about dying. Gradually, he'd come to realise God's love for him. The fact that Jesus had come to set him free began to register. Helped through assorted ministries over a long time, plus near the end a daily verse from scripture, he came to rest his faith in Jesus and died a peaceful man.

I thought about Daddy and his positive influence on my life. How, as a child and teenager growing up on the farm, he'd often taken me outside to study the stars, and how bright they were in that crystal clear atmosphere. He'd pointed out the constellations – his favourite as always was Orion. Dad said it was obvious to him that there was a mind behind this amazing universe – a Creator-God. In my older years, he'd go on to explain that he believed Jesus was a good man, but not God.

This was about to change. With Michael's model, I set about writing out positive verses from the Bible and putting one a day on his breakfast table. Mum and I were amazed by Dad's uptake of these. He was a very slow eater, so we always left him at the breakfast table to finish his meal on his own. A while later, Dad's voice would sound throughout the flat repeatedly, reading aloud his verse-of-the-day.

Transformation
Real faith produces real change of life.
Michael Green: When God Breaks In (pg 81)

As the days went by, Dad became more reflective and peaceful. Christmas was a delight. All his married life, observed by me, he had tended to treat my mother a bit like a Chinese servant – do this or that and he expected it done on the spot. It made me furious and led to numerous rows when I tried to intervene on her behalf. But things changed radically that Christmas. Anxiety left him. He became calm. His relationship with my mother deepened and his appreciation of her was noticeable.

Last Words

And I said to the man who stood at the gate of the year:
"Give me a light that I may tread safely into the unknown."
And he replied:
"Go out into the darkness and put your hand into the Hand of God. That shall be to you better than light and safer than a known way."
So I went forth, and finding the Hand of God, trod gladly into the night.
And He led me towards the hills and the breaking of day in the lone East."
Minnie Louise Haskins, 1908 – from her poem, God Knows

Christmas together was a joy. We celebrated the birth of Jesus and savoured Mother's superb cooking. Dad seemed so well, but a week or so later he developed pneumonia. My return flight to England was booked – a huge dilemma for me. Should I postpone this? But as Dad seemed to be responding to treatment, the doctor told me to stick to my plans. On the night before my departure, I told Dad that I'd be flying home the next day. I was visibly upset. He propped himself onto his pillow, shook his head and sang:

> *God be with you till we meet again*
> *Till we meet at Jesus' feet ...*

I had heard him sing the first line before, but never the second.

The next morning I had to say a final farewell in time for my lift to the airport. I could see Dad was struggling. I dissolved into tears. He shook his head and clicked his tongue several times. Then out it came, his last words to me:

> *We've got to remember*
> *The Lord is with us.*

I frequently think of that sweet bitter moment. I felt happier knowing that Dad was at peace with himself and his Maker.

Orion

To every thing there is a season,
and a time to every purpose under the heaven:
a time to be born and a time to die.
Ecclesiastes Chapter 3 (KJV) written circa 970 to 931 BC by King Solomon

I landed in England. Dad died peacefully in hospital three days later. Of course, I was on the next plane back to South Africa.

On my return flight I experienced an extraordinary moment. The blinds had been drawn. Wishing to think alone, I silently slid mine open to dwell amongst the stars. There it was: Orion!

Close up image of Orion's Belt - ESA/Hubble

The belt merged with the light on the plane's wing. It was a sign. All was well with Daddy. It was a TOTT time to thank God for what Dad had done with his life and for all he'd given me.

Mother told me Daddy had slipped into a coma for two days before he died. She continued to talk to him:

Freddie, stretch out your hand and God will take it.

Moments before he died, Fred raised his right hand up high. Ethel tried to hold his hand. Fred pulled away. A few moments later, he repeated the movement. It was then it dawned on Ethel. Her Fred was reaching out his hand to his Maker as he silently slipped from this world to the next – his permanent abode.

Ethel's Heartfelt Prose

This handwritten text was amongst Ethel's papers

*Every mood of impatience,
every slam of the door – impatience;
every hurried exit – rudeness.*

*Every little neglect and careless gesture came back
at every turn and moment of the new life without him.*

*She was free.
How she had longed for freedom –
to be free as the birds,
to be alone with no interruptions, no demands,
no responsibilities or ties.*

AND NOW

*The misery of the new found freedom was coagulating
into a solid, cold block of utter desolation and aloneness.*

*Voices were there,
the presence felt
but no companionship.
The human touch, the familiar sounds were gone forever.*

*'Oh for the touch of a vanished hand
for the sound of a voice that is still.'*

COPY OF THE
INSCRIPTION IN THE
BOOK OF REMEMBRANCE

25th January

Cope, Frederick
O'for the touch of a vanished hand,
For the sound of a voice that is still.
Into thy hands O'Lord our Fred,
Rejoicing always and T.O.T.T.

And so shall we keep them in Remembrance

Ethel's entry for Frederick Cope, 1890-1979
The Pietermaritzburg Book of Remembrance

Extracts from Tonia's Tribute to her Father
Oxford, 1979

With thankfulness for the life of my Father,

<u>FREDERICK COPE</u>

Born: 5.5.1890 – Wakefield, England

Died: 25.1.1979 – Pietermaritzburg, South Africa

\+

Here follows a thumbnail sketch of a true and beautiful story

\+

Woven into the tapestry of my earliest childhood memories are the bright threads of starlit nights, when, in the farm-stillness, Dad would point skywards to the Southern Cross, Orion and even Venus. That broad band, the Milky Way, did not escape attention. Rather it was the way to unseen galaxies beyond and to Dad's expanding on the amazing Mind behind it all. To lend perspective to the picture he would describe in detail the splendour and perfection of the microscopic desert flower.

\+

Christmas 1978

It was the happiest Christmas we'd had in years. Dad was noticeably and progressively more peaceful. Sounds of his croaky old voice penetrated every room as he sang old Yorkshire favourites, Christmas carols and hymns from his youth. Mother and I were aware of God's gift to Father of more time on Planet Earth. The transformation in Dad was as that in a butterfly freed from its chrysalis. In finding the Truth so long sought, he was visibly freed from the bondage of fear of death.

\+

Eternity is a long time...

Death is a horizon beyond which we cannot see
Sketch by Tonia (1979)

REFLECTIONS

Truth is stranger than fiction
Attributed to, and almost certainly coined by Lord Byron, in the satirical poem Don Juan, 1823:
'Tis strange – but true; for truth is always strange; stranger than fiction'

Although I knew it was Daddy's time to die, parting was far from painless. He had been a stabilising anchor on my life's stormy seas. Dad was always a big thinker, an inspiration, a motivator, but he was no saint! The combination of Fred, a Victorian, twenty years older than my mother, led to disagreements and rows. At times, my father was exasperatingly dominant and, due to his defective hearing, a voluble talker rather than a good listener. Even so, with his heart and mind, he did listen and understood more than I gave him credit for. We'd frequently clashed during my adolescent years, but this stage evolved into a cherished and fascinating adult friendship.

Once the end of writing this biography was in sight, I engaged readers to comment on the draft. Recently one asked:

> *Why have you gone to so much trouble and undertaken such mammoth research to write up this story?*

My answer flowed easily:

> *Because he was my father and quite the most charming, stimulating and fascinating old man I've known. I was his only child. He was fifty-three when I was born. In my eyes he was always an old man! I'd constantly been curious about his life in countries I knew little about. I just had to go on a voyage of discovery. This meant exploring Yorkshire, China and South Africa. I turned up every bit of written, photographic and movie evidence I could lay my hands on. Researching and writing this up has been a long and splendid adventure.*

> *Fred's unique, intriguing and captivating life journey just has to be more widely known. It fell to me to tell it.*

Another question followed:

> *Why did your father leave his prestigious, secure and well-paid job in Johannesburg with the Industrial Development Corporation (IDC) to spend the rest of his working life struggling on a small farm?*

That answer is complex – a mix of situation and opportunity:

> *Fred, a highly qualified Chartered Engineer and Industrial Consultant, was doing a job he revelled in. There were downsides. He did not understand Afrikaans – the main lingo of his IDC job – his hearing was poor and his age against him. In China, he'd mastered the complexities of Cantonese, a tonal language. Then, he had good hearing.*

> *Only weeks after their marriage, Ethel's father died and left Oban to Anna, his wife. A few years later, Anna wrote over the farm to their five children in equal shares. Fred, a serial entrepreneur, saw this as the opportunity to embark on his next venture. With his experience in textiles, he built a factory for the manufacture of ostrich feather goods on Ethel's inherited land. Things did not work out as he'd hoped. He had not foreseen the post-war depression that stifled the sale of luxury goods. The factory closed.*

As far as I know, my father always felt for the underdog and involved himself in the support of such people. In Yorkshire, in his thirties, he became a Freemason and a Rotarian. Both include support for people in need. In China, Fred followed Martin Luther's injunction:

> *If you want to change the world, pick up your pen and write.*

In 1933, he expressed his outsized vision of the world's future by writing a series of articles in the press and subsequently published those articles in booklet form. This booklet is called: *World Crisis – A Way Out: an analysis of the World Economic Crisis - Suggesting its Causes and a Cure – Frederick Cope*

In 1937 he inspired and edited the timely, well-received news magazine for Hong Kong: The *Hong Kong Review*. I inherited Dad's copies. Once this book is published I will make these accessible to the public by donating the originals to The National Archives of the UK at Kew. I have passed digital copies of the Hong Kong Review to China's official Government archives – the *Hong Kong Public Records Office*.

Fred was a forward thinker. In Canton, he foresaw the likelihood of the Japanese invasion reaching the South. Thus he accumulated valuables and packed these in a suitcase with a hidden stash of American Dollars. In 1942, as an exchange prisoner on the Tatuta Maru, he fell dangerously ill. As a result he was unexpectedly disembarked at Lourenco Marques. His nest-egg helped him get going. I inherited his remaining treasures. The richly embroidered silk ladies gown I have donated to *Oxford's Ashmoleon Museum*. This is now in a rotating display of textiles in the Later China Gallery.

No Racist

Fred did not display discrimination or prejudice. In his book, every person deserved to be treated with dignity and respect. He'd made friends from different cultures and countries. Perhaps his experience as a prisoner of the Japanese in China left him without grudges. Instead he came to see his captors in the context of being caught up in an unjust system.

In South Africa, again, he was living under a repressive regime that he did not have the power to change. Apartheid, introduced in 1948, was a violent and unjust system that separated people from each other on the basis of their skin colour. This caused untold misery for many non-whites. Whites had supremacy.

Blacks were denied access to social and educational provisions and forced to live apart in extremely poor conditions. They had no voice. Much to my mother's disquiet, Fred did not keep his views and voice to himself. He argued the toss against apartheid with all who would listen, especially on Saturday mornings in Van Reenen's Green Lantern Inn Pub. She feared that his imprisonment in China could be repeated under the Apartheid regime.

Fred did what he could for those he employed by treating each with respect and paying them above the local going rate. Some neighbours strongly disapproved. He became a mentor to a young intelligent illiterate, Paqua, who grew into the role of Fred's able and indispensable right-hand man.

World Affairs – Focus on China

My father's avid interest in world affairs never dimmed.

1966 stands out in my memory. It was the year we were reunited as a family all living in the same town – Pietermaritzburg. From then on my relationship with Daddy deepened. Endlessly he sought to broaden my understanding of the wider world. My knowledge of history beyond the Boer War (drummed into us at school) was virtually non-existent. It was 1966 the year Chairman Mao Zedong launched the Chinese Cultural Revolution. Dad was horrified. He'd never rated Mao as a leader. In his view, Mao was a ruthless power-driven maniac totally lacking in integrity and causing chaos in China ruining the lives of millions. Fred feared for his Chinese friends.

As I write these concluding reflections, the Cultural Revolution, started fifty years ago, is being flagged up in the media. For instance, *The Guardian* (on line) 11 May 2016, printed an article by Tom Phillips in Beijing that includes:

> *When the mass mobilization kicked off, party newspapers depicted it as an epochal struggle that would inject new life into the social cause. In fact, the*

> *Cultural Revolution crippled the economy, ruined millions of lives and thrust China into 10 years of turmoil, bloodshed, hunger and stagnation. ...*
>
> *An official party reckoning described it as a catastrophe which has caused "the most severe setback and heaviest losses suffered by the party, the country, and the people since the founding of the People's Republic" in 1949.*
> *...*
>
> *... Mao hoped his movement would make China the pinnacle of the socialist universe and turn him into "the man who leads planet Earth into communism".*

No wonder Dad so often quoted:

> *Power corrupts and absolute power corrupts absolutely.*

My father's deep concern for China back in 1966 was justified.

Victorian Values in the Post-WWII Era

Is it ever easy to adapt to the time-period of one's children?

Although Fred embraced change and challenge in his worlds of industry and economy, this did not always translate into life at home. In any gathering bigger than the three of us together, he was firmly of the view that *children should be seen but not heard*. I was never allowed to add to, or correct him, as he conversed with visitors. I had to listen for seemingly hours to what, for me, constituted boring talk. 'Listening' to adults talk sometimes had me drifting off into an Alice in Wonderland world of my own – embarrassing when suddenly a question was fired at me relating to the adults' conversation!

Respect your elders – it is good manners – was something else he drilled into me. Why? Because one day I would be old so I should think about how I'd like to be treated then. Treat old people the way you'd want to be treated when you are old, he'd say. At that, Granny Glaister, my mother's mother, would chime in with agreement.

What was suitable clothing for a teenager living on a farm? Dad insisted on no shorts lest it incite the male farm workers. Well! Shorts in those days were modest shortened longs and not the expose-everything models as in some of today's fashions. Eventually, Mum and I won that battle after I returned from a Durban holiday with her sister and family bearing their gift of two attractive short-sets!

Embarrassing Moments

Without doubt, my most excruciating and embarrassing moment occurred after asking Dad's advice on what I should include in a debate. This was to take place in front of the whole school. I don't recall the title, but remember the flavour included economy. Delighted, Dad was in his element. He not only wrote the whole speech, but insisted on my delivering it verbatim. I did! I lacked confidence and was in awe of him at that stage, to disobey. Lacking conviction on the subject, in words that were not mine, my delivery was dreadful. The blank, bored expressions on the vast sea of faces in the Assembly Hall of Estcourt High School unnerved me. However, the experience taught me a little more of my need to be true to myself and moved me in the direction of standing on my own two feet.

The Visible and Invisible

That which is visible is relatively easy to trace, unlike aspects of life that are beyond the visible spectrum. It is my understanding that throughout his life, hidden in the recesses of Fred's heart and mind, there was a search for the so-called Invisible – Truth.

I realise all too well that many today, especially in the Western World, think that Christians are deluded and bonkers. On occasions they may be right. Human blustering and blunders are sometimes the most visible aspect of 'the church' and obscure the light of God's love for everyone. This, I think, is what had helped to murky the waters in Fred's understanding of who exactly Jesus was. Although facts about Jesus, recorded by both sacred (some eyewitnesses), and secular historians, are often overlooked, even knowing these facts may still only lead to knowing about Jesus. Fred's timely meeting with Jesus – when God broke in during his late octogenarian years, led to him knowing Jesus. Just how this came about is unknown to me. But the result was most certainly visible. Fred was healed from fear – fear of death and the unknown beyond. He was provided with reinvigorating hope – a future to look forward to. Remember Dad's last words to me were:

You've got to remember the Lord is with us.

Legacy

What is a legacy? That word immediately conjures up concepts of inheritance – money, property and assorted assets. This was not the kind of legacy my parents left me. Apart from inheriting Dad's mementos from China and a few family bits and pieces, Dad's legacy (and, in fact, that of my mother) was far more enduring and valuable.

I have their genes and was a much-loved child – nature and nurture. Their example of frugality, productivity and living an adaptable lifestyle, together with values embracing compassion, perseverance and integrity is what underpins my life and constantly challenges me.

Consistently, Dad focussed on thankfulness. He was a deep thinker (look before you leap), a hard worker (no shirker), and balanced his work with play and rest. (How I revelled in those relaxed and fun evening walks on the farm as a family.) Dad was moderate, self-disciplined and persistent. He faced failure head on and started again (never give up).

Dad was not stuck in the past, rather he embraced change. He moved on with energy and hope. So must I. Change may not always be easy, but change we must, if we are to grow. There is a need to stop going over the same ground again and again and move on. One secret I've found is to focus attention on developing new and constructive habits. As John Dryden said:

We first make our habits, and then our habits make us.

Some Personal Struggles

Once the farm was sold, the big wide world seemed to provide little space for recharge. I'd lost much of my security, and spring-back as always happened after holidays at home. Although my parents were alive and well, I felt somewhat rootless. The familiar had vanished.

University exposed much I'd not known existed. One example: A friend who'd been teaching English to Africans in his spare time was arrested and imprisoned. I was young, inexperienced and scared. There seemed nothing I could do to ease the situation of the underdogs in my country – a great burden on me. Later, in my years as a teacher, I reached the point of paralysing burnout. I'd lost all hope of ever doing anything useful for those hampered by the apartheid regime.

I never intended to leave my beloved country but, through unexpected circumstances years later, I settled in England. In 1983, I married Stephen Bowley, my soul mate.

In the mid 1980s, Britain was taking a strong stand against apartheid – sanctions reigned. Our mutual desire to do something for at least some of South Africa's disadvantaged crystallised. Motivated by Nelson Mandela's courageous stand and by many South Africans working to uplift the poor we were prompted, on all sides, to take action. The film *Cry Freedom* was seminal. *Donald Woods'* exposure of the atrocious treatment and death of the anti-apartheid activist, *Steve Biko*, and the Woods' own daring escape to England, to expose the realities of the situation, moved us.

Thembisa

Must here be the beginning of my bliss!
Must here the burden falls from off my back!
Pilgrim's Progress: John Bunyon.

Over Easter, 1988, Stephen and I took a month's leave to travel in South Arica to assess the situation for ourselves. We visited many of the 'small people' doing something for some of the oppressed.

At last! My burden of guilt – a result of hopelessness at not being able to do anything for my countries desperately poor – fell off as Christian's had in Bunyon's Pilgrim's Progress. I realised then that although I couldn't solve the world's problems, let alone those in South Africa, together we, Stephen and I, could do something for some.

Back home in the UK, with the support of our solicitor and likeminded friends, we launched *The Thembisa Trust* – a small charity registered to support grassroots projects in Southern Africa. We soon discovered that we were but the catalysts representing many who cried and longed to do something for the beloved country.

Thembisa is guided and governed by a solid Trustee Team, all working on a voluntary basis. It has embedded in its constitution that 100% of all donations for projects are given to the projects. The few donations given specifically for the administration and running of the Trust enable progress in aspects like Thembisa's upgraded website (launched in April 2016). This website contains information on current and past projects supported, alerts on upcoming events, how to become a member and so on. Naturally the how to donate button is prominent!

Thembisa is the Zulu word meaning to hold out hope.

THE THEMBISA TRUST

Thembisa's logo represents our dream and vision. Though the indigenous Baobab tree is depicted as rooted in South Africa, the charity is registered to operate in Southern Africa – Start small, think big!

It is our hope that in some way Thembisa will prove an inspiration for those struggling throughout Africa.

As the Trust is (still) a small charity, until a few years ago it only operated in South Africa. However, during the last six or so years, it has been in a position to work in partnership with two projects in Zimbabwe that work to uplift children many of whom are orphans.

Over the last twenty-eight years, Thembisa has raised around £340,000 and given support to some seventy-five grassroots projects in Southern Africa where our little goes a long, long way. (When I was at school, South Africa, by then a Republic, forsook the pound in favour of its own new currency, the Rand. Then £1 equalled R2. When last in South Africa, March 2016, £1 was exchanged for R22!)

The joy and the hope brought to the recipients of Thembisa's support – that helped them onto the first rung of the ladder of self-sufficiency, and seeing some of our earlier partnership-projects as now sustainable ventures, no longer dependent on outside contributions for their survival – is rewarding and revitalising. Do visit our new website:

www.thembisatrust.org.

> **The Baobab Tree**
> (Adansonia digitata)
>
> *The Baobab is the undisputed monarch of the savannah trees of Africa. In winter, without their leaves, baobabs resemble petrified octopuses with tentacles groping towards the sky. Almost every part of the tree is useful to man: the leaves can be boiled and eaten as a vegetable, the flower's pollen yields an excellent glue, the seeds are pleasant to suck, or can be ground or roasted to make a palatable coffee, the fruit pods contain tartaric acid (used in sherbet) and the spongy wood can be used to make ropes or paper.*
>
> (Adapted from Readers' Digest Illustrated Guide to Southern Africa - 4th Edition 1985, page 245)

A question:
   So what?
You, the reader, may ask,
   What has Thembisa got to do with Frederick Cope (and his wife, Ethel)?

My reply:
   A whole lot!

I know for certain that Fred and Ethel would be fully behind this venture were they still with us. In some measure, a significant part of their legacy – their compassion for those worst off – is being expressed today in action through Thembisa. The fruits of their lives are being reaped in The Beloved Country years after they have left.

305

In Conclusion

Frederick Cope's life example provides a strong foundation for my life.

In the end, he did meet the Truth he'd so long sought. Truth is not in a religion with its sets of rules, but lies in a person – Jesus Christ. Fred found real meaning in his life when he met with his Creator-God – Truth.

Dad lived up to the Cope Motto:
Always be ready – be present with your mind.

Fred rose to virtually every challenge. For a time, trapped between the rock of suffering and the hard place of the fear of the unknown, he was almost defeated. But, in the end, he was ready to die – ready to meet his Maker as he moved on to his permanent abode.

APPENDIX

Credits

Mine is the hand that penned these lines
Many are the minds that have brought Fred's story to light

Errors that may have crept in are the sole responsibility of the author.

My gratitude goes to those who have contributed to Fred's life-story. Some have been actively involved in the research and editing process, while others have read or listened to Fred's story as it has unfolded week by week.

First and foremost
Stephen Bowley – *my husband, co-adventurer, sounding board, best friend.*
Stephanie Hale – *author, speaker, publishing expert, mentor and much more. The value of your encouragement and guidance throughout my writing thick-and-thins is hard to over-emphasise;*
William Harding – *talented, creative, versatile illustrator who produced the maps in this book;*
Kerry West – *My former able Writers Assistant who for 18 months was an invaluable sounding board and raised my sights on book production and marketing;*

Researchers, readers and editors.
Ruth M. Simpson – *Yorkshire genealogist who unearthed valuable information on Fred's first life and travels;*
Sylvia Vetta – *journalist and author (Oxford & China) for her incisive questions and suggestions;*
Ron Bridge – *China expert who patiently educated me on China as I sought to piece together my father's time there (see page 143);*
Frederick Borchers – *South African section editor who has constantly run more than the second mile;*
Nicholas Newman – *energy consultant and journalist who set my foot on the road of biographical construction at the start of this writing project;*
Elsa MacMichael – *my energetic and visionary cousin who accompanied me on my second visit to China (2014);*
Roger E Nixon – *Military & Historical Searches, London;*
Simon Fowler – *freelance writer and researcher (for China);*
Andrew Judge – *provoking thought and refinement of aspects of the text;*

Family – this includes those who walk with me
Michael and Carol Cassidy – *for over 50 years your friendship, nurture, and example has propelled me along, together with your love of my parents – and for your particular contributions towards this book*;
Frederick (Dick) Cope – *Fred's nephew who remembered Fred on his visits home to England when on holiday from China;*
Susan Riddeford – *who pointed me to aspects of family history;*
Deborah Hennessy – *valued friend who consistently eggs me on;*
Megan Roberts – *family friend who cherished time with Fred in Pietermaritzburg and has contributed to the text on his time in PMB;*
Margie Berry – *a loyal friend who lives at Rosedale, my old home, and has unearthed historical evidence;*
Gillis van Schalkwyk – *South African author who has provided assorted help and motivation;*
Margaret Ann Hobbs, Marjorie Nieuwoudt, Ingrid Joubert, my *encouraging 'Durban' cousins who provided background to Fred's story;*
Louise Young, Bruce Sparks, Roger and Celia Sparks, Joan Andrew, Alan Fuggle and Peter Mac Cullam – *friends dating back to my youth who have encouraged me to keep on writing and/or contributed towards it*;
Fellows, staff and students at St Cross College, Oxford *who, since 1988 when I became a Member of Common Room, have broadened and enlightened me;*
Jenny Camons *for sharing her presentational expertise*;
Gary Wong Chi-him, Clark Friend, Jonathan Mead, Angela Chenyu Zhao, Ami Thomson *for supplying relevant material;*
The home-team who work with us in various roles – Bill Baxter, Billie Hough, Rod Sammons, Tracey Smith, Jackie White, Tony Wilkinson, – *your support, fun and laughter when, as captive audiences, you have listened to my rendering of Fred's story serial style as it emerged. You have helped to keep me on the straight and narrow!*

Institutional research and support has come from The Local Studies Library, Wakefield; Rotary Club of Wakefield; Archivist – West Yorkshire; Library, University of Leeds; The National Archives at Kew, UK; Imperial War Museum; Victoria and Albert Museum; Sotheby's London; Costume & Textiles Specialist at Bonham's, UK; The Gazette – London; Forces-war-records.co.uk; www.findmypast.co.uk; www.archives.presbyterian.org.nz; Jardine, Matheson and Co Ltd, China; The Public Records Office, Hong Kong; Dawn Ingham (Vicar of St Andrews and St Mary's Church, Wakefield); Peter Clark, Secretary to Wakefield Rotary Club; and to all persons who have enlightened me through their contributions to Wikipedia.

Last but not least Grace Townshend – *longstanding friend and medical writer who tirelessly helped shape and edit my earlier books. Your patience and skilled suggestions on this one are much valued.*

No doubt there are those who have escaped mention – thank you too.

Sources and Recommended Reading

With rare exceptions, materials consulted on the Internet are not cited. Below, references are grouped under Fred's three countries though many overlap.

ENGLAND

Beadle, J Brian (1999): Walking around Scarborough, Whitby & Filey
Clarkson, Henry (1889) Memories of Merry Wakefield – An Octogenarian's Recollections, etc
Dinsdale, Ann (2013): The Brontes at Haworth
Green, Michael: World on the Run
Green, Michael: Who is this Jesus?
Green, Michael: When God Breaks In
Hey, David (2011) A History of Yorkshire – County of the Broad Acres
Kellett, Andrew (2008: The Little Book of Yorkshire Dialect
Lindup, Peter (2008): The Little Book of Yorkshire Proverbs
Malam, John (2011) Yorkshire, A Very Peculiar History
Markham, Len: Wakefield and District – An A to Z of local history
Morrison, John: North York Moors – Mini Guide
Newbound, Andrew: Children's History of Yorkshire
North York Moors National Park: Walks around Rosedale Abbey
Osborne, Roger: Discover the North York Moors – Official guide
Packham, Les: Yorkshire in Watercolour
Poems & Poets: Poems of William Cowper (1794)
Skinner, Julia: Did you know – West Yorkshire; A Miscellany
Taylor, Kate: The Making of Wakefield   1801-1900
The Task, Book II – Poetry Foundation
The Guardian, Monday 28.07.14   WW1 re Harry Patch
Wool Board: The History of British Wool
Gong, R. H.; Gong, H.; Wright, Rachel M: Fancy Yarns: Their Manufacture and Application

CHINA

Bunton, Hedley P: Forty years of China   © 1988
Bridge, Ron: British Civilians Interned by the Japanese during WWII
Campbell, Claire: Mail Online 16 May 2009
Chang Jung and Halliday, Jon: Mao: The Unknown Story
Chang Jung: Wild Swans: Three Daughters of China
Chen, Peter: World War II Database
Cochrane, Donald, PCANZ Archives, June 2001
Foreign Office for China 1919-1980
Harmsen, Peter: Shanghai 1937: Stalingrad on the Yangtze

Keswick, Maggie: The Thistle and The Jade:
    A Celebration of 175 Years of Jardine, Matheson & Co.
Mitter Rana: China's War with Japan 1937-1945: The Struggle for Survival
    Mitter Rana: A Bitter Revolution: China's Struggle with the Modern World (Making of the Modern World)
Nathan, Andrew: Jade and Plastic
Presbyterian Church Archives: A Tour of Old Canton
Suzhou Embroidery   ISBN 978-7-119-05980-8
Vetta, Sylvia: Brushstrokes in Time
Xinru Liu, The Silk Road in World History
    ISBN 978-0-19-516174-8; ISBN 978-0-19-533810-2
Yangtze – 1985, China Pictorial ed., Across China
    (Beijing: China Pictorial Publishing Company)

Hong Kong and Southern China

Cope, Frederick: World Crisis – A Way Out 1933 – An Analysis of the World Economic Crisis – Suggesting its Causes and a Cure (out of print)
Cope, Frederick (Editor) The Hong Kong Review – Issues in 1937
    15 Oct Vol 1 No2; 29 Oct Vol 1 No3; 19 Nov Vol 1 No4; 10 Dec Vol 1 No5 (Out of Print. Available for viewing at Hong Kong Central Preservation Library for Government Publications - Public Records Office)
Chang Jung and Halliday, Jon – Mao: The Unknown Story

SOUTH AFRICA

Brand, Christo: Mandela: My Prisoner, My Friend
Briggs, Philip: World Heritage Sites of South Africa: uKhahlamba-Drakensburg Park
Carlin, John: Invictus
Cassidy, Michael: A Witness forever
Cassidy, Michael: The Passing Summer: A South African's Response to White Fear, Black Anger, and the Politics of Love
Cassidy, Michael: Chasing the Wind: Man's Search for Life's Answers
Clark, Nancy L. and Worger, William H. Apartheid
De Klerk, F W: The Last Trek – A New Beginning (The autobiography)
Courtenay, Bryce: The Power of One
Courtenay, Bryce: Tandia
Dugard, Martin: Into Africa – The Dramatic Retelling of the Stanley-Livingstone Story:
Goeda, Wilson: Why Me – A True Story of Reconciliation
Hawkins, E. B.: The Story of Harrismith 1849-1920 (out of print)
Hunt, Keith and Bryer, Lynne – The 1820 Settlers
Keane, Fergal: All of these People
Kirsten, Deborah: Chai Tea & Ginger Beer – My Unexpected Journey: Cricket, Family and Beyond
Mandela, Nelson: Long Walk to Freedom

Mann, Chris: South Africans: A Set of Portrait Poems
Paton, Alan: Cry the Beloved Country
Paton, Alan: Ah, but Your Land is Beautiful
Paton, Alan: Journey Continued: An Autobiography,
Pearce, R. O.: Barrier of Spears: Drama of the Drakensberg
Portsmouth, Henry: The Story of Wyford: 1874–1965
Sparks, Allister: Tomorrow is Another Country
Readers' Digest Illustrated Guide to Southern Africa – 4th Edition 1985
Tutu, Desmond: The Rainbow People of God:
   The Making of a Peaceful Revolution
Tutu, Desmond: No Future without Forgiveness
Tutu, Desmond: God Has a Dream: A Vision of Hope for Our Time
Tutu, Desmond: The Rainbow People of God, with John Allen
Van Schalkwyk, Gillis: About Van Reenen
Woods, Donald: Cry Freedom

Photographs, Maps and Movies

Photographs

Unless otherwise attributed, photographs are from the author's collection that includes those of Frederick and Ethel Cope and some by Stephen Bowley.

@ Tonia Cope Bowley

Whilst every endeavour has been made to trace the owners, if any, of the copyright of the photographs and images listed below, I have not been successful in every case. In some instances more than 70 years have elapsed since the photograph was taken.

Page
Front cover - image Big Red Sun – Karelin Dmitriy/Bigstock.com
9 & 10   **Yorkshire Rose** – Wikimedia Commons GNU Free Documentation License: www.wikipedia.org/wiki/File:Yorkshire rose.svg
20   **WW1 Soldier, Winchester** – Media Image Photography/Bigstock
20   **WW1 Helmet** – Media Image Photography / Bigstock
22   **War Images** –
   1. Soldier – Onepony/Bigstock.com
   2. Sand bags – Havanaman/Bigstock.com
   3. Cemetery – CyclingScot/Bigstock.com
   4. Barbed wire – Shipov/Bigstock.com
23   **Airship R33** – Copyright Airship Heritage Trust collection www.airshipsonline.com
24   **Barlow Railway Station** – 23 April 1961 – Creative Commons Attribution Share-alike license 2.0 – Author Ben Brooksbank
25   **Airship – R33 in hanger** copyright Airship Heritage Trust collection   www.airshipsonline.com

311

27	**Page of Journal of the Institute of Electrical Engineers** (IEE) 1920 (The Journal was published by the IET between 1889 and 1963)
64	**P&O postcard of Malwa** – Reproduced by kind permission of P&O Heritage Collection www.poheritage.com
89	**P&O postcard of Morea** – Reproduced by kind permission of P&O Heritage Collection www.poheritage.comhttp://nla.gov.au/nla.map-brsc67
108	**1920s map of Shameen Island** – From Wikimedia Commons, free media depository.
125	**Stanley waterfront Hong Kong 2014** Donated by Wong Chi-him, Gary
135	**Plan of the City of Canton 1910** – Wikipedia - Public domain – Hosea Ballou Morse (1910) – The International Relations of the Chinese Empire. Volume 1, p. 118.
136	**Aerial photo of Shameen Island British and French Concessions 1935** (source unknown)
154	**Cutting of Kamakura Maru passengers**
157	**Tatuta Maru – Prisoner Exchange ship:** The first Japanese-British diplomatic Exchange - The Japan Times: Attributed to: Shashin Shuho Dec 23, 2006 – image in the public domain under Japanese copyright law. Wikipedia http://ww2db.com/ship_spec.php?ship id=545
186	**Three Glaister Girls in Cosmos field** – contributed by Marjorie Nieuwoudt
221	**Ostrich with head in the sand** – Andrey_Kuzmin/Bigstock.com
221	**Ostrich in a field** – kapyos/Bigstock.com
254	**Photo of Abe Sparks** – contributed by his daughter, Louise Young
274	**Constellation of Orion** – pere sanz/Bigstock.com
291	**Close up Image of Orion's Belt** – ESA/Hubble – Credit: Davide De Martin & the ESA/ESO/NASA Photoshop FITS Liberator

Maps

All maps are attributed to William Harding unless otherwise referenced. Maps of the three countries of Fred's Three Lives from: University of Texas Libraries
http://www.lib.utexas.edu/maps/faq.html

9	**England**
71	**China**
163	**South Africa**

Movies
The Railway Man
Cry Freedom
Long Walk to Freedom

Canton Contacts

Selected letters, invitations and business cards

Letters included in the text:

Page
137   28 September 1939
Shameen Municipal Council to F. Cope, Esq.
Letter of appreciation for services to the food
control regarding emergency reserve supply.

141   1 March 1941
Consulat du France a Canton to Mr Cope
Thanks for improvisation of electric light supply for
the public buildings and the street lighting of the
French Concession during the Canton Crisis period.

Other letters

29 June 1940
The Missionary Sisters of the Immaculate Conception

> Shameen School,
> June 29, 1940.
>
> Dear Mr. Cope,
>
> We greatly appreciate your kindness in giving us the use of the Canton Sailing Club House boat for the Annual Picnic of our Shameen School Pupils. We all enjoyed the day and are most grateful for your service in helping to make this holiday a success.
>
> The Missionary Sisters
> of the Immaculate Conception.
> Sr. St. John Baptist.

25 April 1941
A Friend

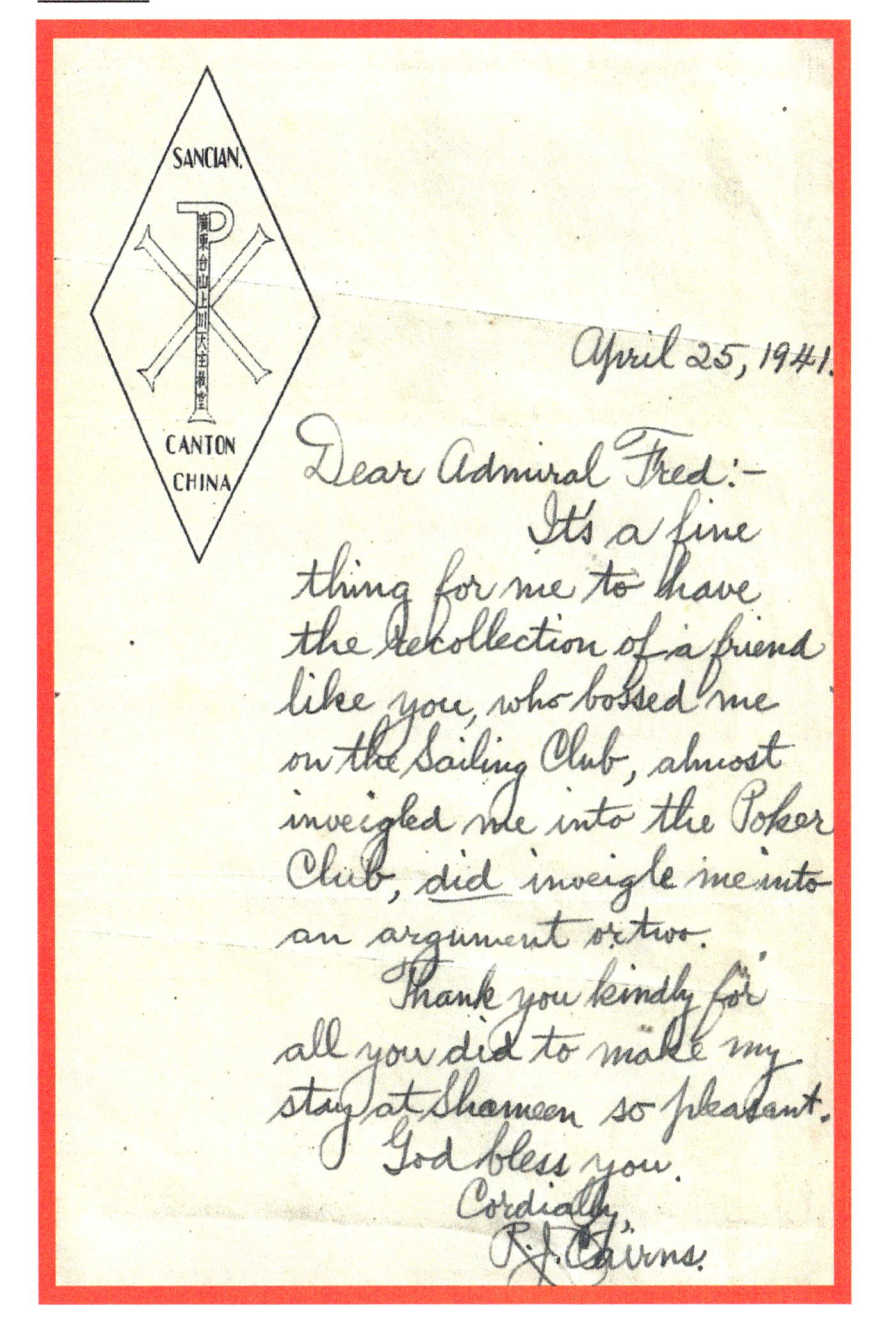

> SANCIAN, CANTON CHINA
>
> April 25, 1941
>
> Dear Admiral Fred:—
> It's a fine thing for me to have the recollection of a friend like you, who bossed me on the Sailing Club, almost inveigled me into the Poker Club, did inveigle me into an argument or two.
> Thank you kindly for all you did to make my stay at Shameen so pleasant. God bless you.
> Cordially,
> R.J. Cairns

Invitations

From Simone Saugon, Consulat du France

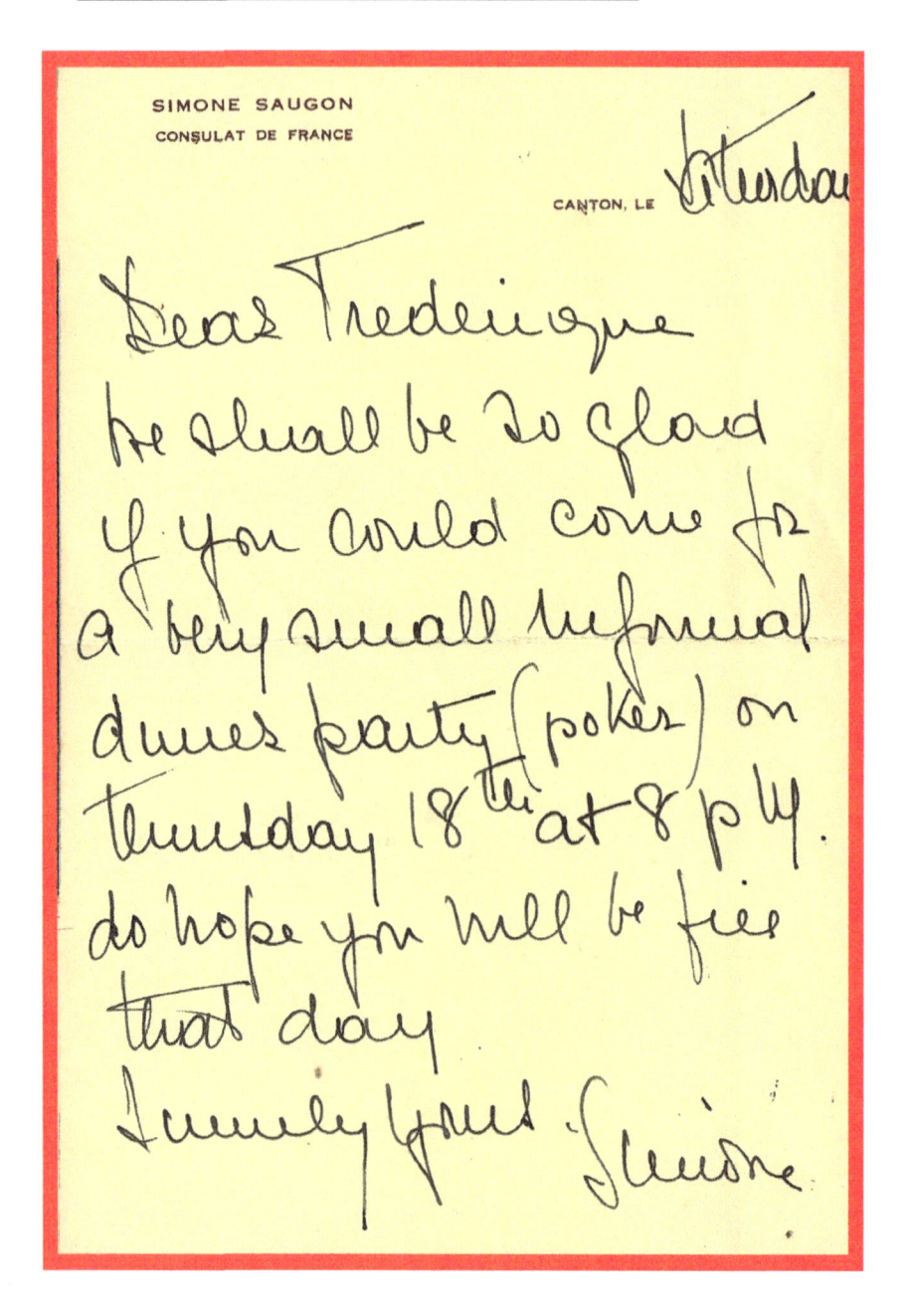

SIMONE SAUGON
CONSULAT DE FRANCE

CANTON, LE Saturday

Dear Frederique

We shall be so glad if you could come for a very small informal dinner party (poker) on Thursday 18th at 8 p.m. Do hope you will be free that day.

Sincerely yours, Simone.

From Mr B. B. Anthony to 'Admiral of Fleet'
(F. Cope Commodore of Canton Sailing Club)

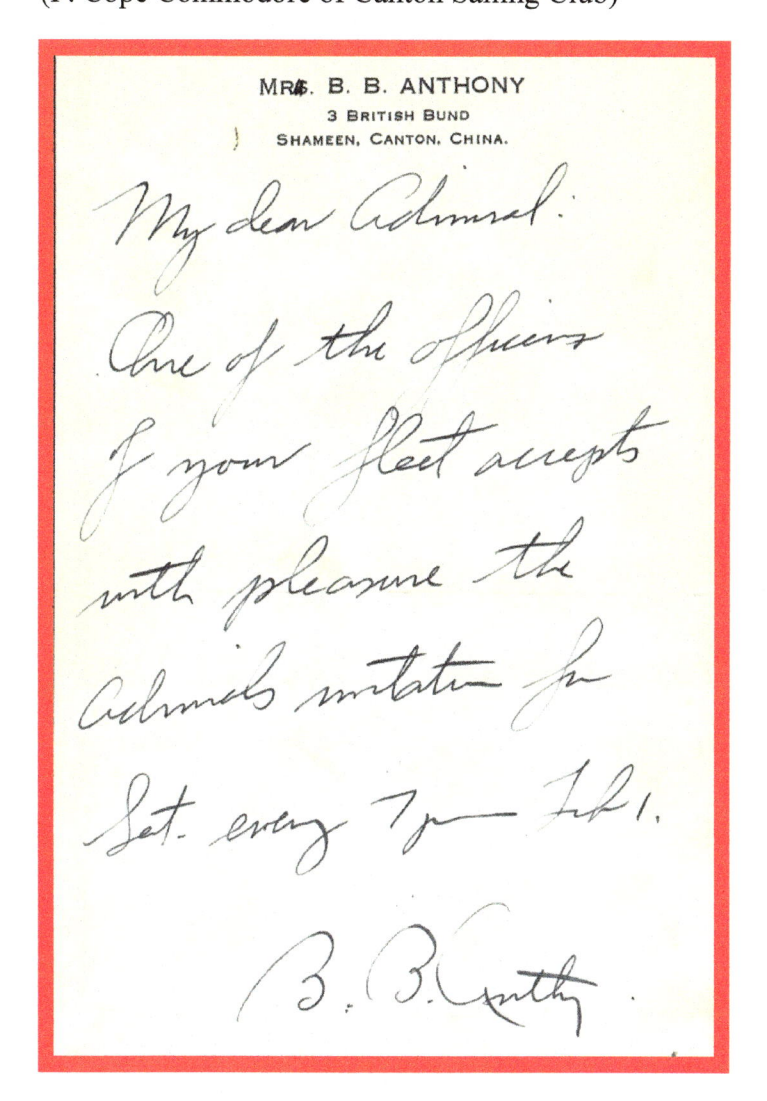

> MRS. B. B. ANTHONY
> 3 BRITISH BUND
> SHAMEEN, CANTON, CHINA.
>
> My dear Admiral:
>
> One of the Officers of your fleet accepts with pleasure the Admiral's invitation for Sat. every 7pm — Feb 1.
>
> B. B. Anthony.

From Captain F.C. Flynn, Royal Navy to Mr Cope
At Home – cocktails 5.30 to meet
Vice-Admiral Sir Percy Noble,

From Mr Walter Smith, USA Consul-General to The Commodore
Cocktails: 7-9   6 August

317

Business Cards

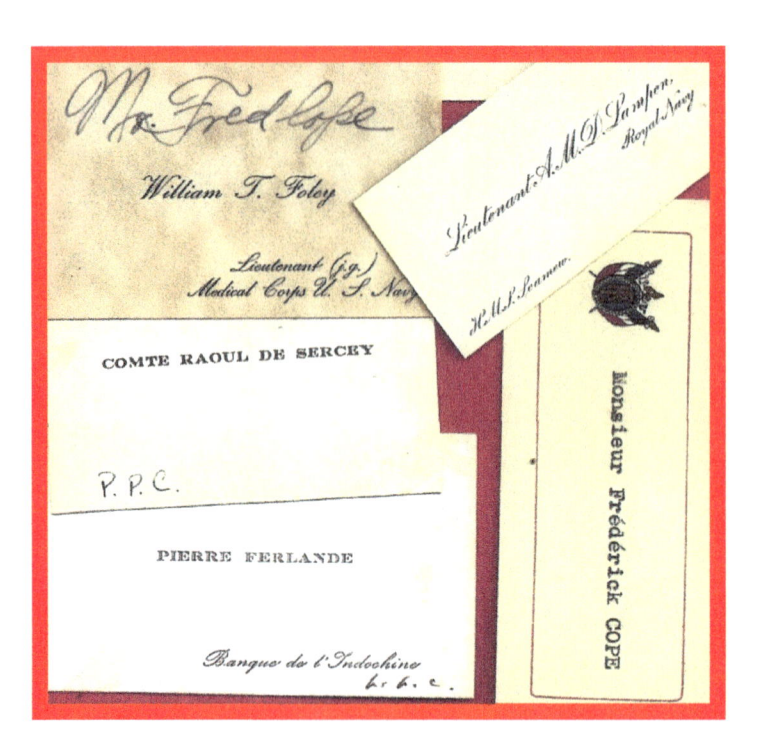

Passport entries
    On Leaving Canton
    And
    On entry to South Africa

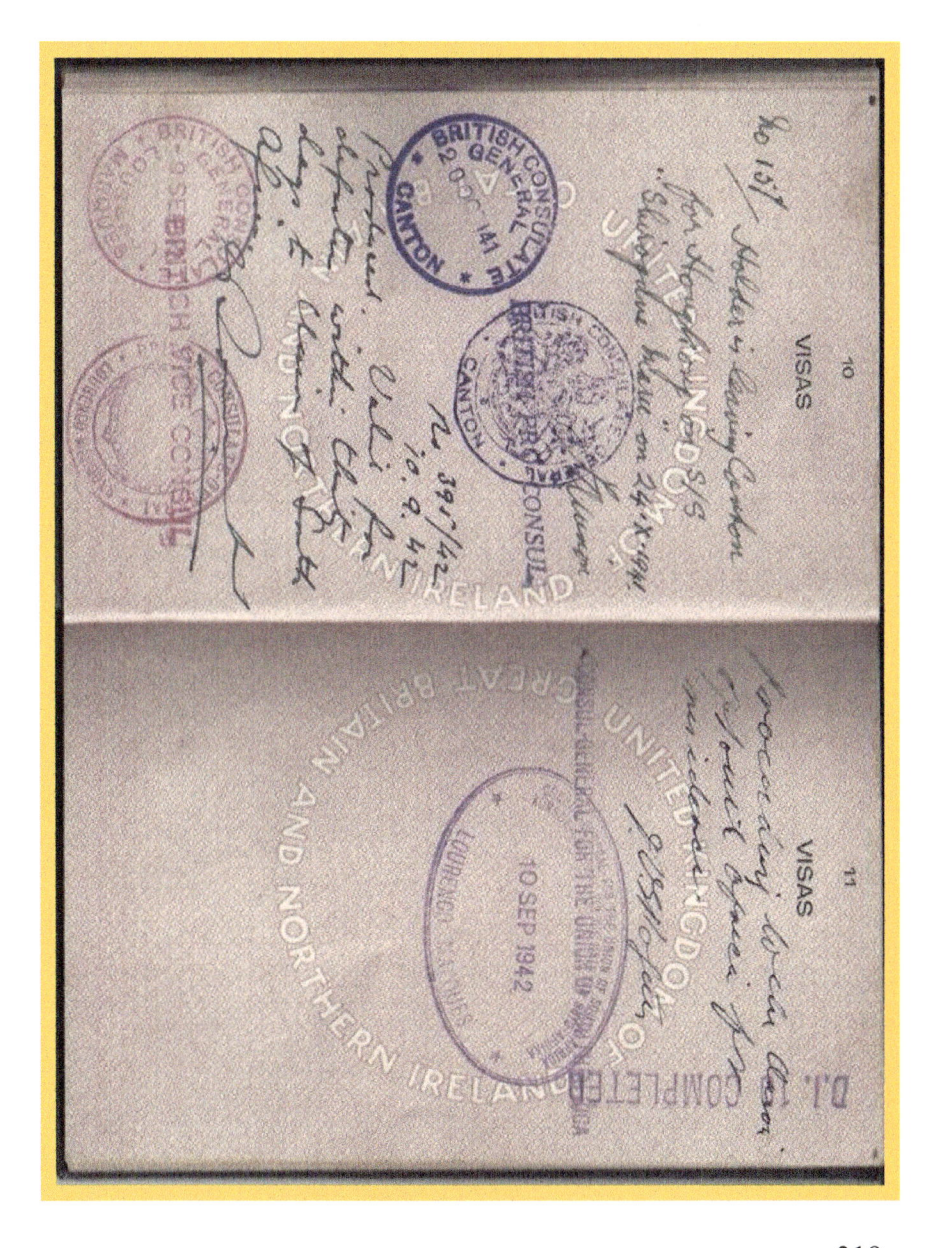

Outline of Experience

Typed by Fred on his portable manual typewriter
page 1

<u>OUTLINE OF EXPERIENCE</u>

of

Frederick Cope.

Chartered Electrical Engineer. Assoc: Member Inst.Elec: Engineer.
<u>Member Assoc: Mining Elec: Engineers.   Industrial Specialist.</u>

BACKGROUND.   Technical education -- Leeds University.
               Training -- under W.B. Woodhouse Esqr.,(Engineer
               and Managing Director of The Yorkshire Electric
Power Company; a member of the Council, and a past President of
the Institution of Electrical Engineers.)

EARLY   After qualifying in Electrical Power Generation
EXPERIENCE.   and Distribution, the writer held various positions
               as an assistant engineer on The Yorkshire Electric
               Power Co., which is a statutory Company, distributing
electricity over an area of over 2000 square miles.
One of these positions was particular experience insomuch as it
conducted a series of special investigations into the working of
a large variety of industries. The investigations were undertaken
for the purpose of ascertaining efficiency methods, and methods
for increasing the rate of production. The industries comprised
small Power Stations and Tramways; Worsted, Woollen, Cotton, and
Silk Mills in their spinning, doubling, weaving, knitting, and dyeing
sections of the Textile Industry: Collieries; heavy and light Engineering works, Chemical, Glass blowing, and Fertiliser factories;
Flour mills; Electrical furnaces etc.
The work in most instances required a close study of the raw materials
and the processes involved.

ELECTRIC   As a departmental head of The Yorkshire Electric
SUPPLY   Power Co., the writer's experience covered the
MANAGEMENT.   development and management of a number of electrical
               undertakings in Yorkshire. These undertakings
               were operated under Provisional Orders of the
Electric Lighting Acts and comprised such industrial towns as the
port of Goole, Castleford, Ossett, Selby, Otley, Sowerby Bridge, Bingley,
                                                                    etc.

WAR   When not on military service in the last War, the
PRODUCTION AND writer was an assistant to W.B. Woodhouse who, as an
NATIONAL   adviser to the Ministry of Munitions and to the
SERVICE.   Admiralty, supervised in his district the speeding
               up policy of work of national importance, work of
               Priority One classification. This experience
covered power problems in connection with National shell, and filling
factories.
For a period the writer was posted to Armstrong Whitworth's Barlow
Airship factory where R.33 was under construction.
Later, engaged on statistics and reports.
Deputed to travel and explain the working of the Heat, Light, and
Fuel Control Order to the various Urban and Rural Councils in Yorkshire.
Afterwards, continued with electrical distribution.

CONSULTANT AND EFFICIENCY ENGINEER. Experience in private Consulting in Wakefield, England. The experience here covered arbitrations, valuations of electric plants for legal transfer and similar purposes; advising on electric supply, also Company directors on new industrial undertakings and on extensions to old plants; efficiency work, mainly in the textile industries, which covered design of progressive layouts, efficient application of power, and specially arranged methods of manufacture

ORGANISATION AND MANAGEMENT. During the same period the writer organised factories from the grass site to the working unit, complete with departmental systems, records, accounts etc. Ownership of industrial interests during this period, a period of ever changing economic and financial conditions, provided considerable experience in factory costing, general financial, industrial, and commercial factory management.

CHINA EXPERIENCE. With the introduction at home of a policy of restriction of production resulting in the breaking up of efficient Plants, of necessity, the writer's consulting activities were transferred to Hong Kong and China. The experience here covered a survey of Chinese industries in Hong Kong, Shanghai, Tientsin, and areas as far north as Harbin. The main experience was in Hong Kong, where, through industrial and commercial interests, contact was made with most of the factories there. During this period the writer prepared industrial reports for a number of China companies, including Jardines and Butterfield & Swire. For a number of years the writer was an Arbitrator for the Hong Kong Chamber of Commerce concerning Textile disputes, (Raw and Semi-raw materials, processes, and finished products are intimate subjects.)

EXPERIENCE UNDER PRESENT WAR CONDITIONS. Rather more than two years ago the writer undertook to put on its feet, the Refrigeration and Ice production plant in Canton of the Hong Kong & Canton Ice Manufacturing Company. A preliminary investigation report had been presented, and substantial economies effected, when the Canton War crisis occurred. The seriousness of the position necessitated an immediate suspension of all investigations and required an instant concentration on the problems of maintaining, under crisis conditions, the supply of Ice, the Cold storage of emergency food, and valuable Red Cross medical supplies. This had to be done by means of improvisations midst extreme difficulties The Canton Power Station was bombed and wrecked, and the public power supply ceased. Regular bombings, gun fire, and explosions of munition dumps disturbed machinery. Constant danger of fire from a blazing City without. Staff problems from a fear of explosions within. Lack of repairing facilities and so forth. During this period the writer improvised a temporary electricity supply for Cold Storage, street lighting and lighting of public buildings for the foreign community.

PRESENT OCCUPATION. The above phase passed, and under the circumstances the writer remained with the Company managing their interests and those of the Dairy Farm, Ice & Cold Storage Company's food organisation. Now a simple job. During this difficult period of Japanese occupation of Canton the writer gave a good deal of assistance to the Concession Municipal Councils on the various problems in connection with essential services and control.

TIMELINE

Time	Frederick Cope	Selected World Events and comments
	ENGLAND	
1890s		
5-5-1890,	Born 94 Stanley Road, Wakefield, Yorkshire	W. B. Purvis patents the fountain pen
28-05-1892	Fred's sister Alice Robbins Cope born	Forth Rail Bridge, Scotland, opened
-09-1893	Fred's sister Alice Robbins Cope died	
1894-1895		First Sino-Japanese War
21-04-1896	Fred's Father - John Henry Cope died	
1899	Mother Martha married William Parkinson	S. Africa 2nd Anglo-Boer War begins
1899-1901		China – Boxer Rebellion
1900s		
1901	Fred at school & a choir boy	N China Boxer Rebellion ends
1902		S Africa – 2nd Boer War ends
1906	Technical Education – Leeds Univ.	International Morse Code Adopted
1907		English suffragettes storm Parliament
1910s		
1910	Junior assistant at Yorkshire Electric Power Company (YEPC) under Mr W. B. Woodhouse (MD)	Ethel Glaister born Union of S Africa formed
1911	Permanent job with YEPC	
1911-1912		Republic of China founded
1913		SA Land Act prevents blacks buying land
1914-1916	Volunteer in WWI Wounded in Left arm / hand – sent home	Outbreak of WWI 1914 SA National Party founded
1918	Assistant Engineer; Associate member of IEE Departmental Head NYEC	WWI ends
1919	Buys into Windhill Mill at Lofthouse	League of Nations created
1920s		
1920	John Sharphouse, Partner of Windhill Mill dies. FC re-conveys the Mill	
1921	FC creates a new wool – wool & artificial silk -named Esmerene Becomes a Charted Electrical Engineer	
1923-1925	Member of Yorkshire Rotary Club Esmerene advertised in Melbourne press by Ball & Welsh	
1925	Industrial Consultant	China; Sun Yat-sen dies – Chiang Kai-shek nationalist party leader
1925/1926	Fred's mother and stepfather to Scarborough	
1926	Voluntary liquidation –Windhill Mill	
25-02-1927	Fred leaves for China	On P&O Melba – London to Shanghai

322

Time	Frederick Cope	Selected World Events and comments
	CHINA	
1930s		
1930	Returns to England visiting his mother	
1930	Sets up consultancy in Hong Kong	8th floor Pedder Building, Pedder Street
1931		Japan occupied Manchuria
1930 / 1932	Residence – 42 FC, Shameen. Canton	
1933	Publication of booklet WORLD CRISIS – A way out	Printed and published by South China Morning Post' Ltd. (Reprinted from FC articles -The Hong Kong Telegraph)
1937		Full Scale invasion of China by the Japanese
1937		China: 2nd Sino-Japanese War Marco Polo Bridge Incident
1937 Oct-Nov	Publication of The Hong Kong Review Frederick Cope initiator and editor	4-5 editions published in 1937
1937		China: Kuomintang and Communists unite against Japan
1937-1938		Japanese invasion of China – start of WWII in the Far East - Hitler makes alliance with Japan – Nanjing Massacre Neville Chamberlain becomes British PM
14-06-1938	Fred acquires new passport C 83909	Issued by Consul General, Canton
22-06-1939- 07-02-1940	Passport entries permitting disembarkation in Hong Kong	
28-9-1938		Japan invades Canton
29-10-1938		Canton surrenders to the Japanese
01-09-1939		Britain declared war on Germany
1940s		
20-06-1940	Passport: Permitted to disembark in Hong Kong	Must report to Registration Dept., 4th floor, Chang Tin Building, Des Vosux Road within 24 hours
15-02-1941	Passport: Vice Consul, Hong Kong approved departure within 30 day	Permission cancelled
24-10-1941	Leaves for Hong Kong on Sharigane Maru	
28-10-1941	Passport – Permission to leave Hong Kong	
07-12-1941	Fred's mentor W. B. Woodhouse dies	Japan's attacks Pearl Harbour US naval base in Hawaii – US enters WWII.
Nov41-July42	Solitary confinement in a police cell Frequent interrogation	Probable date Question – did this include Shanghai?
9-05-1942	Moved by boat to Shanghai	9th May1942.
05-08-1942	Leaves Shanghai, as exchange prisoner	Japan-England exchange – Tatuta Maru
	The boat trip and dysentery – near death	Left from Shanghai
27-08-1942	Put off the boat at Lourenco Marques	Not permitted on Narkunda to England
10-09-1942	Permission to proceed to Union of S Africa	From British and S African Consul

323

Time	Frederick Cope	Selected World Events and comments
	SOUTH AFRICA	
Sep 1942	Secures employment in Johannesburg with Industrial Development Corporation (IDC)	Percy Furness' influence
Oct-Dec 1942	Cathedral Peak Hotel in Natal Drakensberg	
1 Dec 1942	Meets Ethel Glaister	
12 Dec 1942	Engaged to Ethel Glaister	
21 Dec 1942	Married Ethel Glaister in Johannesburg	
Jan 1943	Started working for IDC, Johannesburg	
6 Dec 1943	Daughter born – Esmerene Tonia Cope	
1944	Ethel inherits 1/5 of Oban farm FC resigns from the IDC	
1945	FC & family live at Oban, Van Reenen to help Anna Glaister with the Guesthouse	Hiroshima & Nagasaki – atomic bomb United Nations (UN) formed – successor to The League of Nations
1946	Ostrich Feather Factory at Rosedale	Start of China's Civil War (1945-49)
1948		Apartheid in law in SA; State of Israel
1949	Ostrich Feather Factory closed Return to Oban to manage the Guest Farm	China: Mao Zedong founded People's Republic of China (PRC) Kuomintang (KMT) retreat to Taiwan; WWII end
1950s		
1950		SA-Group Areas Act – ANC civil disobedience, led by Nelson Mandela
1953	Return to Rosedale – farming, Van Reenen	
1954	Chicken farming Sheep farming & cattle farming	
1955	Rosedale farm burnt out	
1957	Secrets of a leather suitcase revealed / tomatoes	Launch of Sputnick-1 starts Space Age
1960s		
1960	Russian comfrey grown for market	SA Sharpeville incident – ANC Banned
1961	Brussels sprouts grown for market	SA a republic – leaves Commonwealth
1963	Rosedale sold – move to Port Shepstone	Ethel returns to nursing
1964	Ethel – Natal Varsity, PMB resident nurse	
1965	Fred joins Ethel in PMB	SA Nelson Mandela life-imprisonment Death of Winston Churchill
1966		**SA** Hendrik Verwoerd assassinated
1966-1976		China Cultural Revolution
1966		SA Soweto uprising – 600 killed
1969		First moon landing; Mao's power ends
1970s		
1970		Millions of black people forced to settled in homelands
1975	Ethel retires – they move to PMB central	End of Vietnam War
1976	Fred & Ethel 3-month trip to England	
1977	Fred's health deteriorates	1st mass-produced personal computers
25-Jan-1979	Fred's death	At rising 89 …

Other books by the author
www.toniacopebowley.co.uk

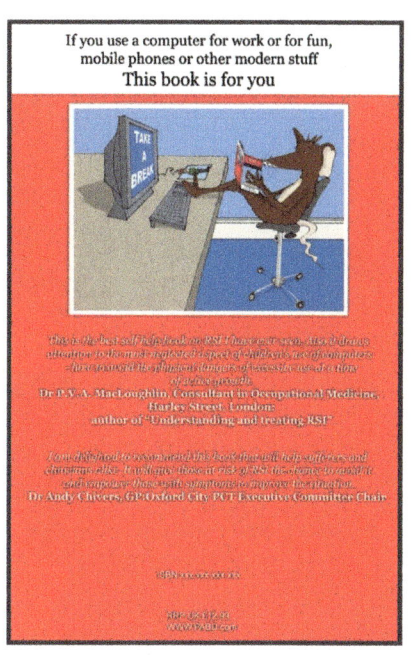

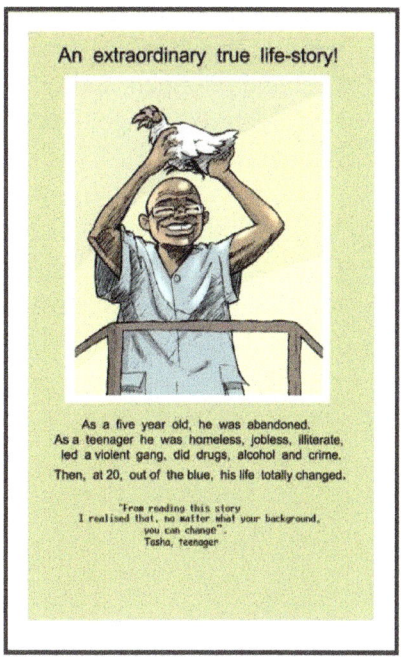

325

ABOUT THE AUTHOR

South African born, Tonia Cope Bowley started writing stories before the age of ten. Her books include: biography, children's fiction, self help and a technical work.
One Man Three lives: The man who would never give up is her fourth published book. (Keep up to date with Tonia's books at www.toniacopebowley.co.uk)

After completing a science degree (Natal) and a teaching diploma (Cape Town) Tonia taught mathematics in Pietermaritzburg for 6 years before spending over a year in Tromsø, North Norway. Then, for almost 30 years, she was employed by Oxford University in teaching and research. In the early years of the advent of personal computers her first published book, *Computing Using Basic: An Interactive Approach*, was a best seller. Since taking early retirement in 2001 she has focused her energies on her writing.

Up to the age of 20, Tonia lived on a small farm in rolling hills near to Van Reenen, Orange Free State. She now lives with her husband Stephen and a couple of King Charles spaniels in an Oxfordshire village, overlooking fields and woods. They have two adult sons.

In 1988, the couple launched a charity, The Thembisa Trust. Over the last 29 years, the Trust has raised over a third of a million pounds to provide support and hope to grassroots projects in Southern Africa, some of which have become self sustaining.

Lightning Source UK Ltd.
Milton Keynes UK
UKOW07f2050160217
294595UK00001B/1/P